POLE, PADDLE
& PORTAGE

POLE, PADDLE
& PORTAGE

Bill Riviere

Drawings by Bill Riviere, Jr.

VNR Van Nostrand Reinhold Company
New York Cincinnati London Toronto Melbourne

Van Nostrand Reinhold Company Regional Offices
New York   Cincinnati   Chicago   Millbrae   Dallas

Van Nostrand Reinhold Company International Offices
London   Toronto   Melbourne

Library of Congress Catalog Card Number 73–76811

Published by Van Nostrand Reinhold Company
450 West 33rd Street, New York, N. Y. 10001

Published simultaneously in Canada by
Van Nostrand Reinhold Limited

3 5 7 9 11 13 15 16 14 12 10 8 6 4

To
Eleanor,
Jo-Anne,
Lee,
Bill.

Foreword

There is very little of the Northwoods atmosphere in this book. The night cry of loons, the skylines of spruce and pointed firs, the resplendent silver of faraway lakes — all of these have been omitted.

They are a part of canoeing, true, but I have tried instead to attain straightforward and detailed descriptions of canoeing and canoe-trip techniques, ranging from simple basics on flat water to more complex and exciting facets such as poling and running rapids. My aims have been to help canoeists of varying ability to improve their skills; to assist summer camp instructors in their work of teaching the young; and to entice non-canoeists to join in this fast-growing and thrilling sport.

Chapter XVII, Canoe Country, is aimed particularly at the latter group. Not intended as a detailed guide to canoeable waters, this section is included to suggest the availability of local waterways; to point out that canoeing is possible not only along Northwoods canoe trails but in virtually every state in the Union and in every province in Canada, often on neighborhood streams, ponds and lakes.

In compiling Chapter XVII, I have drawn freely from the several excellent guidebooks that are listed and recommended in the bibliography. Too, indispensable help came from many who supplied details of local waters with which I could not, of course, have been familiar.

Among these were state and provincial information officers who are expected to supply such data but who went far beyond the requirements of their positions to research and describe for me waterways in their respective regions. Canoe club members, too, responded with invaluable details to which, otherwise, I could not have had access.

Those who plunged in enthusiastically to help were Dave Balfour of the Rhode Island Development Council; John Heuston, travel writer for the Arkansas Publicity and Park Commission; Dudley P. Osborn, boating supervisor for the Nebraska Game, Forestation and Parks Commission; Bill Sizer, Chief of Information and Education, Arizona Game and Fish Department; Bob Burleson, President of the Texas Explorers Club, Temple, Texas; Bill Bickham, member of the American White Water Affiliation, of State College, Pennsylvania; Ron Rhoweder, Conservation Education Biologist for the Oregon State Game Commission; Pershing Carlson, Chief, Information and Education, North Dakota Fish and Game Department; E. Kliess Brown, Chief, Information and Education, Idaho Fish and Game Department; Seward H. Hall, of the Bluff City Canoe Club, Memphis, Tennessee; A Lee Robertson, Information and Education Officer, Utah Board of Fish and Game; Ben Gladding, member of the Sierra Club, of Sacramento, California; Joe Ludiker of the Lago and Whitehead Advertising Agency, Wichita, Kansas; John R. Sweet of the Penn State Outing Club, State College, Pennsylvania; Mark Fawcett of the Buck Ridge Ski Club, Chadds Ford, Pennsylvania, who lent me valuable out-of-print guidebooks; James T. Floyd, Chief, Information/Education, Florida Game and Fresh Water Fish Commission; Ralph Frese, who runs the Chicagoland Canoe Base and who made numerous excellent suggestions, plus supplying important data; and Wolf G. Bauer, of Seattle, Washington, who loaned me his personal maps and other material.

By the time the reader gets to them, I hope that "modern improvements" and "multiple uses" will not have encroached upon waters I have suggested in this chapter. In pointing out canoe opportunities throughout the United States and in Canada, I have tried to foresee the ravages of the dam builders, the road contractors, the shopping-center architects and the housing developers who may have piled tons of fill into a waterway or dammed it to create another lake for water skiing and motorboat racing. Where errors of this type occur in Chapter XVII, I am solely responsible.

I am indebted, too, to my son, Bill, who took time out from engineering studies to do the drawings.

To my wife, Eleanor, go special thanks. Not only did she take many of the photographs but she put to adept use her knack of correctly placing commas and hyphens while proofreading the manuscript and the galley proofs.

Without the unstinting assistance of these people, this book would have remained nothing more than a streamside dream of mine.

B. R.

Contents

POLE, PADDLE
& PORTAGE

Chapter I

The Profile of a Canoe

IT'S TRADITIONAL, when writing about canoeing, to point out that the canoe is the most perfectly streamlined of all watercraft and that the basic lines of the Indian's birch-bark prototype have never been improved upon.

The first half of this statement is probably true, although an argument might be forthcoming from a kayak owner. As for the latter part, if it's interpreted to mean that modern man has never devised a substitute for the canoe it, too, is correct.

However, the twentieth-century canoe boasts a trueness of lines and a flowing of contours that was never attained in birch-bark craft. This is understandable when you consider the crudeness of aboriginal tools and the technological limitations of bark.* The birch-bark was a beautiful, practical and highly versatile canoe and some of the romance went out of the North when it disappeared. Nevertheless, its shortcomings become all too apparent when one considers the durability and sturdiness of aluminum, Fiberglas, or wood-and-canvas canoes.

This isn't to say that *all* of today's canoes are paragons of graceful behavior on the water. Some are, in fact, little better than scows—difficult to paddle, heavy to portage, susceptible to wind, awkward to guide through fast water. It's obvious that some designers have never paddled their own products.

Unfortunately, to the unacquainted, all canoes of any given length look alike. They fail to realize that the canoe is a specialized craft, each type adapted to a particular task. Most first-time buyers decide upon a craft after weighing the pros and cons of aluminum, Fiberglas, wood-and-canvas. Length, price, and weight make up the final criteria. Rarely is

*For a definitive and fascinating study of birch-bark canoes, see Edwin Tappan Adney and Howard I. Chapelle, *The Bark Canoes and Skin Boats of North America* (Washington, D.C., The Smithsonian Institution, 1964), It is available from the Superintendent of Documents, Government Printing Office, Washington, D.C. 20402 ($3.25).

any thought given to the shape of the canoe, its beam, its depth amidship or its fullness, or lack of it, fore and aft. Yet these determine the ease with which it will handle, the load it will carry, the type of water it will navigate gracefully, and the safety it will afford.

Canoe Shapes

Figures 1 and 2 portray an angle from which few would-be buyers view a canoe. Sighting along the keel line is often a revelation. Note that, in Fig. 1, the bottom is relatively flat, this flatness extending well into the sides or chines. The sides, too, instead of rising in a vertical line, curve inboard. This is known as "tumblehome."

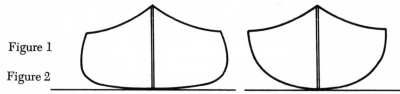

Figure 1

Figure 2

On the other hand, note the roundness of the bottom in Fig. 2 and the sides which rise vertically, lacking tumblehome. The visual difference between these two canoes now becomes obvious, even to a beginner, but what does it mean?

Figures 1 and 2 are somewhat exaggerated for clarity. The canoe in Fig. 1, with its flat bottom, can be capsized only by a concerted effort. The paddler will have to lean out over the side and literally pull the canoe over with him as he falls. Stability, then, comes with the flat bottom. Such a canoe has a shallow draft and handles more easily in flowing water since the current tends to slide under it rather than grasp it. Usually, too, it will carry a heavier load than the round-bottom craft in Fig. 2.

The latter, however, has its place. For one thing, it is faster—witness the rounded lines of a racing shell. Especially when tipped slightly to one side in a racing trim, it will respond more readily to the paddle and is thus ideally suited for racing or as a general-purpose craft for a skilled paddler who likes speed. However, due to its increased draft and relatively limited load-carrying capacity, it is not popular for long-distance cruising.

There are those who argue that "flat-bottom stability is a fallacy." The fact remains, however, that a properly laden flat-bottom canoe is more stable than its round-bottom counterpart similarly loaded. Those favoring the round bottom insist that proper placement of weight will stabilize almost any canoe. This is true. It's also true that proper weight distribution further enhances the inherent stability of the flat-bottom craft.

"Tumblehome" is a delightful word. It makes almost anyone sound like an expert and, probably because of this, tumblehome has been over-stressed by many who insist vaguely that a canoe "must have suitable tumblehome." Invariably, they fail to explain tumblehome or the purpose which it serves. This inboard curvature of the canoe's sides adds struc-tural strength, and the more tumblehome the easier it is to wield a paddle. However, too much tumblehome will allow water to slop over the sides, even in a light blow. Lack of tumblehome means a slightly longer reach with the paddle but, on the other hand, minimal tumblehome, or even sides that flare outward, will prevent this slopping and even turn away small waves.

At any rate, anyone about to buy his first canoe should examine it from the viewpoints of Fig. 1 and 2 —for stability and load capacity, the flat bottom; for ease of handling and greater speed, the rounded hull. However, this is not yet the point of final decision.

If paddling is to be done primarily on lakes or on rivers with slow currents, the lines of the canoe in Fig. 3 should be considered. Note that the keel line is quite flat, following the base line of the drawing for much

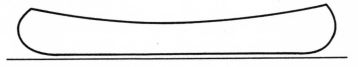

Figure 3

of the canoe's length. This straight keel line minimizes side-drift in a wind and helps to hold the craft on course. Combining the qualities of the canoes in Fig. 1 and 3, therefore, produces a craft well suited to extended cruising on open water.

By way of contrast, the keel line in Fig. 4 touches the drawing's base line only at the center. This is known as a "rocker" design, built for river work usually without a keel. The upswept lines of this canoe (the

Figure 4

drawing is exaggerated for clarity) permit it to pivot readily when dodging obstructions or seeking a passageway in turbulent rapids.

This is one design which corroborates the claim that the white man "has never improved the basic lines of the Indian canoe." The rocker-type canoe is a modification of the birch-bark "crooked canoe" of the Ungava Cree and Montagnais Indians of Canada, built for use in the rapids-filled rivers of the Northeast. Manitou help the poor Indian, though, who attempted to navigate a windswept lake in this craft. The high ends became sails for the wind to grasp and made the canoe an abomination to handle. For use in heavy rapids, however, the design was faultless and has been adapted to modern river canoes.

The craft in Fig. 5 and 6 are the same length and beam, yet their

Figure 5

handling qualities are quite unlike. In Fig. 5, the sharp taper of the hull toward the stem and stern makes for easier paddling and greater speed, especially if combined with a round bottom. Some experts insist that about three-fourths of a canoe's capacity is borne amidship and that the

Figure 6

bow serves only to cut and displace water. They maintain that beam, carried well forward and aft as in Fig. 6, makes for a canoe that responds sluggishly to the paddle and one that is difficult to paddle into a headwind. There may be more than a token of truth in this theory but the bow and stern have a greater function than merely to part and displace water.

For example, a full or wide bow will lift more readily over oncoming waves. Such a stern, too, will rise more easily in a following sea. A narrow bow, in such water, will tend to bite into the waves rather than lift over them; a narrow stern will allow following seas to slop into the craft, particularly when the canoe is heavily laden. I'll grant that narrow lines make for easier handling and greater speed but, for load-carrying capacity in rough water, I much prefer that the beam be carried well forward and aft. The extra energy required to paddle this craft will hardly bring on utter exhaustion.

For a canoe to be used on extended trips, involving a variety of water—large open lakes, swift rivers, possibly occasional rapids—the characteristics of the canoe in Fig. 6, combined with those in Fig. 1 and 3, approach the ideal. For use primarily on rivers, with the certainty of rapids, some degree of rocker, as shown in Fig. 4, should be substituted for a flat keel line.

The lines depicted in Fig. 7 are characteristic of a canoe with a "broken

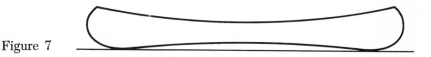

Figure 7

back," usually an abused wood-and-canvas craft. Note that the base line of the drawing touches only at the stem and stern but not amidship. Chances are, ribs have been broken or cracked along the chine line and that the planking has been split. The possibility of such a canoe breaking up in rough water is imminent. "Hogged" in this manner, a canoe is generally beyond repair.

Canoes made for leisurely paddling on sheltered waters often have high peaks fore and aft, as shown in Fig. 8-A. These are graceful lines

Figure 8   A   B

which lend themselves to colorful decorating schemes. This beauty, however, is obtained at a price. On a quiet lagoon high ends present no problem, but on a large lake winds tend to grasp them and buffet the canoe about. By way of contrast, the low profile in Fig. 8-B, characteristic of the guide's or utility models, offers less resistance to wind, even if it is not as pleasing to the eye.

Keels

In order to minimize side-slip, a keel is necessary on windy waters. However, it becomes a nuisance in fast water since it gives the current an added purchase on the canoe and, worse yet, it hinders the canoeman's "side-push," a thrust of the paddle or pole aimed at setting the canoe over broadside to avoid rocks or to seek a passageway. However, only rarely is a canoe confined entirely to lake work or to river travel. Obviously, one without a keel must sometimes be used on open water and, as frequently, a canoe with a keel finds itself in swift currents. Such a compromise is necessary·and not impossible.

The standard keel on a wood-and-canvas canoe is about ¾-inch thick, sometimes tapered to about ⅝-inch and about ⅞-inch deep (Fig. 9).

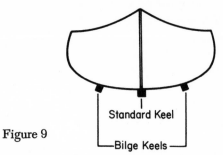

Figure 9

Keels on aluminum canoes are generally about the same depth but considerably thinner (Fig. 10). Fiberglas canoe keels vary greatly,

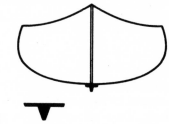

Figure 10

ranging from a slight longitudinal bulge to a pronounced ridge, often molded in primarily to lend rigidity to the hull.

For a "compromise" canoe, the shoe keel, shown in Fig. 11-A and 11-B,

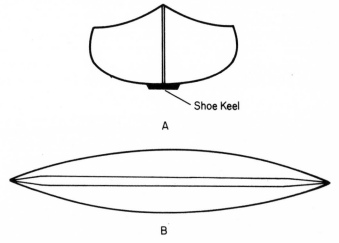

Figure 11

comes into its own. This varies in width from 2 to 4 inches and is usually about ⅝-inch thick. It is, of course, tapered to a point at each end. This keel slows side-drift somewhat yet it permits a canoeman his side-thrust with reduced resistance. It also allows a sharp turn with the canoe, although pivoting is not as easy as with a keel-less craft. The width of the shoe keel is an asset on rocky streams, where it affords protection for a wood-and-canvas canoe. It is available on most canvas canoes and on a few aluminum models.

Bilge keels, shown in Fig. 9 and 12, are rarely seen nowadays but offer

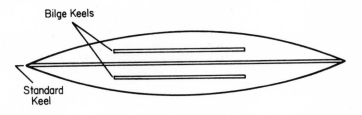

Figure 12

interesting possibilities. They are usually a "do-it-yourself" project among owners of wood-and-canvas canoes. Dimensions vary according to the whims of the canoeman. I've seen such keels 1¼-inch thick, 2 inches deep, and some 5 feet long. They are attached in pairs, one on each side, just inside the chine line, the purpose being to protect the canvas. Trappers use them on canoes that may be dragged over beaver dams or landed frequently on rocky shores. Unfortunately, these added keels make for a canoe that answers a paddle like a barge! At any rate, the coming of aluminum and Fiberglas canoes has pretty well started bilge keels down the road to oblivion.

Makers of aluminum and Fiberglas canoes may be justly proud of their designs, but none has matched the efficiency of the open gunwale provided on wood-and-canvas canoes. This consists of two pieces, one running outside the canoe (outwale) and the other inside (inwale), with the rib ends rising flush between them (Fig. 13). Space between the ribs

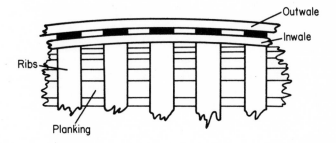

Figure 13

is left open for almost instant draining when the canoe is overturned on shore.

The author and his wife, Eleanor, examine a canoe under construction at the Old Town plant. Note that rib ends have not yet been trimmed, nor outer gunwales attached.

Aluminum and Fiberglas canoes usually have solid gunwales, often of one piece, with small drain holes at strategic locations. Bits of debris, leaves and twigs tend to clog these, however, and complete draining is slow.

Sizes and Weights

One of the most frequent questions is "How big a canoe shall I buy?" There is only one answer . . . the biggest one you can lift gracefully. Unlike other watercraft, canoes are taken from the water when not in use. Because of their relative susceptibility to damage, mooring them at a dock or along a beach is impractical. Too, many are used as car-top craft and, of course, there are portages with which to contend.

Contrary to popular belief, short hulls—purchased because they are light—do not handle well on the water. The shorter the craft, the narrower its proportional beam usually is, the less its capacity, and the lower it will sit in the water when laden. Two men, for example, fishing from an 11- or 13-footer, may find that their angling trip has deteriorated into a balancing act! For one-man use, the shorter canoes are suitable for fishing, hunting, and limited travel, but for two or more persons and their gear, the longer the canoe the better.

Canoes in 11- to 16-foot lengths are generally classified as car-top craft, weighing as little as 35 pounds and up to about 75, depending upon size and hull material. Such canoes can be lifted and carried easily by one man, once he learns the knack of swinging one up to his shoulders. For general sport use, however, the shortest canoes to be recommended are the 15- to 16-footers and, for a family craft, 17- to 18-foot models.

Probably the finest canoe for all-round use is the guide's model, available in wood-and-canvas, aluminum, or Fiberglas in 17- and 18-foot lengths. Most 18-footers will weight up to 85 pounds, although certain aluminum models tip the scales at under 70.

Canoes in the 19- to 20-foot range, weighing about 100 pounds, are suited, in fact, are necessary, for extended or expedition-type trips but it will take a husky expert to tote one single-handedly over a portage. Naturally, if there will always be a second person at hand to assist with carrying and launching, a canoe's weight takes on diminishing importance.

Freight canoes, used in the far North, are made up to 26 feet long, weigh some 160 pounds or more and will carry a pay load of well over a

Indian guides use freighter canoes on James Bay for hauling heavy loads. Canadian Government Travel Bureau photo.

ton, usually to the roar of an outboard motor. War canoes, their proportions not unlike those of the freighters except for a smaller beam, are popular at boys' and girls' camps for pageants, group trips, and for racing.

Two other interesting craft are the North and Montreal canoes, 26 and 34 feet long respectively, manufactured by Ralph Freese of Chicago. These are authentic replicas, in Fiberglas, of the great fur trade canoes that plied between Montreal and the Northwest when beaver was king. Although of glass construction, every detail of birch bark and even the gunwale lashings are simulated accurately. Ralph races these canoes with his crew of nine Indians and doesn't often lose!

One canoe that deserves more than passing mention is the Prospector. This is not a brand-name but a type developed in Canada and still sold extensively in wood-and-canvas construction. It long ago acquired the reputation for being "the workhorse of the North" and is now finding acceptance among sportsmen, and well it might.

My own Prospector, for instance, is a 16-footer (they're available up to 20 feet), is 2 inches wider than conventional 16-foot models and 2 inches deeper amidship. It is capable of loads equalling those of most 18-footers yet it weighs only 75 pounds. Primarily a river canoe without a keel, it is a delight to handle in running water. One of the puzzles of my life is that aluminum-canoe manufacturers have not come up with a similarly-proportioned craft. It could justifiably be touted as the safest canoe afloat!

Capacities

Regrettably, a few manufacturers are willing to give their customers a dunking by grossly exaggerating capacity ratings in their catalog descriptions. Having used one on Maine's St. John River, I've no doubt that a 26-footer will safely haul a ton load, but scaling capacity down proportionally, solely on the basis of length, is dangerous misrepresentation. At a Minneapolis sportsmen's show some years ago, I examined a 17-foot Fiberglas craft with a 10-inch midship depth whose maker claimed a 1,000-pound capacity for it. Such a load would have sunk it at the dock!

When a canoe is overloaded, buoyancy and stability depart hand in hand; freeboard, the distance from the water to the gunwale amidship (Fig. 14), decreases to the point where even small waves slop inboard,

Figure 14

thus adding dangerous live weight. Naturally, such an overburdened craft responds badly to the paddle, fails to lift properly in heavy seas and becomes unmanageably cranky. Trouble mounts progressively.

Length, beam, flatness and width of the bottom, fullness fore and aft all contribute to capacity and steadiness, but even more important is depth amidship. This is where safe freeboard should be determined. Micmac Indians were aware of this and built some of their canoes with a "hogged" sheer, with gunwales 3 to 4 inches higher amidship than fore or aft.

Some canoe makers, vaguely mindful that depth has some bearing on saleability, include "maximum depth" or "extreme depth" in their specifications, some of these ranging up to 16 or 17 inches. Closer examination, however, reveals that these "depths" are measured at the bow or stern peak, not in the vital mid-section where the actual depth is often as little as 10 or 11 inches.

Short of placing a canoe in the water and loading it until freeboard measures about 6 inches, there seems to be no layman's formula for determining capacity, although one oversimplified rule of thumb calls for multiplying the canoe's weight by 10—interesting but probably inaccurate.

As guidelines to canoe capacity, there follow charts of canoe dimensions and capacities as supplied by manufacturers. Generally, these are quite realistic although tending somewhat toward the optimistic. A few are obviously exaggerated and these are so indicated. It should be borne in mind, however, that these capacities are *maximum* ratings in most cases. For extensive travel on open water or for negotiating rapids, the rule of "six-inch freeboard" should apply, regardless of "catalog capacity."

On paper 600 pounds may hardly appear to be a full load for a canoe. In this case, consider that 600 pounds is six times more than the average man can lift; or better yet, visualize 600 pounds as three 200-pound men. The weight-to-canoe-size ratio then becomes easier to grasp.

CANOE DIMENSIONS AND CAPACITIES

Wood-and-Canvas Canoes

Length	Beam	Depth	Weight	Capacity
11 feet	34 inches	12 inches	35 pounds	350 pounds
12	32	12	50	400
14	32	12	60	500
14	34	13	60	600
15	34	12	65	600
15	35	13½	70	650
15	37	12	55	700
16	34	12	70	600
16	36	12	70	700
16	36	13	80	850
16	36	14	75	850
17	35	12	75	650
17	37	14½	85	950
18	36	13	85	1000
18	37	12	80	700
18	38	15	90	1100
20	37	13	105	1300
22	39	14	130	1500
24	40	14	150	1800
26	40	14	160	2000

Aluminum Canoes

Length	Beam	Depth	Weight	Capacity
13	35	13	44	760†
13	35	13	58	750†
13	36	13	57	750†
15	35	12	55	905†
15	35	12	69	890†
15	36	13	69	900†
15	36	12	73	580
17	36	13	60	1064†
17	36	13	75	1050†
17	37	13	78	1060†
17	37	12	86	790
17	37½	13½	72	1050†
18	36½	13	67	1158†
18	36½	13	85	1146†
20	40	14	115	1600†

Note: While capacity ratings marked (†) may not be "grossly exaggerated," they should be considered absolute maximums for travel on sheltered waters only. For extended cruises, on wind-swept lakes or in rapids, these should be reduced by at least 10 percent.

Fiberglas Canoes

Length	Beam	Depth	Weight	Capacity
11	40½	12	45	425
13	35	12	58	575
13½	31	11½	50	400
14	34	12	89	825*
15	34	12	60	850*
15	36	12	69	750
16	33	11½	60	600
16	35	13	70	800†
16	36	12	86	700
16	36	13	99	925†
17	35	12½	68	1000†
17	35½	12½	80	850
17½	34	13	75	900†
18	38½	12	85	1000†
20½	39	15	95	1500

Note: Those capacities marked (*) can be considered exaggerated and should be reduced by at least 20 percent. Those marked (†) should be considered as absolute maximums on placid waters only.

Length, beam, tumblehome, and capacities can all be evaluated quite easily by the practiced eye but one factor which cannot is the canoeman's skill. Another is varying opinion among canoe users.

A skillful paddler can make the most skittish craft behave with the docility of a plough horse. Another expert may consider him a fool for even stepping into such a craft. Some years ago, I spent a few days on my back lawn scraping and re-finishing my 18-foot Kennebec, whose 34-inch beam and fairly rounded bottom made her a delight to handle. My neighbor, a guide for some 30 years, strolled over to view the process. He paused a moment while his eyes roved quickly over the craft. "That," he proclaimed, "is a fool-killer!"

I'd used the canoe for ten years, on quiet lagoons, on wind-lashed lakes and in thrashing rapids. Old *Head Winds,* except on one occasion, had never shipped water dangerously. Opinions vary.

Chapter II

Canvas, Metal, or Glass?

IT COMES as a surprise to many that the North American Indian, in fashioning a birch-bark canoe, framed it with wooden ribs and planking—his design the forerunner of our wood-and-canvas canoes.

It was easier for the Indian to choose a canoe than it is for a modern sportsman. After all, he had the choice of only one fabric—birch bark.* Today's canoeman must choose from among all wood, wood-and-canvas, aluminum, Fiberglas, plywood, and rubber. And, although most of these materials have been used in canoe construction for at least twenty years, misconceptions persist.

For example, there is a general belief that an aluminum canoe is invariably lighter than its wood-and-canvas or Fiberglas counterpart. This is true only in the case of the so-called "lightweight" models whose aluminum skins are about .032-inch thick. Standard weight aluminum canoes, with hulls .051-inch thick, generally match the weight of canvas canoes and are, in fact, often heavier than some of the new Fiberglas designs.

Amazingly enough, the lightest commercially built canoe today is not aluminum, but, rather, an 11-foot wood-and-canvas model weighing a mere 35 pounds, some 9 pounds lighter than any other of its length, and comparable in weight to a fine birch-bark canoe of a hundred and fifty years ago. However, it is planked with relatively fragile ⅛-inch cedar and its capacity is only about half that of an 11-foot aluminum canoe. Obviously, then, there's more to choosing a canoe than consideration of weight.

*Where white birch was scarce or nonexistent, the barks of chestnut, elm, and hickory were sometimes used, although they presented difficulty in forming.

Wood-and-Canvas Canoes

A favorite theme of canoeing writers is ". . . the passing of the canvas canoe . . ."—a premature dirge, in view of the continuing popularity of wood-and-cloth. Although aluminum and Fiberglas canoes far outnumber all others there remains a surprisingly steady demand for wood. Wooden craft offer a far greater variety of models and lengths from which to choose. This variety, in fact, is as great as that of aluminum and Fiberglas combined, although most of the wooden canoes are Canadian-built. It is, for instance, difficult to find a 16-foot aluminum canoe; Fiberglas craft over 17 feet long are scarce. However, there can be no doubt that since wood-and-canvas construction is largely a hand operation marked by spiraling labor costs, wood-and-canvas canoes must someday fall victim to automation.

Some of us accept new ideas reluctantly, or not at all, and this is one reason for the continued production of wood-and-canvas craft. Older canoemen, particularly, sneer at aluminum or Fiberglas but their number is diminishing.

However, there are more valid reasons for the persistence of wooden canoes on our waters. One of these is the craft's inherent quietness. A skilled paddler can slip one along soundlessly, an asset in hunting or wildlife photography. Less tangible, but understandable, is the warmth many feel for a fine piece of wood craftsmanship, the grain of cedar and spruce, the shine of new varnish.

There are very practical aspects to the continued use of wood-and-canvas. Not as buoyant as an aluminum canoe, a wooden craft maintains better headway against wind and is generally less susceptible to its whims. Following a guide's competition in Maine, one of the losers of the single-canoe race—he'd used an aluminum craft for the first time—told me: "Fer every two feet I drove 'er forward, the wind set me back two . . ."

The wooden canoe's ability to stay afloat when capsized is well known. Even when completely awash, it will support the weight of at least one adult *in the craft* and several more clinging to it from in the water, this without the aid of air chambers or flotation material.

Some would have you believe that canoe canvas is little tougher than a lace curtain and that catastrophe lies in wait at every white-water pitch. But a canvas canoe slides off rocks with remarkably little damage, usually leaving only a little paint to mark its errant course. A direct and firm blow against a sharp rock is required to effect an actual cut. Contusions, abrasions, and scrapings are badges of honor on taut canvas, later to be hidden by a fresh coat of paint.

Minor damage is easily repaired. In an emergency, patching the canvas may require only a piece of shirt-tail and spruce pitch. A repair kit, consisting of canvas patches and cement, can be tucked handily into one of the peaks. Anyone moderately handy with tools can effect major repairs, including the replacement of ribs and planking, the latter two available from some canoe manufacturers. Re-canvasing is a tedious chore, hardly a hobby pastime, but not impossible. Many canoemen now replace wornout or damaged canvas with Fiberglas, easier to work and tougher than cotton fabrics. On the whole, however, the sturdiness of wood-and-canvas canoes is greatly underrated.

Planking, in standard models, ranges from $\frac{5}{32}$-inch to $\frac{3}{16}$-inch in thickness, generally of red cedar. Only ultra-light canoes have ⅛-inch planking. However, even $\frac{3}{16}$-inch planking might appear to be flimsy until the rib structure, which backs the planking, is examined. Ribs range from ¼-inch to ⅜-inch in thickness, 1½ to 2 inches in width, spaced as close as 1½ inches apart. For extra strength, half-ribs may be installed at the factory, these being placed between the regular ribs in the midship floor area.

Canvas weight varies according to the size of the canoe and the use to which it will be put. On smaller canoes, No. 8 or No. 6 canvas is applied with the heavier No. 4 fabric utilized on freighters and other larger canoes. This is heavily impregnated with a filler to "kill the weave" for a smooth finish and then coated with marine enamel and varnish. Thus, it can hardly be said that a wood-and-canvas canoe is a fragile thing.

One American canoe maker is currently offering Dacron in place of canvas as an optional covering, thus reducing weight by as much as 12 pounds in a 15-footer. Also available, for added resistance to snags in low-water streams, is a covering of polypropylene-fiber reinforced plastic, somewhat lighter than canvas but tougher.

Despite their enthusiasm for the craft, owners of wood-and-canvas canoes are not blind to the shortcomings of their favorites. They admit that there is a limit to the abuse which canvas will withstand and this limit is far short of that of aluminum or Fiberglas. Without contradicting earlier claims, canvas can be punctured by ramming the canoe against a sharp rock, and repeated blows, even against a smooth ledge, will weaken, split, or crack ribs and planking. Another criticism aimed at wood-and-canvas is that it takes on weight with age. This is true since the cedar and spruce used in the hull will absorb moisture unless kept tightly sealed with paint or varnish.

Maintenance of a wood-and-canvas canoe must be a labor of love. Anyone who doesn't enjoy scraping, sanding, painting, and varnishing should look to another type. One of the annual springtime chores I relished as a guide was the refinishing of my canoe. It marked the end of the long northern winter and heralded the approach of a new fishing and canoe-trip season. The process was lengthy, however, calling for the complete removal of all varnish and paint, inside and out. This was followed by sanding, repainting, and revarnishing. "Making a new one out of an old one," however, won't be enjoyed by everyone. Nor, do all canoemen have the time to devote to this almost annual chore.

A wood-and-canvas canoe left overturned on the bare ground will absorb the ground's moisture. Rot will set in at the peaks and along the ground-touching gunwale. If it is stored for any length of time in this manner, rocks or boards should be placed under the craft at those points where it touches the earth. Nor should one be left outdoors in areas where the snowfall is heavy, at least not without proper support underneath. Deep in Maine's Kennebago country still lie the remains of a canoe I left through one winter, having propped it suitably. When I returned in April to pick it up, I found only torn canvas, flattened ribs and planking. Someone had borrowed the canoe late in the fall, had returned it but failed to replace the supports. The weight of the winter's snow had crushed it.

Another hazard to which a canvas canoe should not be subjected is the hot summer sun. This will cause the paint to check and crack, particularly in the case of canoes left atop automobiles through much of the season.

Rarely seen nowadays but popular two generations ago is the cedar-strip canoe, probably one of the loveliest of all watercraft. Ribbed like a conventional canoe, it has planking of thin cedar strakes over which no covering is placed. Instead, the wood is sanded smooth and varnished to a high gloss. Waterproofing is attained through craftsmanship, by matching the planking strakes snugly. Usually built in 16-foot lengths with a 30-inch beam and weighing about 85 pounds, this canoe is used primarily for flat-water racing. It is not a craft to be left out under a hot sun or propelled recklessly in rock-strewn waters. The seats are laced with rawhide rather than conventional cane.

Following World War II, considerable hullaballoo accompanied the introduction of the plywood canoe but it never attained great popularity. Nonetheless, it is available and in some demand.

Two models are offered; one a 16-footer with 36-inch beam and 12-inch midship depth; the other a 17-foot craft with 32-inch beam and 12-inch depth. Weights are 65 and 57 pounds respectively, the greater weight of the shorter canoe due to its thicker mahogany plywood. The longer craft is constructed of two layers of mahogany veneer and two inner layers of birch, this type of construction is extremely sturdy for its weight. Since these are varnished inside and out, without fabric covering, they present some of the maintenance problems of the cedar-strip canoe.

Aluminum Canoes

Unquestionably, aluminum canoes outnumber all other types. An outgrowth of the World War II aircraft industry, they have caught the imagination of thousands, and for good reason.

They can be dragged across gravel bars or bounced off rocks with little, if any, damage. Maintenance is practically nil. They never need painting unless a change of color is desired, and rot need not be feared. Leaving one exposed to weather indefinitely creates no problems, although I suspect an extremely heavy snow load might crush one. Aluminum, of course, cannot take on weight through the absorption of moisture and, contrary to the belief of some, use in salt water does it no harm.

Evidence of the advantages of aluminum was obvious during the 1966 sportsmen's shows throughout the country when the Grumman Company displayed the "oldest aluminum canoe in existence." In service some twenty years at the hands of an active Maine sportsman, it had evidently seen hard use yet it was still sound in every respect.

Probably no modern watercraft answers the helm as readily as an aluminum canoe. Paddling one from a kneeling position amidship is a delight, so far as maneuverability is concerned, unless there is a stiff head wind. The craft will pivot, leap ahead, or stop with the agility of a superbly trained quarter horse. Most have good lines—ample beam with fullness carried well fore and aft—so that they ride heavy seas well. Unlike wooden canoes, they are self-righting when tipped and, thanks to foam-filled compartments or air tanks in the peaks (under the seats and along the gunwales in some), they are unsinkable.

Aluminum is not without sin. For one thing, it is noisy. In a ripple, even if you paddle cautiously, the small waves slapping against the sides are a fair imitation of a distant machine gun; a blow of the paddle against the gunwale is not unlike the boom of a base drum. To most canoemen, however, this is of little consequence. In fact, one white-water paddler pointed this out as an asset. "When I hear a hollow thump ahead of me on the river," he said, "I know somebody's hit a rock or log and this puts me on my guard. . . ."

Because the lightened bow—necessary when poling upstream in rapids—is easily buffeted about by the wind, an aluminum canoe is not ideal for poling. Another annoyance is the metal's propensity toward sticking on rocks upon which it may be driven. Too, aluminum's ability to conduct heat and cold is somewhat of a shortcoming. Left under a hot sun, the metal is not pleasant to contact and, conversely, paddling in a kneeling position shortly after "ice out" will bring a quick chill to the knees. Knee pads will overcome such drawbacks of course, and generally the other annoyances are shrugged off by most canoemen, the advantages by far overshadowing these relatively minor deficiencies.

The aluminum canoe's ability to right itself almost instantaneously can have serious consequences, however. A strong wind may blow it out of reach before the dunked canoeman can grasp it.

The durability of an aluminum canoe borders on the incredible but it does have limitations. Like any other canoe fabric, it is not indestructible.

Because of the craft's reputation for sturdiness, inexperienced canoemen are sometimes lured by a false sense of security and attempt foolhardy stunts. During the summer of 1966, a young camper drowned in the Penobscot River while attempting to run rapids around which I prefer to carry. When his canoe was retrieved, its bow had been folded upward as if it were tinfoil! All in all, the aluminum canoe is a marvelous development in watercraft but completely lacking in the characteristics of the bulldozer.

Fiberglas Canoes

Fiberglas canoes got off to a poor start and, regrettably, there are still more bad designs than good ones. Early models, and some current ones, include awkward and graceless gunwales and keels of cast aluminum. Even if their ugly appearance could be forgiven, their weight is impossible to overlook. Also, laminations were not always the product of proud craftsmen and all too frequently peeled following slight damage. However, Fiberglas seems to have found itself and better designs are appearing.

The Lincoln canoe, for instance, has proved itself in wild, "hellahoopin'" white-water competition. The unique Indian brand Fiberglas canoe of simulated birch bark is attractive, has good lines and is of reasonable weight. Old Town's placing of polyurethane foam in the gunwales as well as in the peaks has produced sensible distribution of flotation material. More and more, Fiberglas canoes are approaching the excellent designs of the better wood-and-canvas and aluminum craft.

What's more, they are as maintenance-free as aluminum craft. Fiberglas won't deteriorate through exposure, although if repeatedly dragged up onto a gravel beach, the exterior finish may wear away, resulting in the parting of the laminated layers.

One little-known material coming into use for canoe construction is a thermoplastic laminate which makes possible a one-piece, seamless craft, comparable in weight to others of similar size. Quite frankly, I've not tested one of these but the material, developed by U.S. Rubber Co., is reported to be more rigid and resistant to impact than either aluminum or Fiberglas. Color is "built-in" and a "uni-cellulor" core makes the canoe unsinkable. A 16-foot model, with 36-inch beam and 12½-inch depth, weighs 65 pounds. The seats are Fiberglas as are the decks and thwarts. The gunwales are vinyl.

Several firms offer canoe-building kits which include pre-cut frame members and covering fabric. While this kit-construction may be suitable for leisurely paddling on sheltered waters, it does not attain the sturdiness required in a canoe to be used on rough water.

All makers of canoes are naturally prone to glowing claims for their products but, despite these, no canoe material is indestructible and each fabric has qualities not found in the others. Specific requirements must govern individual choice.

Generally, though, an aluminum canoe is ideal for all-round pleasure use. For the canoeman with some degree of skill and a penchant toward the romantic, wood-and-canvas most closely approaches the Indian's birch-bark craft. For general use, and for rough-and-tumble canoeing—shooting rapids for thrills and in competition—and where canoes will be subject to other abuses, the choice rests between aluminum and Fiberglas. And, of course, for the paddler with special yearnings, the all-wood, strip or plywood craft may have greater appeal.

Chapter III

Trim for Travel

TO ANYONE who has heaped camping gear into a station wagon, loading a canoe would seem an equally simple and uncomplicated task. The modern car will handle a considerable load before its road trim or balance is affected but this is not true of a canoe. Proper loading is important not only to safety but to ease of handling and to portaging.

Many canoeists pile duffel into a canoe as if they were storing clutter in an attic. Two or three packs are deposited approximately amidship and around these are tucked dozens of items—axe, fishing rods, extra clothing, cook pots, binoculars and whatever else can't be jammed into a pack. The result is a canoe that sails with the grace of a leaky coal barge and is just about as easy to unload for a portage. Such haphazard loading techniques are a mark of the greenhorn.

Loading

Loading a canoe begins long before you reach the water's edge. It begins, in fact, during the planning stages when equipment and supply lists are made up. The first step is to eliminate non-essentials mercilessly, particularly if the cruise is to be an extended one; a diary that won't be written in or binoculars that won't be used, these should be culled.

Once all of the gear is assembled it should be sorted into two or three "departments." One, for example, should include food, cooking utensils, first-aid kit, waterproof matches, and other related items. A second should comprise the tent, sleeping bags and clothing, plus miscellaneous gear such as fishing tackle and camera. If necessary, a third pack may be organized but two are preferable.

The advantage of systematic organization becomes apparent when landing to make camp or to portage. At a campsite, one man unloads the "kitchen" pack and starts supper underway while his partner, deploying the second pack, sets up camp. On a portage, one partner "heists" the

Compact organization of camping gear eases the work of the portages. The author about to cross a carry with a full ten-day outfit. Photo by Eleanor Riviere.

lighter of the two packs and the canoe; the second man totes the heavier pack, plus the spare paddle, fishing rods, or rifles if these are included on

The author and his wife reload their canoe at the end of a portage, with the craft fully afloat and parallel to shore

the trip. All in all, system makes travel easier. One of my early canoe partners stated the case clearly: "One trip over a carry is a genteel sufficiency!"

Once actual loading is about to begin, the canoe should be placed parallel to the shore if at a beach, and fully afloat. Water provides an even support of weight and this is vital to the lifespan of a wooden canoe. Putting a heavy load aboard a partially beached craft strains the unsupported midsection and will eventually break the canoe's back. Fiberglas and aluminum canoes will stand such abuse but it is, nevertheless, poor canoemanship. Pushing a loaded aluminum canoe over gravel into the water will do little harm beyond scratching paint but treating a Fiberglas canoe in this manner will result in abrasive wear to its outer finish and subsequent peeling. As for canvas canoes, such treatment is downright abusive. Another advantage of loading with the craft fully afloat is that trim can be adjusted as gear is put aboard. When loading at a dock, the canoe should be tied at both ends, parallel to the dock.

If you've managed to pack your entire outfit into only two packs, the task of loading is simplified. These are placed amidship, centered so that the canoe does not list. If heavy rapids are anticipated, it's wise to tie them in. However, if there are several packs—and this may be necessary for a long-distance cruise—the heaviest is placed on the bottom just over the keel line. Smaller or lighter packs are then located about it in such a manner that the craft does not list. If possible, the packs should not protrude above the gunwale line, thus presenting a low profile to crosswinds. The packs may be covered with a light tarp and tied in.

A well loaded canoe—gear compactly stored amidship and securely tied in. Grumman Co. photo.

A 50-foot length of ¼-inch manila or ³⁄₁₆-inch nylon rope should be standard equipment in all cruising canoes. Dozens of uses will be found for it in camp but, afloat, it becomes inexpensive insurance. None of us plans to capsize and a well handled canoe will not, but there's always the possibility. Tying in the gear will guarantee that it will remain in possession: Rounding up runaway sleeping bags, tent, and grub along a mile or two of brush-lined riverbank doesn't add much to the pleasure of a canoe trip!

If lake travel lies ahead, with strong winds and heavy oncoming seas, stow the gear so that the bow rides slightly higher than the stern, taking into consideration the weight of the paddlers. A light bow will lift more readily over the waves. The same trim applies to loading for upstream travel. With the bow slightly out of water, the current has a less effective grasp on the canoe and it becomes easier to guide it into passages or around obstructions. For downwind travel on large lakes an "even trim" is best, while a light stern is preferable for downstream running in swift currents.

Freeboard has already been discussed, but at shoving-off time the temptation to overload may arise. The recommended 6-inch freeboard may then shrink to 5, or possibly 4 inches—an invitation to disaster. Don't forget, 6 inches is an appallingly short distance between gunwale and cold water! Anything less is foolhardy. For a graphic illustration of this, hold a ruler vertically on a desk or table and note the 6-inch mark.

Loading in the quiet of a lee shore is, of course, working under ideal conditions—not always possible. A strong onshore breeze may be kicking up a nasty surf, in which case it's best to wait for the wind to abate. If it's absolutely necessary that loading and departure take place, the canoe may then be partially beached with its bow (or stern) pointing directly into the surf. It should be far enough up on the beach so that it does not bob or rock. It is then loaded as quickly as possible. With one partner on each side, the canoe is then grasped amidship and lifted slightly to clear the beach and slipped into the water. Without releasing the canoe, both partners then clamber aboard. This means wet feet, of course, but soggy moccasins have never deterred eager canoemen!

Flying spray and rain may eventually build up a puddle in the bilge possibly soaking through the packs. Several solutions are possible. The entire outfit can be wrapped in a lightweight plastic tarpaulin. Lacking this, the tent may be used as a wrapper. A wet shelter can be dried and erected with some inconvenience but wet sleeping bags or a soaked grub supply present far worse prospects. A third solution is to lay three or four poles, 5 to 6 feet long and 2 inches in diameter, in the bottom of the canoe. The duffel bags are then placed atop these. Bilge water may slosh between the poles but wetting of the gear will be minimal.

Boarding

Contrary to the preachings of some safety experts, boarding a canoe is not a tightrope act nor should the craft be looked upon as a skittish cow pony eager to toss its rider. Exaggerated caution usually results in outright lack of confidence and often a dunking. This "be sure to step in the middle" advice continually being dinned into the public mind is nonsense.

At a sportsmen's show some years ago, I watched a pair of Red Cross "experts" demonstrate canoeing technique in the show's tank. The audience, typically ignorant of canoeing, was highly impressed as each demonstrator carefully held the craft for the other as he boarded. They stepped gingerly into its exact keel line and slowly lowered themselves into kneeling positions. The two then paddled about the tank with the spirit of slow-motion robots. They disembarked with equal deliberation. The remarks I heard from watching Nova Scotia guides were not flattering! Slated for a jousting event to follow, one of them leaped nimbly aboard the same canoe, paddle in hand and with hardly a waver, streaked around the pool in a standing position. It was a grandstand play by an extroverted guide, I'll grant, but he did manage to undo some of the misleading teachings of the "experts."

All of which is to say: "Board a canoe as if you expected to succeed!" It's not necessary to step into the exact centerline nor do you need to hold your breath. The Nova Scotia guide's technique isn't recommended for all but there is a middle ground.

Traditionally, and for practical reasons, the stern man holds the canoe while the bow paddler steps aboard, adopting either a kneeling or sitting position. Then he, in turn, steadies the craft while the stern partner boards. When disembarking, the stern man alights first. This sequence isn't imperative but, since the stern paddler is generally considered "in charge" it is up to him to see that the canoe is ready to shove off or properly poised for landing. If a passenger is to be carried, he boards first, followed by the bow man, then the stern paddler. In landing, the passenger disembarks last. Experienced canoemen go through this procedure automatically, rarely giving it a second thought.

In boarding at a beach or gravel bar, one of the little niceties that is also automatic with experts, is the rinsing of sand and grit from shoes. One foot at a time is "swished" in the water for a moment so that the soles are washed clean. This eliminates gritty sand or tiny pebbles which might otherwise scratch a varnished or painted surface.

Landing

A favorite landing technique of novices, particularly in boys' and girls' summer camps, calls for driving a canoe up onto the beach. On a rocky shore or pebbly beach this is devastating to the bottom's finish! The canoe should be brought slowly to the beach or dock for a parallel landing. This doesn't mean a wide, sweeping approach. Experts paddle directly to the landing site and, just before contact is made, opposite sweeps of the bow and stern paddles swing the canoe into landing position. Skilled paddlers perform this landing with ease, often coming within an inch of the dock, yet not touching it.

Occasionally an emergency landing must be made, sometimes on a windward shore. Running before a severe windstorm may not allow time for a proper landing, particularly if heavy seas are breaking. It's wiser to seek a lee shore, of course, but this is not always possible. This, then, is another occasion that calls for wet feet in preference to a damaged or swamped canoe. As the craft enters shallow water, headed directly into shore, both paddlers brake its headway. The stern man then steps out holding his end of the craft. The bow man follows. The two move amidship on opposite sides of the canoe. It is then lifted slightly and eased up onto the beach, out of reach of the waves. With good timing, the waves will actually assist this maneuver. Attempting to land on a windward shore in the conventional manner is almost sure to result in damage to the canoe or a wetting of a duffel. Better wet feet than a wet bilge!

Needless to say, whenever a canoe is left on the beach, even for a few minutes, it should be pulled up out of reach of the waves or current. To do this easily, lift the shoreward end of the canoe waist-high and pull it in until the stern strikes bottom (gently!). Then set the bow down and the craft will stay in place. For an overnight stop or if large waves are breaking, the canoe should be retrieved from the water's edge entirely.

On the Kennebago River in Maine some years ago, I wished someone had given me that advice. Several canoeloads of guides and "sports" had gone ashore for lunch and I'd pulled my 18-foot *Head Winds* up onto a narrow beach.

"You plannin' to walk home tonight, Bill?" one of the other guides asked me casually, a few minutes later.

"No. Why?"

"I just saw your canoe headin' downriver. . ." Then the guffaws broke out as I glanced up to see my canoe sweeping gracefully around a bend, empty! It wasn't the half-mile pursuit in a borrowed canoe nor the subsequent upstream struggle with two canoes that bothered me, however. It's simply that I was never allowed to forget my carelessness.

For overnight stops, placing the canoe within the shelter of trees is better than overturning it on the beach where an unexpected night wind might roll it into the water. Lacking such shelter, it's wise to tie it down. Incidentally, a wooden canoe left overnight in bear country should be washed clean of any bits of fish viscera or scales which might linger following a successful day's angling. Bear love these tidbits and have no compunctions about tearing a canoe apart to get them!

Chapter IV

"Put the ash to 'er...!"

ROUNDING A wind-swept point and close-hauling into a stiff blow one canoe partner inevitably shouts to the other: "Put the ash to 'er. . . . !" It's not meant to be an order but, rather, a cry of exuberance; an acceptance of the challenge of the wind. It is heard at canoe races, at daredevil white-water competitions. Even in the far North as a canoe approaches a bend around which awaits the roar of wild water, someone cries out: "Put the ash to 'er. . . . !"

The cry is the same whether the paddles are ash, maple, birch, spruce, or even aluminum. In fact, cedar and pine occasionally find their way into paddle stock, sometimes as laminates. Most blades, however, are ash, maple, or spruce.

Paddle Construction

Though heavy, maple is the sturdiest, practically unbreakable even under the stress of a brawny paddler's arms. Maple is resilient too, with a limberness which canoemen often seek. Though not quite as sturdy as maple, ash is also limber and considerably lighter, hence the choice of many experts. Whether ash or maple is chosen, nearly all agree that a limber paddle is a must. Hand any knowing canoeman a paddle and he'll test it for springiness by bearing down on the shaft, propping the blade tip against one foot. If it gives appreciably, chances are he'll grunt approval.

He knows that with the start of every paddle stroke a slight almost imperceptible shock is transmitted to arms and shoulders, and the more flexible the paddle is (within reason, of course), the more this shock is absorbed by the springiness of the shaft and blade. This may seem a minor matter and some have pooh-poohed it, but it's a valid point, readily apparent at the end of a long day following stroke after stroke, hour after hour, mile after mile of paddling. Many canoemen like to give the paddle

27

blade an extra "flip," or final surge of power just before withdrawing it from the water. In order to attain extra flexibility, some even thin down the shaft at the throat where it joins the grip.

Maple and ash paddles are commonly available commercially although birch, which has much the same qualities, is difficult to find. Indians occasionally made paddles of cedar, and once in a while a pine paddle is encountered. Brittle and easily broken, neither is very satisfactory.

Racing canoemen, who maintain a fast prolonged pace, frequently choose spruce paddles for their lightness. These, however, are not the run-of-the-mill "store-bought" spruce paddles. Rather, they are of special design (Fig. 15), sometimes laminated for added strength.

Figure 15

The common solid spruce paddle, highly varnished, has earned the name of "pudding stick" among wilderness canoeists who fear its brittleness. However, the spruce paddle isn't to be discounted completely. It serves well in the hands of women who would tire quickly wielding a heavier blade and whose strength isn't likely to break the shaft. Youngsters, too, find the spruce paddle adequate and easy to use.

In recent years there have appeared clumsy imitations of laminated racing paddles. These are cheaply turned, often of inferior stock whose defects are hidden by a coat of paint or disguised by the over-use of varnish. They are the true "pudding sticks," stiff-shafted with heavy blades whose edges are almost a half-inch thick, guaranteeing a noisy "plop" every time the paddle is dipped. These are generally found in sporting goods stores, stacked helter-skelter in a drum. Whether of maple, ash, spruce, or laminates, the best paddles are generally obtained from canoe manufacturers or from dealers who are themselves canoemen first, salesmen second.

Developed from World War II life-raft paddles, aluminum blades with hollow shafts and wooden grips are becoming popular among racers and those who ride the wild waters of spring freshets.

Emergency or improvised paddles may, of course, be carved of almost any wood, depending upon skill with axe and knife. *Life* magazine once carried a photo series showing a Canadian Indian carving a paddle from a white-birch log, the entire operation from tree-felling to smoothing with a knife requiring only a half-hour! Few of us are such masters of the axe and knife. Nonetheless, a suitable emergency paddle can be carved from softwood such as spruce, or sturdier birch, in a reasonable length of time by a canoeman of moderate skill with cutting tools. How badly the paddle is needed will probably govern the skill which can be mustered!

The need for improvisation can be eliminated, however. Simply carry a spare.

The subject of blade-width has kept many a campfire discussion going far into the night. A wide blade will tire the paddler quickly, one side claims; a narrow blade, opponents counter, will take longer to get you there. Both are correct, of course.

Without doubt, it takes more energy to draw a wide blade through the water but, by the same token, the larger bearing surface will propel the canoe with greater speed, thus diminishing travel time between two given points. A canoe will also answer more quickly to a wide blade. The narrow blade is more than adequate, although not producing as much thrust, and it's easier to wield. Actually, such discussions, entertaining as they might be, are largely hypothetical. But lest I be accused of fence-straddling, I prefer a wide blade.

These range from 7 to 8 inches in width and are likely to be the choice of Northeastern canoemen, undoubtedly influenced by the early designs of the Micmac, Passamaquoddy, and Malecite Indians of eastern Canada and Maine (Fig. 16). Midwestern and Western paddlers are prone to

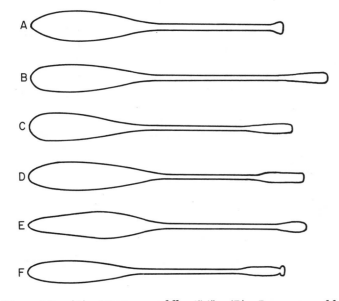

Figure 16   (A) Micmac paddle 5'4"; (B) Passamaquoddy, 6'4"; (C) Malecite, 5'7"; (D) Passamaquoddy, 5'11"; (E) Passamaquoddy, 6'; (F) Malecite, 5'6".

narrower blades which the western Cree, Ojibway, and Koutenai Indians favored (Fig. 17). Present-day blades range from 5½ to 7½ inches and are widely distributed so that choice can be made irrespective of geography. Depending upon the overall length of the paddle itself, blade lengths range from 26 to 30 inches.

The shape of the blade also comes in for its share of arguments even

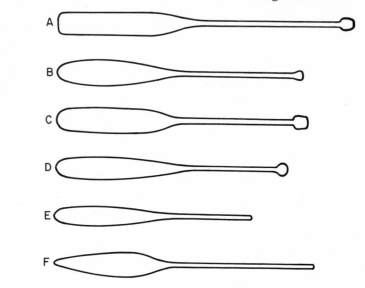

Figure 17   (A)   *Cree Indian paddle, 6'4"; (B)   Tetes de Boule, 5'3";*
              (C)   Ojibway,   5'4";   (D)   Western   Cree,   4'10";   (E)
              Western Cree woman's paddle, 4'3"; (F) Koutenai, 5'5".

though there are only three basic styles, with variations from these. The Maine Guide blade (Fig. 18-A) is closely patterned after the Micmac

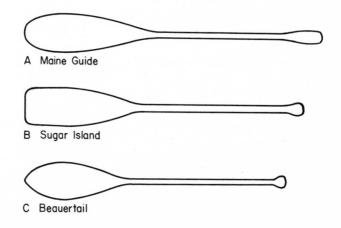

A Maine Guide

B Sugar Island

C Beavertail

Figure 18   (A)   *Maine Guide blade; (B)   Sugar Island blade;*
              (C)   Beavertail blade.

maple blade, not surprising since the Indian canoe builders of eastern Canada traveled in what is now the Pine Tree State. The Sugar Island blade (Fig. 18-B) somewhat resembles the Cree blade and is favored by racers. The Beaver-Tail (Fig. 18-C) seems to boast no traceable ancestry although it is not unlike the Maine Guide type. Many of the current crop of laminated and solid "pudding sticks" follow somewhat the lines of the Cree and Ojibway paddles, hardly flattering to some of the world's best canoemen!

For general use or cruising, the Maine Guide or Beaver-Tail is entirely suitable; for racing, the Sugar Island seems better to fit the quick beat used in competition. Any further statement regarding desirability of one or the other would be nothing more than added fodder for far-into-the-night but unresolvable discussions!

An examination of grips, however, takes on validity since these determine comfort of the paddler's hand and the efficiency with which he handles the paddle. One of the most comfortable is the Pear grip (Fig. 19-A) found on most paddles. Because of its rounded shape it can be grasped comfortably from almost any angle and affords a firm hold. Racing paddles are usually topped by a T grip (Fig. 19-B) which lends a still firmer grasp. The Flaring grip (Fig. 19-C) is quite flat-topped with a

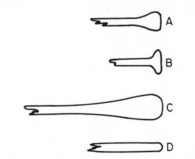

Figure 19

(A) Pear grip; (B) T grip;
(C) Flaring or flat-top grip;
(D) "Hoe handle" or In-
dian grip.

wide flaring of the shaft at the throat. This flaring is thinned considerably to add resiliency. Understandably not popular is the "hoe handle" grip peculiar to certain Indian paddles, this being nothing more than the absence of a grip (Fig. 19-D).

Heaping further fuel on the fire of contention is the matter of paddle length. The most frequently advanced theory calls for blades to reach the stern paddler's eyes; the bow paddler's chin. When Abraham Lincoln commented that a man's legs should be long enough to reach the ground he might well have applied the statement to canoe paddles. They should be long enough to reach the water without regard to a canoeman's eyes or chin, with which he does very little paddling.

For stern paddling, I prefer a 6-foot paddle, 1 inch longer than my height. With this I can conveniently paddle while standing, sitting, or

The author demonstrates that for paddling while standing a 6-foot paddle "is long enough to reach the water." Photo by Eleanor Riviere.

kneeling. It is long enough so that when I dip the blade, its entire surface, not just two-thirds of it, is in the water working. The long shaft affords excellent leverage and a greater reach for sweeps. It is equally important for the bow man to use an adequate paddle. With sufficient reach he can perform wonders of maneuvering not possible with overly-short paddles. All in all, I believe that canoemen will find their canoeing ability upgraded by the use of paddles whose lengths equal approximately their own height. At least, they should be long enough to reach the water!

Certain rules for choosing and caring for paddles are justifiably arbitrary. When buying a paddle, sight along the shaft toward the blade, making sure the latter is not off-center, a defect which appears frequently and subsequently leads the paddler to think that he's paddling with a hockey stick! Be certain, too, that the grain of the wood runs straight with the shaft and blade. A slight cross-grain makes the paddle an early candidate for kindling wood. As already pointed out, many "store-bought" paddles are highly varnished or painted. If such a paddle appears to have a straight grain and you like its "heft," buy it, then remove the finish from the shaft and grip with paint remover, followed by sanding.

If you feel that your paddle should have a protective coating, soak it thoroughly in water, then allow it to dry. This will raise the grain of the wood, which is then sanded again. Repeat two or three times or until the grain fails to rise. After the final sanding, rub the surface thoroughly with boiled linseed oil. Such a finish will not raise a crop of blisters. The process should be applied only to the shaft and grip, however. The blade is best protected by varnish or paint.

Keeping the blade tip from fraying will make for quiet and craftsman-like paddling. Such fraying or "fuzzing" results from poling with the paddle. Should this occur, the fuzzy edge can be trimmed with a sharp knife, then sanded for a smooth finish, followed by paint or varnish.

It is not surprising that more paddles are broken ashore than afloat because of the common habit of laying them on the beach. All too often someone steps on the shaft or blade. Paddles should always be leaned against a tree, pack, or the canoe to protect them from this hazard. Wet hardwood blades left to lie in the sun will warp almost immediately; they should be kept in the shade if possible. Storing paddles for extended periods calls for hanging them to eliminate the chance of warping. A temporary screw-eye, inserted atop the grip, can be slipped over a nail on a wall so that the paddle hangs freely. During woods trips paddles should be kept out of the reach of porcupines, which like to gnaw the grip and throat for the salt deposits left there by perspiration. The paddles can be brought into the tent or tied in pairs by a 4-foot length of twine and draped over a tree branch.

Paddling Techniques

Solo canoeists are much like churchgoers; they tend to gravitate to the rear seats. While this does not necessarily depreciate the value of worship, a lone canoeman in a 16-foot canoe finds himself with the bow in the air, in effect paddling a 10-foot canoe with a 6-foot bow overhang, about as precarious as standing on the gunwales! Because most canoes are

Paddling solo from the stern seat raises the bow dangerously high, in effect converting a 16' canoe to a 10' craft with a 6' overhang. Photo by Eleanor Riviere.

equipped with seats, beginners feel they must use them. Some, aware of the awkwardness and danger of paddling solo from the stern seat, perch themselves on the bow seat, facing astern. Since the bow seat is nearer amidship, this levels the canoe but paddling is difficult due to the wide beam at this point. Seats serve a purpose, but when a canoeman is alone he should shun them.

Pseudo-experts suggest that a heavy rock be loaded into the bow to balance the paddler's weight—the height of absurdity. If the suggestion were sound, the canoeman would have to lift rocks almost equal to his own weight before attaining suitable trim. In the event of a capsize, such a rock(s) might lodge under the bow seat and drag the bow down, leaving only the stern pointing skyward, for the paddler to cling to. Round stones might shift and throw the craft off balance, to say nothing of marring or gouging the interior surface. Finally, why propel needless dead weight?

Paddling solo from the stern seat is practical only when a passenger is carried or when a canoe cruising outfit is stowed forward. In an otherwise empty canoe, however, there are only two practical positions. One of these is the "cruising position," which calls for kneeling just aft of the center thwart, thus raising the bow only slightly. Kneeling should not be

directly over the keel, however, as this will level the craft and make paddling awkward. Kneel, instead, somewhat off-center so that the canoe lists to the paddling side. The degree of list, of course, depends upon the paddler's skill and, initially, it should be minimal, at least until he "gets the feel" of the craft. Paddling in this position is not only easier but results in greater speeds. When complete confidence is acquired, try it with the gunwale almost awash for the ultimate in canoeing!

The second midship position is the racing stance, the paddler on one knee, the other leg straddling the center thwart. This position results in

The single racing position. Photo by Eleanor Riviere.

better control and makes possible a hard drive with the paddle. It too calls for a list to the paddling side; the greater the list, the greater the speed.

Neither of the midship kneeling positions is difficult to learn but they should first be practiced on placid waters. Wooden-canoe ribs may be hard on the knees and there's little comfort afforded by Fiberglas or aluminum although foam pads may be used for cushioning. Lacking these, try a folded sweater or heavy shirt.

The safest position, though not necessarily the most efficient (for white men, at least), is that used by Indians before they traded their paddles for outboard motors. Birch-bark canoes had no seats and the paddler knelt on the bottom, thighs resting on calves, feet turned in and the rump lodged on the instep. Canoe Indians, of course, had been conditioned to this position by endless generations of canoe handling and they could squat in this manner hour after hour without ill effects. For a white man, this position becomes torture within a few minutes, however well adapted it was to Indian techniques.

Canadian canoes formerly provided an improved paddling position. Few realize that the gunwale-height seats common on today's canoes are an American innovation, now adopted in many Canadian craft. However, north-of-the-border canoes used to be equipped with wide thwarts, set some 5 inches below the gunwales. A paddler could then kneel forward of this thwart, slip his feet and calves under it and wedge his rump against the cross-bar. This approximated the Indian position but eased the weight from the knees and feet by allowing the paddler to lean into the thwart. In fact, Canadians outdid the Indians since this position solidly welds the canoeman's body to the craft and, at the same time, permits full use of muscles in the arms, shoulders, back, waist, and thighs.

The double cruising position. Stowe Canoe Co./Orvis Co. photo.

An expert, aboard one of these canoes, could drive it with the power of a small farm tractor!

This same position has been adapted to American-style canoes with their gunwale-height seats and it has become known as the "cruising position," not to be confused with the single-paddler cruising position described earlier. The paddler kneels in front of the seat and leans backward onto its forward edge, giving him nearly the same purchase and free use of muscles afforded by the Canadian placement of thwarts. On extended trips, I have found this position far more comfortable than the seemingly restful full-sitting stance.

Actually, the dangers of using seats have been exasperatingly overemphasized. Canoe seats have their place and the misguided suggestion that they be removed for safety's sake is nothing more than impractical theorizing by "experts" unaware of a canoe's true capabilities. I grant that

Although apparently doing a good job, these boys should be in kneeling position when running rapids. Michigan Tourist Council photo.

the kneeling position is a must when running rapids or paddling in heavy seas. However, when the waters turn placid and a seventh-inning stretch is called for, there is no reason why canoemen cannot slip up onto the seats and relax leg muscles. It's not necessary to be miserable to enjoy a canoe trip!

During a Minnesota canoe trip in an ancient Peterborough canoe carrying a heavy load amidship, I found that paddling from the stern deck, back of the rear seat, was delightfully relaxing and, due to the considerable weight in the center section, remarkably stable. Skill and judgment should govern canoeing positions, not hard and fast rules.

Paddle Strokes

Outdated notions die hard. As so often happens at a summer camp waterfront, I once got embroiled in a heated discussion with another canoeing instructor who insisted that both of a paddler's arms should be fully extended and rigid through the full sweep of each stroke; the arms acting much like the spokes of a wheel with the shoulders as the hub. For a water-carnival pageant, I conceded, this presents graceful movements to watch, but during a long trip atrophy of the wrists and elbows is inevitable. We never did reach an agreement and the old stiff-arm concept still prevails among some canoeists.

Common among the untrained is the opposite view, calling for constant flexing of both arms and ignoring the power of back muscles. The upper hand starts close to the face or shoulder, elbow fully bent, the lower arm extended to dip position. The upper hand then pushes forward while the lower arm is flexed to draw the blade back. This style of paddling places the entire burden of effort on arm muscles only. It can be improved greatly by keeping the lower arm semi-rigid through the stroke, thus increasing leverage and bringing into play powerful back muscles. This, in fact, can be considered the basic stroke of canoeing, in which the paddle grip is not lifted above eye level through the stroke.

Skilled canoemen can paddle for hours on one side of the canoe, but to break the monotony and to distribute the work load among body muscles, most partners switch sides periodically, usually without missing a beat. The bow man sets the pace and paddles are plied in unison, except when navigating heavy seas or rapids. When either calls for a shift, the switch is made following the next complete stroke. Each pulls his paddle up smartly, changes hand positions on the shaft and dips into the next stroke without wasted motion. Some suggest that the stern man switch his paddle over the stern to avoid flipping water into the canoe but this makes for an awkward shift. The few drops of water that may drip into the canoe are of little consequence.

Paddling calls for rhythm. Unconsciously, each paddler dips, pulls, and recovers at precisely the same moment, with a slight pause just before the blade is plunged back into the water. Otherwise, a frequent change of pace or the repeated breaking of the rhythm makes paddling difficult and creates annoyance. Many a case of "bush fever" has been aggravated by a lack of coordination between partners!

Recovery of the paddle from each stroke—that moment before the dip is made for the next stroke—is actually a rest period and, brief though it may be, it is vital. For an abbreviated moment, between strokes, muscles get a respite as the paddle is flipped forward for the next stroke. Feathering the blade, as it is lifted over the water also eases the chore.

Underwater Stroke

Also known as the "Indian stroke", this is not actually a separate stroke but rather an underwater recovery, in which the blade is not lifted from the water but feathered and brought forward soundlessly, edge first, parallel to the gunwale. Whether its popular name "Indian stroke," is romantic nonsense I don't know, but I suppose Indians used it for sneaking up on an unsuspecting moose just as modern hunters, wildlife observers, and photographers do.

Indian Stroke

The true Indian stroke is rarely seen nowadays, probably because the aborigine's low position in his craft is pretty much out of style. This low stance made it possible for the Indian to roll the shaft of his paddle on the gunwale as he drew the blade back with semi-rigid arms, in effect using the gunwale as a fulcrum to attain a J stroke. This is a short, choppy stroke, deceptively effective; one, in fact, that will outrun any of the white man's strokes. That it wore out gunwales and paddle shafts worried the Indian little. He could always whittle new ones quickly!

Cruising Stroke

The simplest and easiest of all bow strokes to learn, the Cruising stroke serves solely to propel the canoe forward without turning. The blade is brought forward, dipped and drawn backwards, the path of the blade paralleling the keel—not the gunwale, as beginners are prone to do. The paddler must reach away from the canoe slightly and sweep back at a slight angle toward the craft's side (Fig. 20-A). Unskilled paddlers

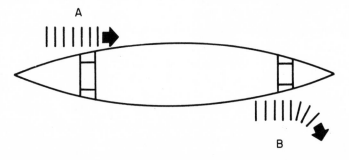

Figure 20   *(A) Cruising stroke; (B) J stroke.*

tend to draw the paddle along the gunwale's curvature, which drives the canoe into a turn away from the paddle.

J Stroke

The J stroke is used by the stern paddler or by a single canoeman. To execute the stroke, he reaches forward and dips the blade close to the gunwale and draws it back parallel to the keel. Since the stroke causes the canoe to veer from the paddle into a turn, the paddler compensates with his backward sweep of the blade by twisting it and pushing it away from the craft to form a "J" or hook (Fig. 20-B). This keeps the bow from swinging too far off course or, if it has deviated, the "J" pressure brings it back into line. This may appear to be a case of zigzagging to remain on a general course, and with beginners this is often the case. However, experienced canoemen paddling tandem strike a "balance of power" between them so that neither "fights" the other. Their craft stays on course with little noticeable weaving. An expert paddling alone leaves no evidence of weaving in his wake. It's a matter of practice.

My sole criticism of the J stroke is that after a few miles the pressure on my right shoulder joint begins to tell, and my left arm tires. I much prefer the Canadian or the Pitch stroke, which is easier to execute and which calls for a slightly slower beat.

Canadian Stroke

Sometimes mistaken for the J stroke, the Canadian stroke affects the canoe's behavior in much the same way. Once acquired, however, the Canadian stroke is the less tiring of the two. Following the stern paddler's backward sweep, the paddler feathers his blade instead of pushing the blade outwardly to execute a "J", brings it forward underwater, and withdraws it at a point opposite his hips. This is not an easy stroke to master but it is efficient in that it keeps the canoe on course without slowing its headway. The J stroke, on the other hand, slows it slightly.

Pitch Stroke

The Pitch stroke is a little-known but marvelously effective stern maneuver. It is started conventionally, but as the blade passes the hips, it is turned to form a rudder which, as it sweeps back toward the stern, terminates with the flat of the blade parallel to the canoe's side (Fig. 21). It is important that the blade be kept fully immersed for full effect. It is

Figure 21   *Pitch stroke.*

withdrawn from the water in its feathered position at the completion of the sweep toward the stern, thus offering little resistance to the wind. It can, in fact, be flipped forward almost effortlessly into position for the next stroke.

Sweep Strokes

The extreme maneuverability of the canoe becomes apparent when Sweep strokes are used. The Full Forward Sweep is effected by reaching forward with the blade fully immersed and edge down, in much the same position as that of an oar. It is then swept in a wide arc just below the surface of the water until it returns to the side of the canoe (Fig. 22-A).

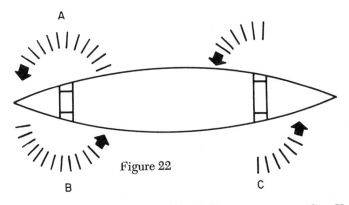

Figure 22

Sweep Strokes: (A) Full forward sweep; (B) Full reverse sweep; (C) Half or quarter sweep.

A Full Reverse Sweep is the same, except reversed, so that the blade starts its sweep in back of the paddler and progresses in an arc to a point in front of him (Fig. 22-B). Tandem paddlers, each executing a full forward sweep on the same side of the craft will send it into a wide turn, away from the paddles. However, if the stern paddler effects a forward sweep and the bow man a reverse sweep on opposite sides, the canoe will pivot within its own length. A single paddler poised amidship can pivot the canoe in either direction with a forward or reverse sweep. The so-called Half-Sweep and Quarter-Sweep (Fig. 22-C) are simply abbreviated versions of the Full Sweep.

Inverted Sweep

The Inverted Sweep is used by a single paddler, usually from a midship position to swing the canoe sharply to the side on which he is paddling. He reaches out with the blade, some 45 degrees off his bow and draws it toward him. As the blade nears the canoe's side, he then swings it away from the craft, much as in the J stroke (Fig. 23).

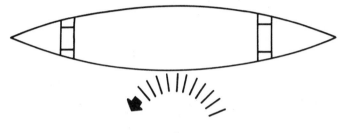

Figure 23   *Inverted sweep.*

Backwater Stroke

The Backwater stroke is merely the reversing of the Cruising stroke, serving either to stop the canoe's forward motion or to reverse its direction.

Hold or Jam Stroke

The Hold or Jam stroke consists merely of "applying the brakes" and can be performed in tandem or singly (Fig. 24). The paddlers literally

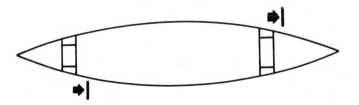

Figure 24   *Hold or jam stroke.*

"jam" their paddles into the water at right angles to the canoe in a vertical position. This will stop the craft's forward momentum quickly but requires a strong pair of arms and wrists if the canoe is well underway.

Draw Stroke

The Draw stroke is used for slipping a canoe broadside or, if applied on opposite sides, for turning it sharply within its own length. The paddler reaches out at right angles from the craft and, with the flat of the blade facing him, draws it directly toward him in a vertical position. It is a particularly handy stroke for a single paddler working amidship or for tandem paddlers landing at a dock.

Push Stroke

The Push stroke is the reverse of the Draw stroke although it is not as easily performed. The blade is dipped close to the gunwale and pushed away from the canoe. It is rather an awkward maneuver and some recommend that it be eased by using the paddle shaft as a lever against the gunwale (See Pry stroke). It is useful, however, when the canoe must be slipped broadside and there is not time enough in which to flip paddles to the opposite side for a Draw stroke. Tandem paddlers, using the Push stroke on opposite sides, will pivot the canoe but it is not a graceful performance.

The Pry Stroke

The Pry stroke serves the same function as the Push stroke but much more quickly and effectively. Developed by white-water canoemen who find the Push stroke slow and ineffective in running water, the Pry stroke will quickly set over the bow or stern. As the stroke's name signifies, the paddle is used to pry the canoe sideways around an obstacle or into a channel. The blade is dipped, full depth, with its face parallel to the keel, the shaft resting against the gunwale, at a point just in front of the paddler. He then pulls the shaft inboard so that the flat of the blade thrusts outward, thus setting the canoe over. Needless to say, the stroke calls for a rugged paddle. Many canoeing instructors, accustomed only to flat-water canoeing where the Pry stroke is little used, frown upon it as an abuse of paddle and canoe. Nevertheless, to a white-water paddler the Pry stroke verges on the indispensable.

Sculling Stroke

The Sculling stroke, of which there are several variations, is probably the most versatile of all. It can be performed repeatedly without withdrawing the blade from the water and with it the canoe can be pulled to one side, stopped, turned, or even reversed, depending upon how the blade is angled. It is started much like the Draw stroke. However the blade, instead of being drawn directly toward the paddler, is zigzagged back and forth, first one edge leading, then the other, with constant pressure applied (Fig. 25). The blade may then be feathered underwater and

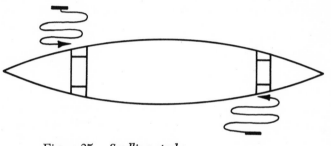

Figure 25   *Sculling stroke.*

returned to the starting position, or it can be converted to the Push stroke. Old-time canoemen called this stroke "fish-tailing," an apt term!

Throw or Lift Stroke

This stroke is not for amateurs! Properly executed by the bow man, it will throw the bow to the opposite side abruptly. Improperly done, it may pull the paddler into the water, break the paddle, or wash it back under the canoe. Few women can execute this stroke because it requires muscular arms and wrists.

The blade is thrust into the water vertically, close to the gunwale and with the face of the blade parallel to the keel. The grasp on the paddle by both hands must be firm and the lower arm braced stiffly. The leading edge of the blade is then turned toward the canoe. With the canoe traveling even at moderate speed, the rudder-like move will throw the canoe's bow over sharply. The bow man who executes this stroke gracefully and effectively is one who can judge the canoe's momentum, the correct angle at which to set the blade—and his own strength. The Throw or Lift stroke is a challenge and it should be practiced by beginners in quiet water and at slow speeds.

The Low Brace

This is a riverman's stroke, at its best in preventing a capsize or in steadying the canoe in a banked turn—a technique used in entering a swift current from an eddy. The canoeman leans with the craft, his paddle fully extended to the side with the flat surface of the blade thrusting downward. At the same time, the knees draw the canoe toward the paddle. It is not an easy stroke to perform well, but since it is invaluable to a skilled canoeman, a beginner should practice it, preferably under the guidance of an expert.

The High Brace

As the name implies, the High Brace is related to the Low Brace. It varies in that it is used not only to stabilize the craft but also as a draw stroke. The canoeman again leans with the craft, dips his paddle at an angle into the water as far out as he can reach and pulls the flat of the blade toward him. The paddle grip is held high and the blade fully immersed for full effect. The High Brace calls for great skill and is probably the most difficult of all canoe strokes to perform properly. With this stroke, a single canoeman can swiftly spin his craft from swift water into the quiet of an eddy, or vice versa.

Bow Rudder

The Bow Rudder is not difficult to execute but requires considerable strength in the outboard arm and wrist. As the name implies, it enables the paddler to turn the canoe from the bow position. The sharpness of the turn can be accented if accompanied by a Full Forward Sweep by the stern paddler, on the opposite side. The bow paddler thrusts his blade into the water at about 30 degrees off his bow (Fig. 26), extending the

Figure 26   *The Bow rudder.*

blade as far as he can reach, making sure, too, the face is vertical—like an oar. His lower hand and arm should be *in back* of the paddle so that they act as braces. The blade should be kept just below the surface of the water, not thrust deeply as in a conventional stroke.

With combinations of various strokes, a canoe can be maneuvered quickly, gracefully, and with complete control. With practice comes an instinct for using the correct strokes, and combinations of them. Some of the more useful basic stroke combinations follow:

Traveling straight ahead
> *Bow—Cruising stroke*
> *Stern—J, Canadian, or Pitch stroke*

Wide turn to right
> *Bow—Cruising stroke on right*
> *Stern—Full Forward Sweep on left*

Sharp turn to right
> *Bow—Draw stroke or Bow Rudder on right*
> *Stern—Full Forward Sweep or Draw stroke on left*

Very sharp turn to right
> *Bow—Lift or Throw stroke on left*
> *Stern—Draw stroke on left or Full Reverse Sweep on right*

Full pivot to right
> *Bow—Full Reverse Sweep on right*
> *Stern—Full Forward Sweep or Draw stroke on left*

Quick stop
> *Bow—Jam stroke*
> *Stern—Jam stroke*

Reverse and right turn
> *Bow—Back stroke on right*
> *Stern—Full Reverse Sweep on left*

Only maneuvers to the right have been cited among these suggestions but, naturally, movements to the left will result by executing the suggested strokes on opposite sides of the canoe.

Chapter V

Poling a Canoe

THAT WE'RE living in an increasingly overprotective society doesn't come as news to the adventuresome. We're told when and where to cross the street; we're persuaded to wear tin hats while riding motor scooters and to wear ugly "signal yellow" or "flame orange" garb when hunting. One of these days, we'll be required to wear life jackets when driving across bridges! For "our own good" we're being deprived of our self-reliance, our ability to think for ourselves, and our prerogative to make our own judgements.

It's not surprising then that so few canoe owners have learned to pole their craft in fast water—not when you consider that ever since one of the Pilgrim Fathers swiped Squanto's birch-bark canoe and flipped over in Massachusetts Bay, "experts" have been crying: "Never stand up in a canoe!"

Pseudo-experts have wailed this advice for so many years that the general public has come to believe that the ability to remain upright in a canoe is a mysterious gift allotted only to full-blooded Indians in the employ of the Hudson's Bay Company! The truth is, standing in a canoe, properly done, is as safe as the front pew in church. Moreover, poling is a comparatively easy skill to acquire. Ron Kloepper, the 1966 winner of the National Poling Championship on Missouri's Meramec River, had never tried poling until some two months before the competition!

For years, on rivers close to my former home in southern New Hampshire, I'd grudgingly retreated whenever I encountered a set of rapids. I knew that getting through them with a paddle was impossible, particularly upstream, but being thwarted in this manner rankled. The chortling rips seemed to taunt me, and there always was the nagging thought that beyond the rapids lay miles of idyllic waters and riverbanks, coves to explore, deep holes harboring big trout, alder runs overpopulated with woodcock, big bucks skulking hard-to-reach swamps bordering the river.

I'd tried portaging, of course, and often the carry path was passable. Not infrequently, though, none existed and I ran into a tangle of impenetrable brush. I'd dragged and lined the canoe through several rips but this was not easy and repeatedly produced a bootful of water and sopping britches.

Then, in 1941, I was assigned by the U.S. Border Patrol to Fort Kent, Maine, where there were more canoes than automobiles, the town being the terminus of the famed Allagash and St. John River trips. Here, Willard Jalbert, a fellow patrolman who'd teethed on a canoe thwart, gave me a taste of white water. Wielding a 14-foot ash pole through rough-and-tumble St. John rapids, while I alternatingly cowered and exulted in the bow, Willard explained the basic technique. He was convincing. I could never match his skill, of that I was sure, but I borrowed a 20-foot Skowhegan canoe and a pole. For two months before winter set in, I wobbled up and down quieter stretches of the river, gradually tackling faster and faster rips. There's been a pole in my canoe ever since.

Poling, either upstream or down, is easier and faster than paddling. Several years following my initiation on the St. John, I accompanied a Boy Scout upstream canoe trip on the St. Croix River which forms the boundary between Minnesota and Wisconsin. Below Taylor's Falls we found the water swift, flowing over a shallow, sandy bottom. Repeatedly, and annoyingly, my paddle kept striking the sand bars and the powerful current swept the blade by me. The boys were in similar trouble, none of us making any notable headway. We put ashore and cut poles of alder— there was little else available. The scouts rocked and splashed hilariously as they stood in their canoes but we doubled our speed. Safety experts would have wailed, I'm sure. However, no one tipped although none of the scouts had ever before used a setting pole. All, of course, were good swimmers.

Poles

The poles we cut that day were far from ideal. I would have preferred spruce or tamarack. A stump-dried tree—one that has died but not yet started to rot noticeably—about 2 inches at the butt and 12 to 14 feet tall, is a prize. If any bark remains, it should be peeled and the knots smoothed, lest they skin or blister the hands. To the lower end should be attached a soft-iron "shoe" which grips rocks and ledges with a minimum of slipping. Some shoes are equipped with a steel spike, blunt-ended, about a ½-inch in diameter and 2 to 3 inches long. Anything longer might lodge solidly in a crack, leaving the canoeman with the choice of parting with his pole or his canoe!

For poling where the bottom is soft or muddy, the metal shoe is a drawback since it offers little purchase. During a canoe trip ino Oke-

*In Okefenokee Swamp, the author found the still, shallow water ideal for poling.
Photo by Eleanor Riviere.*

fenokee Swamp in Georgia I discovered that "swampers" there cut
hardwood poles and attach two short, curved sticks, 8 to 10 inches long,
so that they form a fork. This proves effective in the gooey, peat-moss
bottom of the great swamp. Available commercially, is a "duck-bill" shoe
of galvanized iron which opens automatically to provide a bearing
surface when downward pressure is applied. It closes when drawn
upward.

Poles of ash, maple, or hickory, although heavier than spruce or
tamarack, are tougher and springier. Ready-made versions, equipped
with shoes, are sold by some logging equipment manufacturers who turn
out lumberjack's pike poles. Like paddles, these may be treated with
boiled linseed oil. However, I've never treated any of mine and one
lasted twelve years. Frequent use will generally maintain a hand-polished
finish.

Competitive poling is bringing about new concepts in pole design.
When Ron Kloepper won the 1966 national championships, he used a fir
pole wrapped with Fiberglas and saturated with polyester resin. This lent
the brittle fir strength and flexibility. To the pole was added a 4-foot rod
of ½-inch steel, this in turn fitted with a shoe. Aluminum poles are also
appearing in competition; these should not be the usual rigid metal but
rather an alloy that will not retain curvature when it is "sprung" under

pressure of poling. Bamboo poles have also been used and, I suppose, are adequate.

Poling Technique

Traditionally, the hand-over-hand "climbing the pole" technique has been used by Northwoods polers. However, competitive poling has seen the development of the "quick jab" style and the "quick-change-over" method. The "quick jab" user performs with a 10- or 12-foot pole on one side of the canoe only, standing so that he faces the side of the canoe, feet well apart for balance. Without moving his hands on the pole, he gives quick jabs against the bottom, sweeps the pole forward a short distance and repeats the jabs. This style has the advantage of keeping the canoe under continuous forward motion, as there is only a slight lull between push and retrieve. However, the method lacks the power of the "hand-over-hand" or "quick-change-over" methods.

The latter calls for a longer pole, 14 to 16 feet long. The pole is dropped into the water at a point just back of the poler's position and pushed against the bottom, with a hand-over-hand action as the canoe moves forward. At a point some 5 feet from the top, hand position is shifted and the pole is quickly flipped to the opposite side, plunging the *top* of the pole into the water for the thrust and hand-over-hand climb on that side. This style would undoubtedly draw guffaws from old-time canoemen but it is effective where speed and power are the utmost considerations. After all, it was this stroke that won the 1965 championships!

However, both the "quick jab" and the "quick-change-over" technique would be exhausting if maintained for more than the few minutes required for a race. There can be no doubt, either, that a canoeman using the traditional "climbing the pole" method, on one side only, would outlast another using either racing style over a lengthy course. The "climbing the pole" technique is accomplished with a slow, rhythmic plunge of the shoe-end of the pole into the water, a hand-over-hand follow-through, then the retrieve. I must confess, however, that on several occasions when the outlook for staying upright in a rough stretch was not bright, I've combined all three styles of poling. On the whole, though, the traditional Northwoods, hand-over-hand style is preferable. The canoe maintains good momentum yet the pace allows time for choosing a route among obstructions, either upstream or down.

For the initial attempt at poling, try a lakeshore with firm bottom and gradual drop-off; a swimming beach during the off-season is ideal, preferably one sheltered from the wind. A single passenger, sitting on the floor just aft of the bow seat will help stabilize the craft, in which case take a position just forward of the stern seat. If alone, stand slightly forward of this station.

Poling isn't a high-wire act, so you won't have to poise gingerly over the keel. With the canoe fully afloat and parallel to shore, step aboard confidently, placing your left foot slightly off-center with the calf of the leg thrust lightly against the stern seat or thwart. The right foot should then be placed forward and to the right, so that you face about 45 degrees off the port bow, assuming you are right-handed. If left-handed, reverse the position to face the starboard side.

Grasp the pole about midway of its length, right hand uppermost, the left about 18 inches below. Thrust the shoe end into the water, just back of your left foot and as close to the canoe as possible. Be sure of firm footing, then apply a light back-thrust with both hands, swinging into the pole with your arms and shoulders. As the canoe moves ahead, continue a steady thrust, using the hand-over-hand motion, "climbing the pole" until your hands reach the top. Go into a slight crouch and give a final, firm—but not sudden—thrust. Although your initial shoves with the pole will be gentle, perhaps even groping, be prepared for a spurt of speed which you've never experienced while paddling. A canoe propelled by a pole is a lively craft; hence the need for the semi-crouch to prevent the canoe from darting out from under you!

As the canoe darts forward, lift the pole smartly from the water with an upward flip, toward the bow. Never drag it through the water during the retrieve as this will turn the craft from its course, much as if you had used a backwater stroke with a paddle. Before momentum is lost, take another purchase with the pole and repeat, always on the same side and striving for a smooth, rhythmic beat. You are now poling a canoe! Basically, it's that simple.

The craft should be kept parallel to shore, avoiding deep water where the pole is useless. If the canoe tends to turn in one direction or the other, or skids broadside, alter the thrust of the pole to compensate. A half-hour of this sort of practice on a lakeshore and you'll be ready for stream work. However, before graduating to flowing water, practice "snubbing."

Snubbing

Snubbing is used for slowing or stopping the canoe in running water. With the craft underway, reach forward with the pole for a firm bite on the bottom at a point approximately amidship and as close to the gunwale as possible. As the pole finds bottom, lean into it, flexing your knees slightly. At slow speeds this will bring the canoe to an abrupt halt and may at first throw you slightly off balance. At greater speeds, or in a

The various positions of the canoe pole as the craft is pushed upstream. Photos by Eleanor Riviere.

fast current, you may have to snub several times before coming to a standstill. Practice snubbing until you can perform it smoothly and confidently and you will have acquired the basic skills for poling.

Poling Upstream

For further practice, seek out a shallow, slow-running stream, relatively free of obstructions. Initial efforts here should be upstream, noting the effects of the current on the canoe's behavior. You'll immediately observe that the current's pressure tends to steady the craft as long as the bow is headed directly upstream. Veer from this course, however, and the current will swing the bow toward shore. To counter this, alter the thrust of the pole so that the canoe is always directly parallel to the stream's flow.

In probing for a toe-hold, your pole may occasionally wedge itself between two rocks or in a crevice. If this occurs, snap it upward quickly. If this fails to dislodge it and you can't stop the canoe's motion, release the pole. You can always fall back upon your paddle for retrieving it.

One of the quirks of running water you'll encounter is that, when poling diagonally upstream, the force of the current will drive your canoe toward shore. Experienced canoemen put this phenomenon to work whenever they want to "set over" or "ferry" cross-stream. This technique

The quieter stretches of streams are good practice waters for beginners at poling. Photo by Eleanor Riviere.

calls for care, however. Don't allow the canoe to drift with the current but, rather, apply pressure with the pole—not enough to make upstream headway but sufficient to hold your own against the flow. This will set you over.

Don't underestimate the power of flowing water; remember, that it never ceases working. It's far better to overshoot on the upstream side than to ram a downstream boulder broadside. Should you lose control momentarily and end up with the canoe broadside to the current, it's easier to shove the stern downstream than to try to force the bow into it. Failing this, simply pole directly ashore or into slower-running water where you can regain full control.

Having gotten the feel of running water, try a section of the stream where Nature has strewn a few boulders about. Before starting up through, drop your pole into thrust position and hold the canoe at a standstill while you plot an upriver course. Failing to do this may lead you into a rock-flanked dead end from which retreat may be neither graceful nor easy.

First inclination is to stick to the main channel but this isn't necessarily the easier course. The mainstream current may be too powerful or too deep to afford purchase for the pole. On the other hand, boulders produce eddies and swift runs create backwaters which will actually carry you upstream for short distances. An alert canoeman takes advan-

The author on Maine's Kennebago River, upstream and down. Photo by Eleanor Riviere.

tage of these instead of bucking the full brunt of the current. Plot your course to utilize all quiet stretches of water below rocks, blowdowns, or other obstructions. Stop at each to determine your next move. This rock-to-rock system is an easy one to master and a labor-saver. Of course, there won't always be convenient boulders strategically deployed for your benefit. Nonetheless, tackling one eddy, one sluice, or one run at a time eventually adds up to conquering an entire set of rips.

As you attempt poling in swifter water, more powerful thrusts must be used and at an accelerated pace. Because the canoe is so nearly perfectly streamlined, the current can't get a strong grip on it as long as the bow is headed directly into the flow. It follows then that as long as you exert a greater pressure on the pole than is exerted on the canoe by the current, you will make headway. However, a good canoeman recognizes a superior force when he meets it. When you find yourself losing ground or at a standstill despite brute-strength effort and the little tricks you've learned, you're in water too powerful to be overcome with a pole. Retreat is indicated.

Poling simultaneously, two men can make headway where a lone poler would be stymied. Tandem poling is usually done with both poles on the same side of the canoe (although this rule is not inflexible) and requires fine coordination between the partners. In heavy water one man generally holds the canoe while the other obtains a fresh purchase for his pole, then the two push in unison. They may also alternate their strokes. At any rate, tandem poling in fast water is tricky work even for experts who know each other's canoemanship well.

Poling Downstream

Snubbing is used in downstream poling, and here too you should seek out a slowly flowing current for initial practice. As with upstream poling, study your proposed route, this time from the head of the flow, where you'll get a more accurate picture of the problems than is possible from a

Proper position for snubbing or slowing the canoe in a downstream run. Photo by Eleanor Riviere.

shore position. If you can hear the rumble of heavy water below, beware. The gentle rips you now face may be only a preliminary drop into dangerous rapids. In this case, go ashore and scout the entire length of the white water. If the rapids appear impassable, or even if there is a slight doubt in your mind, avoid the run. Caution is indicated too in choosing a channel, so that you don't find yourself trapped in a down- stream dead end, far more difficult to work out of than the upstream variety.

Once decided upon a course through the rips, apply only enough pressure to the pole to start the canoe. It's often pointed out that a canoe's speed must exceed that of the current in order to maintain steerage way. It's also true that a slower speed, particularly when poling, affords the same steerage way. Downstream poling, like downhill skiing, requires complete control at all times. If your canoe doesn't do exactly what you intend, you're out of control and in danger. Even when running an apparently clear channel, it's good insurance to go through the motions of snubbing as you descend, applying only enough pole pressure against the bottom to keep the speed within the limits of your skill.

Downstream technique differs from poling upstream in that the current aids the pole in propelling the canoe. The pole, is used primarily to slow, stop, or guide the canoe. Unless it's too rough or too deep, take advantage of the current's power in the main stream. Not only will it carry you at the expense of less effort but it will also help guide the canoe. To see proof of this, toss a small stick into the flowing water and watch it ride. The water will carry it around rocks without its touching them. To some degree the current will do the same with your canoe, but bear in mind that your craft is considerably heavier than the stick and has greater momentum. Your bow will swing gracefully by rocks but the stern may follow only if aided with slight thrusts of the pole. However, if you run faster than the current, momentum will overpower the force of the current and you'll leave paint on the rocks!

It should be remembered, too, that the midship section of the canoe and its stern may not follow in exactly the course set by the bow, even with the aid of a pole. In dodging an obstruction, particularly in a sharp turn, allow room for the stern to swing somewhat wider than the bow.

If your route suddenly becomes impassable, don't make a hair-trigger decision to change it. Snub the canoe to a full stop instead and appraise the possibilities of another course before going on. As experience is acquired, you'll make these reappraisals on the run, but in the meantime pause to be sure. If it will help—and it's considered cricket—wedge the bow gently against a smooth rock to help hold the canoe while you search out a new passage.

In changing course, especially in a stream heavily strewn with rocks, avoid traveling diagonally across the current, bearing in mind that the current carries you downstream even as you traverse. In such water, keep the stern upstream at all times, dodging obstructions by setting the canoe over broadside with a side-thrust. In other words, cut square corners.

Canoemen generally agree that the canoe should be light in the stern for downstream running, thus giving the current a less effective grip on it. This means that the poler in an empty craft must work from near amidship, possibly astride the middle thwart to attain proper trim. With cargo or with a passenger aboard, he can work from a more convenient station further aft.

Hall Grant, who'd poled and paddled as a guide on Maine rivers for sixty-one years before he died in 1963, didn't agree with this theory. He preferred to keep his stern slightly lower than the bow so that, he explained, the current helped him swing the bow into passageways he chose. One or two thrusts with the pole, he said, then aided the stern to follow. A heavy bow, according to Hall, is difficult to direct from the stern, either with a paddle or pole. I've tried his method and, where there is sufficient depth for the lowered stern, his technique is valid.

Poling on quiet streams can be done with almost any type of canoe, but where close maneuvering may be necessary or in heavy rapids, a keel-less craft is best suited. Short canoes, under 16 to 17 feet, are more difficult to handle too, since they sit lower in the water and answer pole thrusts less readily.

Soft-soled shoes, moccasins, or tennis shoes help the feet to fit the inside contours of the hull and contribute greatly to good balance. My favorites are soleless moccasins with 6-inch tops, for which I searched

Soleless moccasins are the most comfortable footwear for canoeing and contribute to good balance when poling. Photo by Eleanor Riviere.

unsuccessfully for years in the United States, finally locating a pair in New Brunswick. Heavily-soled, stiff boots have no place in a canoe. You feel less nimble of foot wearing them; they're hard on interior finish and hamper a swimmer in the event of a spill. Wear loose-fitting clothing, especially through the back and shoulders, for here are the muscles that do the work in poling.

I've cited only basic techniques in describing poling technique. Obviously, the use of a setting pole cannot be learned entirely from reading a book. Practice and experience make a skilled poler. No two sets of rapids are alike, no two poling situations the same. Evaluation of any one set of rips must be based upon conditions at hand as well as upon general theory.

Poling doesn't mean, however, that you'll spend endless hours dodging boulders or appraising seething caldrons of white water. Often you run into a sluice or chute, obviously clear of obstructions and gliding swiftly over a smooth bottom. This sort of water doesn't rumble or threaten—it laughs. Head the bow into it and "put the ash to 'er. . . . !"

Chapter VI

Reading and Running White Water

I'M A RAPIDS APPRAISER. Driving along a road which parallels a river, I'm likely to tie up traffic while looking over a rocky pitch from behind the steering wheel, or, if the rapids seem especially challenging, I'll pull over for a more thorough inspection. It's a compulsion with me. I'm an addict, irresistibly drawn to tumbling water.

Naturally, I enjoy viewing lacy ribbons of froth dancing among the rocks or spray flinging high into the air where miniature rainbows hang, but this isn't my purpose. My sole concern is navigability, upstream and down. I plot canoe courses. Could I, for example, snake my Prospector through without leaving an undue amount of paint on the rocks? Maybe, along that left bank to that big boulder, then a set-over to that ledge with the big eddy below it. . . . I've navigated thousands of streams in this manner without even getting my feet wet! It's a completely hypothetical approach to white-water canoeing, of course, but such assessments are good practice and even afford some degree of vicarious excitement.

In appraising a set of rapids prior to actually running them, care should be taken to look them over from as close to water level as possible. Viewed from a high bank, for example, rips will appear easier to run than they actually are; height tends to flatten pitches, just as the earth looks relatively flat from an airplane. Examination from water level will give a truer picture.

Rating of White Water

However, far more scientific and thorough evaluations of fast water have been made for canoeists; for instance, the Standard International River Classification System included in the safety code of the American

Shooting the rapids. Grumman Co. photo.

White-Water Affiliation. Also known as a "difficulty rating," the system rates white water in general and in guidebooks is applied to specific rapids. The various classes of rapids are graded as follows:

Grade I. Very easy. Waves small, regular; passages clear, sandbanks, artificial difficulties like bridge piers, riffles.

Grade II. Easy. Rapids of medium difficulty, with passages clear and wide; low ledges; spray deck useful.

Grade III. Medium. Waves numerous, high, irregular; rocks; eddies; rapids with passages that are clear though narrow, requiring expertise to maneuver; inspection usually needed; spraydeck needed.

Grade IV. Difficult. Long rapids, waves powerful, irregular; dangerous rocks; boiling eddies; passages difficult to reconnoiter; inspection mandatory first time; powerful and precise maneuvering required; spraydeck essential.

Grade V. Very difficult. Extremely difficult, long and very violent rapids, following each other almost without interruption; riverbed extremely obstructed; big drops; violent current; very steep gradient; reconnoitering essential but difficult.

Grade VI. Extraordinarily difficult. Difficulties of Grade V carried to the extreme of navigability. Nearly impossible and very dangerous. For teams of experts only, at favorable water levels and after close study with all precautions.

While these are blanket ratings applied to all rapids, actual classification may change according to water level. A rise of 1 foot, for instance, might alter a Class II rapids, normally considered easy, into a Class III or possibly even a Class IV pitch, altogether too rough for beginners. Inversely, a 1-foot drop in water level might convert a difficult-to-negotiate Class IV run into a relatively easy-to-handle Class II ride. Nevertheless, the International River Classification is an accurate indication of what a paddler may expect from a given set of rapids.

With these variables in mind, however, Randy Carter of Warrenton, Virginia, devised the Randy Carter River Marking System, which is in use in many sections of the eastern United States, particularly in Virginia, eastern West Virginia, and in the Great Smoky Mountain region.* Not only does Randy's system take into account the International River Classification System but it also expresses navigability in terms of actual water height available to canoeists. Ratings under this system start at 0, the lowest possible water level at which a stream can be run by a canoe, in this case about 3 inches of water. Graduations above this level are in 1-foot increments, up to 5 feet. Above this level, most rocky streams are considered unsafe for canoeing except by the most daredevil experts.

Nor is Randy Carter's system entirely a "paper classification." Yellow paint markings have been placed on bridge piers, boulders, ledges, and other riverside points, many visible from nearby gasoline stations and roadside stores whose owners have agreed to answer telephone inquiries regarding water levels. Under a gentleman's agreement, canoeists send 35 cents in stamps to reporting stations whenever they obtain information! Thus, canoemen can obtain on-the-spot reports without driving needless miles.

Another means for assessing the navigability of streams whose water levels fluctuate is the U.S. Weather Bureau River Gauging System, part of which consists of small concrete towers located along riverbanks and housing automatic devices which transmit readings to nearby regional Weather Bureau stations. Like the Randy Carter system, government readings start at 0. However, while the Carter zero designates a minimum of 3 inches of water, the government's zero is set *below* the stream bed so that a Weather Bureau reading of 1½ feet is required to equal the 3-inch or 0 Carter reading. A reading of less than this would indicate dry going!

In a general way, navigability can also be determined through the use of U. S. Geological Survey maps. On these, contour lines follow constant elevations, so when one or more of these crosses a stream, an appropriate drop in gradient is indicated. Contour intervals may vary among the various quadrangles, with the more popular 15-minute quadrangles using a 20-foot contour interval.

It is generally considered that streams having a gradient of 60 feet per mile are navigable, at least for canoes. However, when the gradient approaches that mark, the stream is likely to be Grade IV or worse. On

---

*For a more detailed description of this system and of the canoeing waters of this region, See Randy Carter, *Canoeing White Water*, 5th edition, 195 p. It is available from the author, 158 Winchester St., Warrenton, Va. 22186.

the other hand, an extreme gradient may consist of a single waterfall around which a portage is possible, with the rest of the river offering smooth paddling.

Close examination of these maps will reveal the location of major rapids on larger streams. Those less than 40 feet wide on 7½-minute quadrangles and less than 80 feet wide on 15-minute quads are shown as single blue lines. Rivers of greater width are shown as double blue lines. All in all, while the Geological Survey maps will not give you a detailed picture of what to expect in the way of fast water, they are useful for preliminary appraisal.

Guidebooks are invaluable since they describe, in considerable detail, entire riverways, one notable example being the Appalachian Mountain Club canoeing guide.* Another is *Appalachian Water,* in two volumes, by Walter Frederick Burmeister and published by the Canoe Cruisers Association of Washington, D.C. Unfortunately it is out of print at this writing but copies may be available at local libraries or from white-water canoemen. Several other excellent guidebooks, usually regional in scope, are available and listed in the Bibliography. Many canoe clubs issue bulletins describing river trips and anticipated water conditions. Several state tourist promotional agencies, fast awakening to canoeing's resurgent popularity, publish variously detailed booklets on trip possibilities. These publications and the addresses of their publishers are included in the Appendix.

Apart from the difficulty rating and the water level, choosing canoe water involves other factors: the distance between put-in and take-out, arranging for a car shuttle, travel time, campsites en route, and, of course, aesthetic values. While on the map a river may fling a challenge at a canoeman, it's hardly a delight to paddle or risk a dunking in a waterway so polluted that it is an open sewer, nor do smoke-belching industrial plants lining both shores offer much attraction.

Further, the ability to appraise a set of rapids according to the International River Classification doesn't make a competent canoeman of the average canoeist. There's the matter of reading the "set" of the water (its temper so to speak), its volume and its power, plus a knack for interpreting "trail signs" on the surface. The same set of rapids may differ from day to day, evidenced by a change in the tone of its roar. A skilled canoeman evaluates his prospects according to conditions of the moment.

There is a tendency to refer to all fast-flowing water as "white," "swift," "quick," or "fast." Where one draws the line between each is difficult to pinpoint. True white water, most agree, tumbles with varying degrees of force among and over rocks, boulders, ledges, gravel bars, and other obstructions, natural and man-made. There is no question about its being

*The A.M.C. New England Canoeing Guide, Appalachian Mountain Club, 5 Joy Street, Boston, Mass. 02108. 500 p. $5.

"white water"; it foams, froths, and roars! The term cannot honestly be applied to those stretches of river which flow, albeit with great force, smoothly and silently, only occasionally obstructed by barriers. Such water is worthy of respect and might rightly be termed "fast" or "swift."

Single Obstructions

Obstructions to be encountered by today's canoeman may include rocks, large boulders, ledges, sunken logs, stumps, gravel and sand bars, bridge piers, washed-out dams, and, in timber country, "dead heads" or "dead men." These are logs anchored at the upstream end and afloat at the other, sometimes barely protruding above the surface and ever a threat to hard-driving canoes. In these days of indiscriminate construction, it's not unusual to find streams littered with old bridge timbers, steel beams, and broken concrete abutments. Such obstructions affect river currents, of course, creating chutes, pitches, sluices, eddies, sharp drops, billowing waves, and any number and combinations of cross-currents, all challenges to canoemen. A wise beginner accepts the challenge of streams which present only occasional obstructions, these fairly widely spaced.

One of the common "trail signs" to be read on the water is the riffling of the surface in the form of a V pointing upstream. You'll find a rock or other obstruction, barely submerged, at the apex of the V, or a short distance above it. A similar V, but pointing downstream, indicates that the current is flowing between two submerged, or partially-submerged, objects. If the V is wide enough, chances are you can travel through it safely.

A more subtle danger is evidenced by an upward bulge in the water, not unlike a large, bubbling spring. This is trickier to gauge, since the obstruction causing it may be anywhere from a few inches to 2 feet underwater and up to 15 feet upstream, depending upon the volume and power of the current. A common mistake is to avoid the bulge, only to strike the obstruction! There is little need to mention the obvious hazards, rocks that protrude above the surface clearly, ledges and trees overhanging the bank or fallen into the stream.

Whenever a pair of lake canoeists seek to avoid an obstacle, they are likely to swing wide of it, often with sweep strokes. Such a leisurely turn has no place in fast-flowing water, however. As already pointed out, the current continues to carry a canoe downstream even as the craft is turning. Keeping the canoe aligned with the current is important. Whenever an obstacle looms ahead, instead of sweeping right or left around it, paddlers simply apply simultaneous draw strokes, both on one side of the canoe, thus setting it over broadside without losing headway (Fig. 27).

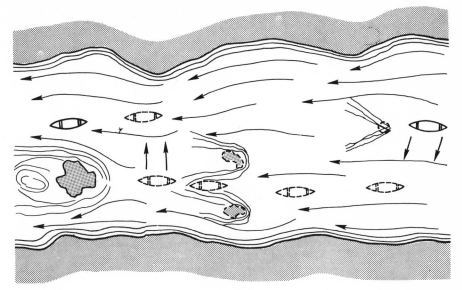

Figure 27

The canoe should be "set over" broadside, or nearly so, to avoid obstacles in running water.

River Bends

Almost invariably, the current is swifter and deeper on the outside of a stream bend. To complicate matters, sub-surface waters follow the channel as it sweeps through the curve, but surface waters may flow directly crosswise toward the curve, where they are deflected back into the mainstream or rolled under. As a result, many a canoeist attempting to follow the channel with sweep strokes is surprised to find himself swept directly into the outer bank or, worse yet, into overhanging bushes or tree limbs. The sharper the bend and the swifter the current, the more likely this is to occur. The inclination on most bends is to take a short cut across the shallows which almost invariably mark the inside of a stream turn. Often this course is feasible but there's also the possibility of going aground.

As innocuous as a slick-water river bend may appear, a definite technique exists for navigating it. This calls for swinging the stern toward the inside of the bend placing the canoe nearer to broadside of the main current but, actually, more in alignment with the surface cross-current (Fig. 28). As the canoe sweeps into the bend at this angle, the bow is gradually pulled downstream, probably with draw strokes. In effect, the canoe becomes the spoke in a great wheel, with the outer bank the rim.

As the craft eases out of the bend, the bow is then swung back into the mainstream, once again aligning the canoe with the current.

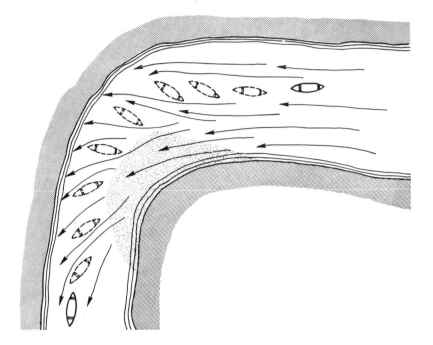

Figure 28

Sweeping around a bend. Cross hatching indicates shallows.

Shifting Channels

Channels do shift, veering from one side of a river to the other, sometimes abruptly. For example, paddling down a swift but clear channel along the left bank, you may suddenly encounter a barrier of boulders lying dead ahead. These will, naturally, prevent your passage, even though a substantial flow may continue through the barrier. A quick appraisal reveals that the main channel is now near the right bank. What to do? We have seen that a sweeping turn in flowing water may result in a pile-up on the very obstacle you're trying to avoid. The solution lies in setting over or ferrying.

This is a matter of putting the current to work for you. The stern of the canoe is edged out into the current so that the canoe is at an angle to the main current (Fig. 29). In downstream travel, the stern is always angled in the direction you wish to travel. The degree of angle varies according to the power of the flow. There can be no arbitrary rule. It's a matter of

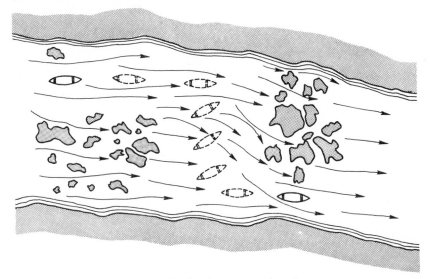

Figure 29   *Setting over or ferrying.*

experience. The canoe is held at this angle while both paddlers back-water just enough to keep the current from carrying them downstream. This will force the canoe to edge, almost broadside, toward the opposite riverbank. The principle is the same as that used by old-time river ferries which were guided by an overhead cable and powered by the current striking the ferry's angle-side. Once the canoe is set over and arrives at the head of the new channel, it is then re-aligned with the current and proceeds downriver.

Riffles

Riffles are really miniature rapids, characterized by small waves and water slipping rapidly over a shallow bottom. Such a pitch may be obstruction-free and deep enough to be run, but larger rocks may occasionally obstruct passage, at least partially. Riffles do not have the power of heavy water, and if there is a clear channel they afford a pleasant ride with little danger. The very shallowness, however, presents problems in that paddles cannot be used as such without striking bottom. The stern paddler can convert his blade into a shallow rudder, but unless headway is faster or slower than the current's speed, such a rudder is next to useless. To a canoeing purist, it's considered sacrilegious behavior but paddles can be used as poles, pushing against the bottom to control speed or for steering. In such water, I prefer to bring the paddles inboard and use my setting pole for snubbing.

Riffles often prove that the stern should be somewhat lighter than the bow for downstream running. So shallow are some that the stern may bump along the bottom if proper trim hasn't been maintained. All in all, however, riffles present few dangers beyond the scraping of paint. They're excellent practice water for beginners.

The Sluice or Chute

This is a swiftly-flowing channel, usually on a relatively steep gradient, constricted between narrowing banks, boulder fields, or ledges. A comparatively large volume of water must find its way through a channel smaller than that through which it has been flowing. Breaks in abandoned dams often provide this condition, resulting in a sharply dropping chute which generates great power.

Usually such channels are fairly clear, the force of the water, especially at flood stage, having prevented the deposit of rocks or logs. The head of the sluice is often deceptively smooth—inviting, in fact, with scarcely a ripple showing on its surface. As it enters the raceway, however, small waves develop, these growing in size until the foot of the chute is reached. Here, the fast-flowing water strikes relatively still water and much of the chute's power is dissipated in large waves known as "standing waves" or "haystacks." If evenly patterned and regular, these haystacks generally indicate deep water. Any noticeable break or irregularity in their pattern is a sure sign of a hidden obstruction.

Whether or not a sluice can be run by novices depends much upon the size of the haystack at its foot and the possible presence of obstructions. Barring the latter, even an open canoe can probably "shoot the chute" without danger if the standing waves are little more than a foot high. Larger haystacks, however, call for a spraydeck and skilled canoemanship. Very large waves, 2 to 3 feet high, are the expert's territory. Obstructions of any kind should deter beginners and cause advanced canoeists to examine the run closely before attempting it.

Running the sluice itself is not difficult, as a rule, except that steerage way must be maintained. To broach in such a situation is disastrous. The popular belief that a canoe's speed must exceed that of the current may be in error during this type of run. Speeding up the canoe substantially beyond the current's rate of travel will cause it to plunge into the haystack rather than ride over it, a guarantee of a lap-full of water coupled with the strong possibility of swamping. Running a sluice in this manner is foolhardy for all but experts and even they will do it only when riding a decked canoe.

A more reasonable and safer approach is to slow the canoe so that it will not plunge too sharply into the standing waves but, instead, will ride up on them. It probably will not climb completely to the crests, but at least it will not "submarine." Climbing the haystack at an angle, rather than head-on, will afford the bow even more lift (Fig. 30). At any rate,

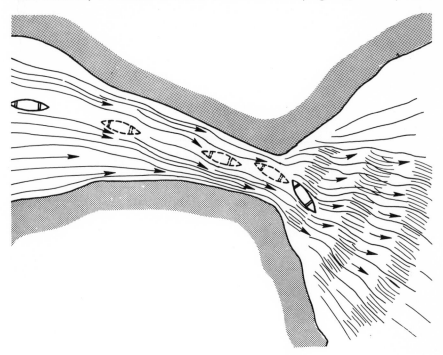

Figure 30 *Running a chute*

the canoeist who tackles such a chute can expect an exciting ride. How much water comes aboard depends upon his skill, and upon whether or not his canoe is decked.

Eddies

Eddies are quickly recognized by the circular flow of the current, usually adjacent to a relatively swift run. Almost invariably, eddies are found immediately downstream of rocks, boulders, or other obstructions; some moving in leisurely circles, others whirling with such speed that whirlpools form at their centers. Eddies are useful to white-water canoemen. Downstream paddlers use them as rest stops or as observation posts from which to appraise channels to be run. As pointed out earlier, upstream polers use them similarly and also take advantage of larger eddies to carry them upriver. In most instances, eddies found in Class I, II, and III rapids present few problems to paddlers who've mastered basic white-water skills. Eddies created by heavy water plunging wildly among rocks are another matter.

Newcomers to fast-water canoeing are unaware that there is an "eddy line" between a chute of swift water and the eddy itself. This is the demarcation line between the chute's turbulence and power and the eddy's quiet water. There is a surprise in store for any canoeist who thinks he can ease his canoe from a powerful run into a lazy eddy from upstream. As the bow enters the eddy, the main current still has a strong grasp on the stern and the craft will be spun quickly broadside to the current, possibly even completely turned end for end, to be carried downriver stern first and probably out of control.

On a turbulent or particularly powerful current, "white eddies" are treacherous. These are swiftly rotating currents, highly aerated and heavily foamed, much less buoyant than the main channel; they require the paddlers to dig their paddles deep and hard to obtain purchase.

Two techniques are used for entering an eddy from upstream in a swift current. One calls for driving the bow into the eddy at substantial speed, almost grazing the obstruction forming the eddy, so that the current has little time in which to swing the stern downstream. The hard drive is continued into the quiet water where "brakes" must be applied immediately, usually with jam or backwater strokes.

The second technique sees the canoe remaining in the main current until its entire length is opposite the eddy and close to the eddy line (Fig. 31). The stern is then set over quickly into the eddy and the bow

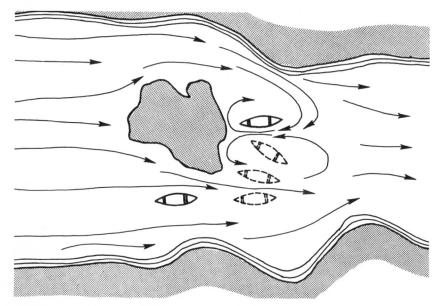

Figure 31   *Entering an eddy.*

paddler pulls in his end of the craft, aided by the current.

At any rate, both of these eddy-entry methods, because they must be used when the situation is critical, are for experts. Novices, to whom the maneuvers may appear easy, should practice them in safer waters!

Leaving an eddy to enter a strong current is, at best, difficult. Nosing the bow into the mainstream from the quiet of the eddy may cause the canoe to spin out of control as the current grasps it. It may simply be pushed back into the eddy however, if the paddlers are having a lucky day.

Proper technique requires that the canoe be angled upstream into the current with powerful strokes. As the current strikes the craft, paddlers lean to the downstream side, bracing themselves and the canoe by hard digging with paddles on that side. Exposing the forward end of the craft's bottom to the power of the current will then snap the canoe around quickly into alignment with the main flow. Obviously, this is a maneuver for advanced canoemen.

Some General Rules

As I've described them, some of the foregoing river conditions and techniques can aptly be termed oversimplifications. After all, eddies, chutes, riffles, and haystacks do not occur in the orderly manner in which for clarity I've tried to describe them. Nature distributes them helter-skelter. Where, when, or how they will occur or in what combinations is impossible to enumerate or anticipate. This is the fascination of white water. No book, no matter how detailed, can imbue its reader with skill. It can only alert him to the possibilities. Nor can any amount of reading replace coaching from an expert or experience attained while actually running white water. The basic situations I've described are intended only to give a beginner some idea of what to expect—along with a few hints as to how he can acquire necessary skill.*

White-water canoemen generally agree that an open canoe can be used safely in rapids up to Grade III, at least by paddlers of experience. For waters of Grade III or greater turbulence, a decked craft is a definite advantage. Temporary decking may include little more than a canvas covering attached to the forepeak and gunwales and running back to the bow seat with provisions for the paddler. For especially heavy seas, decking covers the entire canoe except for paddlers' cockpits. Perhaps the

*Three outstanding books dealing with the forces of white water and the techniques for handling it are: John T. Urban, *A White Water Handbook for Canoe and Kayak* (Appalachian Mountain Club, 5 Joy St., Boston, Mass. 02108); Peter Dwight Whitney, *White Water Sports* (New York, Ronald Press, 1960); *Basic River Canoeing* (Buck Ridge Ski Club, 32 Dartmouth Circle, Swarthmore, Pa. 19081).

finest craft for white-water running is the European "banana boat," a cross between a kayak and a canoe, with solid, full-length decking which provides three cockpits, two for paddlers and a third through which duffel can be packed aboard. Removable "skirts" which embrace the paddler's waist make the banana boat practically waterproof. This is an upswept-keel craft, not unlike the design of Eastern Cree's crooked canoe.

During lake—or "flat water"—travel whether the stern or bow is in charge of the canoe is pretty much a matter of mutual agreement. Generally, the stern man directs, since he does much of the steering, and since visibility immediately in front of the craft is not critical. In white water, however, the bow paddler is in a better position to appraise obstructions lying ahead and to choose a passage, particularly when a quick decision is required. He heads the bow into the channel and the stern man sees that the stern follows. The stern partner is not without responsibility, though. He needs to grasp quickly his partner's intentions and to correlate his paddle efforts. Such understanding comes from long practice together and is born of necessity. There simply isn't time for even a short conference.

Whenever the river channel appears divided, either by an island or rocks, chances are the main channel, where the flow is heaviest, will see you through. If it involves more turbulence than you choose to tackle, follow along its edge. Presented a choice between a swift-flowing course and a leisurely flow, overly cautious canoemen may be tempted to choose the quiet water, especially if both channels appear to be clear as far as they can see. The swifter channel is probably the surer route. Comparatively dead water, in the midst of rips, usually indicates obstructions

White-water canoeists on Vermont's West River. U.S. Army Engineers photo.

ahead which have dammed that particular channel. Chances are it's a dead end from which you'll have to back out. Stay within the main current if possible.

Even in a relatively mild Grade I pitch, paddlers should kneel. Sitting positions are for leisurely travel on flat water, not running rapids. The kneeling position is not only safer but grants the paddlers much greater purchase with paddles.

Wilderness canoe travelers usually combine the use of the pole and paddles for negotiating rapids, thus attaining the ultimate in control and precise maneuvering. In fact, whenever possible, most Northwoods guides prefer poling downstream runs, especially where the water is swift but shallow. For a thrill ride through a wild pitch, though, paddles cannot be matched.

Lining or Tracking

Canoeing literature is rich with descriptions of techniques for lining or tracking a canoe through swift water by means of tow lines. Actually, the need for such a chore is less frequent than is implied. However, a stretch of water is occasionally encountered where the depth is too great for poling or the canoeman lacks the necessary skill for this; also the current may be too swift for paddling. Normally, such a situation calls for a portage. However there may be no portage trail, or the carry may wind tortuously over a dangerous or difficult cliff. It may be that the canoe is so heavily laden that towing is an easier alternative than unloading, carrying, then reloading.

Some suggest that a 100-foot line of ¼-inch rope be attached to each end of the craft, to be kept coiled for ready use. This is fine if it doesn't somehow get overboard and snag into a rock or fallen tree, thus bringing the canoe up short unexpectedly. The 100-foot lines are sound suggestions but they should be attached only when needed.

An exception to this is the running of violent water when shorter painters, possibly 20-feet long, should be attached and allowed to drag. These help retrieve a canoe which might spill.

Situations requiring tracking or lining vary. For example, where water is swift but shallow, the single-line method is used. The tow line is attached to the craft's towing ring if this is located at its cutwater, just above the water line. This location causes the bow to lift slightly when being towed, as it should. However, if the tow ring is located on the forward deck, towing from this will cause the bow to sink slightly and the canoe to "hog" or waver erratically. This type of tow ring should be ignored and a towing harness rigged.

This is simply a short length of line running from one gunwale under the craft loosely to the opposite gunwale, just forward of the bow seat. At a point along the keel, the tow line is attached to it. Thus, when pull is exerted on the tow line, the bow tends to lift.

The canoeman then steps into the water, throws the line over one shoulder and wades upstream pulling the canoe after him. For downriver travel, the procedure is reversed, the canoeman wading behind his craft and guiding it.

For deep or very swift water the two-line method is more effective. For this the canoe should be trimmed about level so that it will pivot amidship. One line is attached to the gunwale just forward of the bow seat; the second line close to the stern seat. One man handling both lines and walking on shore can pull the canoe upstream, but a two-man tow operation is easier, one man to each line.

The canoe can be steered by remote control, by alternating the pull on the lines. For instance, pulling in the stern line and slackening the bow line slightly will cause the canoe to veer from shore. Slackening the stern line and tightening the bow rope will pull the craft closer to shore.

At best, though, this is a tedious and slow process, especially if the shoreline is rough or traversed by ledges, or if there are overhanging bushes and thick woods.

It is possible for one man to handle the towing while his partner guides the canoe from the stern seat with a paddle or pole. However, this can be tricky. A sudden tug of the tow line may well unseat him.

Chapter VII

Across "Dusty" Waters

IN SOME PARTS of the North, when a large lake heaves mightily with great seas and whitecaps cast plumes of spray downwind, the lake is said to be "dusty." Tossing waters aren't confined to the North, however, nor to the vast expanse of giant lakes. All points of the compass see this condition occasionally and even relatively small ponds are sometimes slashed by winds before which white caps run like drifting snow.

On the other hand, who hasn't seen the broad sheet of tarnished silver that is a lake on a warm, summer morning just after the fog has burned off, where the flash of a canoe paddle can be seen miles away?

River canoemen refer to lakes or quiet streams as "flat water," not intended in a deprecatory manner. It's simply to differentiate these from the wild pitching of heavy rapids. "Flat water," however, is a misnomer. It refuses to stay flat!

When my wife and I left Pine Island in Maine's Upper Richardson Lake on a September morning, the only ripples were those trailing our 18-foot Kennebec. We dawdled most of the 3½ miles to Upper Dam Carry, fascinated by the sandy bottom as it slipped slowly by under the canoe. At the carry, a slight breeze rose out of the northwest. An hour later, well out into the broad expanse of Mooselookmeguntic Lake, we found ourselves bucking waves, 20 feet between crests, with no let-up during most of the 7-mile distance to Haines Landing. At times, Eleanor even had difficulty reaching water with her paddle as the bow climbed onrushing waves. Hardly "flat water!"

Rapids are generally consistent in their turbulence. Apart from variations in water level which might alter the choice of channels, there is little change, at least from hour to hour. Not so on a lake, particularly a large one. Within a matter of minutes, its surface can change from mirror-flat to "standing on edge!" For canoeing on such water, give me not a white-water specialist, but a skilled "flat-water" canoeman.

Small craft, particularly canoes, cannot maintain an even keel where waves are a foot or more high. In fact, a canoe in rough water, can be likened to a Navy destroyer battling 40-foot seas, for in both cases the bow and stern are alternatingly lifted out of water. There the resemblance ends. The destroyer, provisioned and depending upon mechanical power, can "ride 'er out," until the storm abates. Not the canoe. Relying on muscle power, the canoeman must make headway into a lee shore before he tires to the extent that he loses control, or run downwind to shelter.

With a canoe properly trimmed, two canoemen of moderate experience will have no serious difficulty heading their craft into foot-high waves. It's simply a matter of pointing the bow into the blow and paddling steadily, absorbing the slight rocking and pitching in their strokes. Paddlers can adopt a rhythmic beat and switch sides occasionally to relieve tiring muscles.

Off a point of land or at the mouth of a large river, an offshore wind or incoming tide may develop a "cross-chop"—waves running in two directions and colliding, thus losing their regular pattern. This will cause the canoe to bob erratically.

When waves exceed a foot in height it's generally wiser to seek a lee shore for travel, even if this means several additional miles of paddling. The long way around may well prove to be the shortest distance, considering the savings in energy.

This is not always possible, of course. For one reason or another, it may be necessary to buck a headwind to reach a destination, or a couple of adventuresome canoemen may choose to test their mettle, a venture which only skilled paddlers and strong swimmers should attempt.

To Windward—Two Paddlers

They will find that, as the wind rises and waves climb higher, an increasing degree of paddle finesse is called for. It's no longer sufficient to point the bow into the wind with hard-driving strokes. You must "quarter." Each wave is now treated as an individual adversary, the canoe climbing it at an angle away from the wind. This angle may be as great as 45 degrees when there are giant rollers.

Shorter strokes are in order, too. There isn't time for the leisurely sweep of the blade. Nor is it always possible for the two paddlers to dip simultaneously; they may find, in fact, that alternating strokes will keep the craft on a steadier course. With a strong wind off the bow, both may stroke on the lee side to offset wind pressure.

Some experts suggest that the stern man dip his paddle deeply and retrieve it with an upward and backward sweep of the flat of his blade so that he tends to lift the bow. This is much like picking up a fishing rod from the tip end! The leverage isn't very effective. Also, this would call for a long stroke, and a slow one—definitely not feasible when great seas are rushing at you.

In such water, it's important not to drive the canoe hard against oncoming combers lest it nosedive into the waves. Give the bow a chance to lift. Particularly as the canoe reaches the crest of a wave, it must be under full control, since it will tend to swing downwind into the wave's forward trough, with the danger of broaching. The stern paddler should apply sufficient power to his stroke and to his rudder to hold the canoe on its course. Here, too, a skilled bow paddler comes into his own. As the bow crests, his stroke should pull into the wind.

As the midsection glides over the crest the stern will lift. Then, the entire craft slides down the back slope of the wave. Any excess paddle pressure at this time will drive the canoe into the next wave, rather than over it. There can be no pat formula dictating suitable paddle pressure in such water. The prime aim is to climb and descend each wave without slopping water aboard; the secondary aim, to make headway.

Even with the canoe properly trimmed for lake travel, the bow may be slow to lift if the overall load is heavy, with some water slopping over the forward windward gunwale. A highly skilled bowman can alleviate this considerably. As a wave approaches, he flexes his knees upward, raising his own weight in a low "jump" from his position, as the canoe starts to climb an oncoming wave. This is much the same maneuver used to "bob" a canoe. The upward motion of the bowman's body literally lifts some of his weight from the canoe. A true artist in the bow can, at the same time, reach forward with the flat of his blade thrust into the onrushing crest and bear downward, adding to the forward lift. Such a maneuver calls for the timing of a high-wire flyer but it will lift the bow beautifully. It should not be a quick, abrupt movement but a smooth motion, accomplished so that the paddler is back in paddling position as the canoe slides over the crest into the following trough.

This is no trick to be stored in a convenient memory nook for use when the need arises. It's too late to learn it, then. Practice it on smaller waves near shore. An ill-timed move, a momentary loss of balance—almost inevitable when learning—are not critical in shallow water. On a 3-foot roller, a mile from shore . . . that's another matter.

To Windward—Single Paddler

A lone canoeman tackling rough water from a kneeling position amidship finds his canoe highly susceptible to strong winds. By the same token, the center position affords greater maneuverability. From this point he can pivot his craft up or downwind.

Facing a powerful wind and mounting waves, a lone paddler should angle his craft into the blow so that he can paddle entirely on the lee side. Position here is important. If he kneels directly amidship, his paddle's center of effort will lie just forward of the center of the canoe.

The wind will then have a greater bearing surface against the canoe at the rear than at the front, hence will actually help keep the craft on course. In an extremely strong headwind, the paddler may move forward even more, thus increasing wind pressure at the stern and decreasing it further at the bow.

Basically, paddling technique in rough water is much the same for a single canoeman as for a tandem team. Timing, however, is more critical. For instance, as the bow rises over a crest, it is more likely to swerve downwind. Therefore, the lone paddler must have his blade in the water on the lee side, applying rudder and forward thrust as his bow mounts the wave. If he loses this grip momentarily and his canoe starts to broach, he can quickly regain his course and control by pivoting the craft into the wind just as the midsection rises to the crest. At this point—and his opportunity will be brief—both his bow and stern are relatively free of the water's grasp. This seemingly complicated move becomes instinctive with experience.

With a single paddle, too, lengthy, time-consuming sweeps are not feasible. Short, quick, powerful strokes are needed.

Occasionally, it may be necessary for a pair of paddlers, or a lone canoeman, to run cross-wind and this is possible. In moderate seas, a canoe can safely run almost parallel to the waves, rising over crests and dipping into troughs rhythmically. The secret is to edge the bow slightly upwind just enough so that white caps do not slap at full right angles to the gunwale. Otherwise, they might slop enough water inboard to require bailing.

A single canoeman has an advantage here. By paddling on the lee side and giving his canoe a downwind list, he can ride over foamy crests and keep a relatively dry bilge, since he increases his freeboard on the windward side. Also, with his upwind gunwale raised, white caps tend to slide under the canoe rather than strike its side.

Where a cross-wind traverse seems necessary yet wind and wave threaten trouble, the alternative is to tack, in the manner of a sailboat. Quarter, perhaps a half-mile into the wind, then come about and paddle a similar distance, quartering with the wind, always in the general direction of your ultimate goal. The angle of tack depends, of course, on the velocity of the wind, the height of the waves and the skill of the paddlers. Of course, the smaller the angle of tack, the more direct your route will be.

Running Downwind

Running before the wind in high seas can be thrilling but should be reserved for those who know their way among wind and waves. It is not unlike surfboarding for long distances. It may be deceptively easy at first.

On a large lake, waves which are initially 2 to 3 feet high, exciting but not yet dangerous, may gradually progress in size to 6-footers from which there is no turning back! The further downwind you travel, the bigger will be the waves.

In such water there's little need for vigorous paddling but it's wise to angle slightly away from the course of the wind. A slight tack, to one side then the other, will keep you on course and eliminate climbing the waves at a direct right angle. Here the stern paddler's work is critical and it functions primarily as a rudder.

It won't take you long to discover that, once your canoe has climbed a crest, you can hold it there for a few moments, surging ahead at great speed, a passenger aboard the wave! "Surfing" a canoe is a master maneuver which requires precise timing.

Should you gain too much speed and outrun the crest slightly, the canoe may pitch suddenly downhill ahead of the wave. Deft maneuvering and great strength applied to the paddles can save you from broaching. This can happen only if you "over-paddle." Generally, it's impossible to remain atop a big wave for a lengthy free ride. Relatively lightweight surfboards accomplish this, but the waves will invariably overtake and pass a laden canoe with its greater weight. The trick is to remain in the crest as long as possible.

As each giant comber pulls away and the canoe starts to drop into its following trough, the stern paddler should have his blade firmly in the water, using it as a rudder. The stern will drop first, of course, and the canoe will seem to be sliding downhill—backward! This is not the case. It is simply settling, stern first, into the trough.

Once it has dropped, the stern is already in the grasp of the next wave, even while the first comber has not yet completely released the bow. This is where the danger of broaching occurs. Every ounce of power in the stern blade should be applied as rudder to keep the canoe on course. The bow man, too, can help by keeping his end of the craft downwind.

Occasionally in great seas it seems impossible to keep the canoe aligned with the wind, so great are the waves. Canoeists in this situation are in danger and should rig a sea anchor. This calls for deft handling of the craft by both paddlers while one of them rigs the anchor. A length of rope, 20 to 30 feet long, is tied to a simple water bucket, metal or canvas, to a cook kettle, or to any receptacle with a bail handle, the bigger the better. The other end is tied to the gunwale as far astern as possible. Then the pail is heaved overboard. This will immediately drag the stern into the wind and hold it roughly in that position. It's a wise canoeman who rigs his sea anchor *before* attempting a rough downwind passage.

All in all, downwind running can be a delight because it requires little paddling to maintain headway. The waves and wind supply this; the paddles keep the craft on course.

How heavy a sea will a canoe withstand? Chances are, as long as the wind allows it to remain on the water it can hold its own. However, winds exceeding 40 to 50 miles-per-hour make canoeing impractical, even for experts.

Few will deliberately tackle water such as I've described. Occasionally, though, some may be caught out in an unexpected blow; or an emergency may require disregarding the wind. Almost invariably though, the expert seeks a lee shore along which to travel and he'll take advantage of the quiet water that lies downwind of islands and points of land. If this is not possible, he'll outwait the wind. The loss of a few hours, or even a day, while wind-bound is trifling compared to the risks of travel in mountainous seas. In fact, being wind-bound can be a pleasant experience. My wife and I once spent four days on a small island in a 17-mile lake which "stood on edge" before a southerly storm wind. We pitched a snug camp and "let it blow itself out." We could have left the island from its lee side and gone downwind to the far shore, but there we would have run into tremendous surf and more wind. We remained on the island and enjoyed the storm.

Night Travel

An alternative to chomping at the bit on a wind-bound island is to travel at night. In most parts of the country, westerly and northwesterly winds, even if ferocious by day, will abate at sunset or shortly thereafter. Easterly or southerly winds usually do not. Barring the latter, travel by canoe at night is entirely practical providing you are familiar with the waters or have some navigational ability, using either a compass or the stars. If there is a bright moon the matter is simplified, since the outline of any surrounding hills will keep you posted as to your position. Nonetheless, caution should be used. Travel at moderate speeds so that striking a reef or rock won't spill you into the lake.

On wilderness lakes, night travel is relatively safe, so far as other craft are concerned, but it's a wise plan to have a flashlight at hand. At the sound of an approaching motor, flash the beam around and continue to do so until the power boat has left the vicinity. Don't travel with the light on. Its brilliance will blot out the surrounding landmarks and make it difficult for you to see the stars. On "civilized" waters, of course, night-time travel without a light is foolhardy and, on many waters, illegal.

Navigation at night is relatively easy even without a compass, providing there is no cloud cover. Anyone who can recognize the Big Dipper can find the North Star and there is no better directional sign visible on the earth. On a cloudy night, travel without a compass is risky. It's wiser to stay ashore.

Chapter VIII

Portaging

BLESSED INDEED is the canoeman who completes a long trip without having to tote his entire outfit, including the canoe, over a portage. This is a rare experience. Few extensive trips are without obstructions which must be bypassed by a portage. However, a carry—as it is known in the Northeast—is not completely without compensation.

Day after day of paddling on a seemingly endless river or through a lengthy chain of lakes may become monotonous, and a portage often comes as a welcome break in the routine. Leg muscles, long cramped in the canoe, get a stretch; a new spirit imbues the paddlers, a sort of what-lies-beyond-the-portage wondering.

The need for a portage is usually obvious: a dam, a severe set of rapids or a ridge between two lakes. In most instances, there's no question about the need for carrying, although most professionals will portage only if absolutely necessary, the prospect of unloading, toting, and re-loading having little appeal. Occasionally, a compromise is arrived at. One partner may tote the outfit over the portage while the other runs the rapids with the empty canoe.

For novices, however, or even those canoemen of moderate skill, the ground rule is: "When in doubt, portage." A well beaten portage path is also eloquent advice!

During river travel, start looking for the portage trail as soon as your map indicates rapids or other obstruction ahead. Lacking a map, watch the shore closely, particularly as the rumble of heavy water comes into earshot. The portage trail may be on either side of the stream, but generally the early canoemen who established the carry trails chose the shortest path; so if there is a bend in the rapids, the portage trail will be along the inside of that bend, providing the terrain on that side is passable.

The portage trail may not be obvious, but usually there is a natural landing place, possibly a smooth ledge or beach with signs of human use—campfire ashes, cut poles, or, in this age of desecration, even litter!

*Narrow runs between lakes may eliminate the need for a portage but these may
be tricky. Manitoba Department of Industry and Commerce photo.*

In some areas, such as the Superior-Quetico Boundary Waters, signs indicate the portage.

The portage trail between lakes isn't always as easy to locate. Lacking
a map, look for a dip in the surrounding skyline. Early canoemen sought
not only the shortest possible route but one involving as little climbing as
possible. A valley or notch in the hills is usually the portage route.

Old-time canoemen were guided by a "lob-tree." This was usually a tall
pine whose uppermost branches had been lopped off by a high-climbing
axeman, so that the trunk protruded high into the air above the lower
branches. Most of them have long since disappeared.

Some portages get relatively little use. Not only are these difficult to
locate but they may also be blocked by blow-downs,—trees knocked
across the path by storm winds or lightning. Because of this, the first man
across should carry the axe.

The easiest of all portages—the author sliding his outfit over a beaver dam. Photo by Eleanor Riviere.

Those among the older generation who used to read Robert Lincoln Page's exploits in the Canadian canoe country may recall that he designated the length of all carries in "chains." Some maps still use this designation. A "chain" is a surveyor's measurement, equal to 66 feet.

It has already been pointed out that the ideal two-man canoe outfit consists of the canoe and two packs, so that one partner can heft the canoe and the lighter of the two packs. The second man takes the heavier load—and the axe. This rule is not rigid, however, when the carry trail may be steep or difficult. Two trips may then be indicated.

Psychologically, it is unsound to dally at the beginning of a portage. Procrastination sets in easily! Dreading the heavy work ahead, canoemen sometimes decide to "rest before tackling the carry." Unless prior travel has been particularly wearying, it's best to take only a few minutes to stretch muscles. Then, load up and hike out. Get it over with! Rest is so much sweeter at the far end of a portage.

I haven't intended to convey the impression that a portage is a fiendish form of torture. Toting 60 to 100 pounds over a woods trail is hard work but, with a properly-rigged outfit, it need not be an altogether fearsome chore.

Yokes

Among the aids are "store-bought" carrying yokes for the canoe, usually of hardwood or aluminum with fixed or adjustable pads to cushion the

Commercial carrying yoke for portaging. Grumman Co. photo.

shoulders. The yoke is attached to the canoe at its midship balance point, with the stern only slightly heavier than the bow. It may be attached permanently, replacing the center thwart, or by means of wing nuts and bolts which allow its removal. Not all such carrying yokes are suitable. For example, at least one has the padding block attached to the wooden crossarm by means of wood screws which invariably pull out and render

Ready-made carrying yoke causes canoe to ride high on shoulders but this increases visibility. Balance is not seriously affected. Grumman Company photo.

the yoke useless. My first commercial yoke developed just this trouble. Replacing the screws with brass stove bolts and nuts solved the problem but not until I'd been tortured on one carry.

There are those who object to the "store-bought" variety of yoke. "The canoe rides too high," they claim. Actually, the difference is only about 2 inches, hardly enough to throw the canoeman off balance! Before buying a commercial yoke, however, it's best to try it on for fit, lest the pads not rest properly on the shoulders. Bear in mind that up to 100 pounds will be pressing on a relatively small area of the anatomy! The commercial yoke is generally satisfactory if ruggedly assembled.

Some prefer a hand-carved carrying yoke of light but strong wood such as spruce, such a yoke resembling that used by early farmers and pioneers for carrying water to livestock. Anyone that dedicated to canoeing, willing to spend hours with knife and chisel, can carve himself a beautifully fitting, custom-made yoke. However, I doubt that the small increase in comfort justifies the long hours of carving and whittling.

A frequently used yoke is one improvised with paddles. Where the canoe lacks a center thwart, the paddles are lashed between the forward and stern thwarts. Since the shafts, rather than the flat of the blades, rest on the shoulders, a sweater or other padding should be used to relieve some of their gouging effect.

Because the flat surface of the paddle blades rest on the shoulders, this type of yoke is one of the most comfortable. Photo by Eleanor Riviere.

Probably the ideal yoke results when paddles can be lashed to a center thwart. The flat of the blades will protrude forward of the thwart so that when these rest on the shoulders, the canoe is slightly tail-heavy. This makes it easier to raise the forward end for better visibility on the trail. Resting one or both hands on the gunwales in front of the carrier counterbalances the stern weight, so fore and aft control is nearly perfect. With the flat of the blades, instead of the shafts, resting on the shoulders, greater comfort is attained.

The lashings for such a yoke should be securely tied so that the paddles cannot slip fore and aft, nor from side to side along the thwart. Either of these motions could throw the canoe off balance. In case of a fall along the portage, there is some danger of injury from the paddle-edges being so close to the carrier's neck—another reason for a slow, careful pace along the carry trail!

Another type of yoke, in little use nowadays, is the tump line. This is attached to a center thwart close to the gunwales or, lacking a center thwart, to the gunwales themselves at midship point. A broad band of leather or heavy canvas, fitted midway of this line, rests on the carrier's head. Enough slack must be maintained in the line to allow the head to fit comfortably without raising the canoe too high. At the same time, the line should be taut enough to prevent the head from striking the canoe's bottom. Sometimes the tump line is used in conjunction with a paddle

Smaller canoes can be carried easily without a yoke, for short distances. Stowe Canoe Co./Orvis Co. photo.

yoke so that the toting chore is shared by head and shoulders alike. The tump line, however, is an instrument of torture to anyone not accustomed to it!

In the case of lightweight canoes—50 to 75 pounds—no yoke is necessary for short carries, provided there is a center thwart. In lugging my 75-pound Prospector from streamside to the car, or over a short portage, I rarely bother to rig a yoke. Needless to say, this would be painful over a long haul, since the center thwart lies directly astride the back of the neck.

Very small canoes, 13-footers in the 35- to 40-pound class, can be carried "basket-style" for short distances. One arm is slipped under the center thwart and the portage made much the way a housewife might carry her market basket. At best, though, this is awkward, and I prefer the conventional carry.

Lifting the Canoe

For the pick-up at the beginning of a portage, the canoe should be drawn up on shore far enough for its midsection to be on dry land. The craft can be lifted directly from the water, but I prefer dry feet on which to walk across a portage!

For a one-man pick-up, roll the canoe on its side, the interior facing away from you. With the craft balanced fore and aft, reach down with one hand as far as possible to grab the center thwart or the yoke. With a forward shove of the knees and an upward pull with the lower arm, toss the canoe upward. Don't try to lift it in a slow, deliberate manner. This is dead weight. Try, instead, to heave with an upward rolling motion so that as the canoe reaches shoulder height, it is nearly upside down. At this point, duck your head into the yoke or into position along the thwart. The canoe will then rest gently into position, ready for the carry.

Your first attempt will seem awkward, but after a half-dozen practice lifts you'll find yourself tossing the craft to your shoulders without a second thought to the mechanics involved.

In order to relieve some of the dead weight, it's important to shove outwardly with the knees against the bottom when the lift is initiated. This will get the canoe underway in its rise to your shoulders without straining back or arm muscles. At the same time, both hands propel the canoe upward, literally tossing it into position on the shoulders—actually much easier than it sounds. The secret lies in *tossing*, not lifting!

This is the method of the professional canoeman or the expert. Few guides tolerate help from a second person in lifting a canoe. They've too much pride in their work. On several occasions at public landings, I've had well-meant offers of assistance from bystanders who have never seen

Lifting the canoe for a portage—Step One.

Step Two.

Step Three.

a canoe lifted. Invariably, I've turned down these offers, as gracefully as possible. I suppose I must have offended many a would-be helper, who probably assumed that I merely wanted to display my prowess. But a one-man lift is actually easier, and if the second man is unfamiliar with the technique, there's the added danger of dropping and damaging the canoe.

There is another lift method for the single canoeman. The canoe is placed on the ground, right side up. The carrier grasps the gunwales forward of

Step Four, ready for the carry.

the bow seat and rolls the craft into an upside-down position, with the stern peak resting on the ground and the bow lifted over his head. He then backs into position amidship. This maneuver is far from graceful and it marks the amateur on the canoe trails, but it is, I suppose, a legitimate lift for anyone not sure of himself with the conventional lift.

Still another technique is to have a partner lift the bow high while the stern rests on the ground, the canoe upside-down. The carrier can then crouch into position under the yoke and complete the lift from there. This is also a novice's technique which professional canoemen would scorn, but it isn't to be sneered at, especially if those involved are new at the game.

Still another method which one man can accomplish alone is to raise the bow, upside down, and rest it in the crotch of a tree or on a low limb. He can then move back into position for the lift.

All in all, though, when a one-man carry is involved, the canoeman should learn the conventional midship lift; it is easier in the long run, less likely to damage a canvas canoe, and, not unimportant, a point of pride among experts.

For a two-man carry, the lift is relatively easy, performed with the canoe right-side-up on dry land. The bow man stands by the craft just forward of the front seat, the stern man slightly ahead of the rear seat. At a signal, each bends down and grasps the gunwales at his station. In unison, they lift the canoe, rolling it over as it rises. In most cases, the seats serve as carrying yokes with the forward edge resting on the carrier's neck, not a comfortable position unless padding is used. However, the carrier's hands are free to raise the canoe slightly by the gunwales, thus relieving weight from the neck. The forward carrier's visibility is limited unless he occasionally raises the craft for a glance ahead.

Another two-man carry combination is for the men to tote the canoe right-side-up, the ends of the canoe resting on one shoulder of each man. With a keel-less canoe this works well but if the craft is equipped with a keel, it may cut painfully into the carriers' shoulders. On such a carry, some gear may be left in the canoe.

For a short portage, the canoe may be carried knee-high and right-side-up, each man taking a finger grasp on the edge of the decks; for a waist-high, right-side-up carry, they wrap one arm around each end, with fingers folded over the lower cutwater or bang plate. Neither of these carries is very satisfactory over a lengthy portage. In fact, except where absolutely necessary, the two-man carry is far less desirable than the midship portage by a single carrier.

Difficulty can arise, especially on a long carry, from an uneven rhythm of the two men's footsteps. Unless these are coordinated—a difficult accomplishment on rough terrain—the canoe will bounce erratically, a temper-fraying annoyance during a long, hot portage. Also, if one man is shorter than his partner, he'll bear the brunt of the weight and the bouncing.

Even a lone carrier soon learns that a "bouncy" stride causes the yoke or thwart to cut into the shoulders or into the back of the neck. Most experts learn to walk with "swivel hips" when toting the canoe, adopting a slinking stride which covers ground and involves a minimum of vertical rise with each step.

Lowering the Canoe

Having lifted and carried the canoe over the portage trail, how does one set it down? The procedure is exactly the reverse of the lift. In the case of a single-man midship carry, the carrier simply lifts one gunwale, ducks his head out from under the yoke or thwart, and rolls the canoe over and down. As the canoe turns right-side-up, he grasps the center thwart or yoke and lowers it gently to the ground. Care should be taken to maintain fore and aft balance, so that one end of the canoe does not strike the ground too hard. With practice, the carrier can learn to drop one end into the water so that the canoe is partially afloat when the drop is completed. For a two-man drop, a similar reverse of pick-up procedure is called for.

Don't Overdo It

Voyageurs of the early fur trade took fierce pride in their portaging prowess. I've not been able to authenticate the story, but an oft repeated yarn on Minnesota canoe trails concerns pioneer canoemen who toted four 90-pound bales of fur and supplies by means of tump lines over 2-mile carries at a dog-trot! Whether they actually trotted or whether or not their loads actually weighed 360 pounds is immaterial today, but the story does illustrate that a conditioned carrier can tote tremendous loads. It also points to the lively rivalry that existed among canoemen and canoe brigades. Some of this rivalry, scaled down somewhat, still exists. Many modern canoemen pride themselves on the great loads they can carry. To those for whom this is a way of life—the professionals—this is well and good, but for the average vacationing canoe traveler, overloading or hurrying is foolhardy.

A typical husky canoeman, in good health, should be able to lift and portage a 75-pound 16-footer; possibly, with more frequent rests along the trail, he can handle an 80-pound, 18-foot canoe. Beyond this point, the possibility of strain or injury is too imminent to risk. No arbitrary rule can be adopted. Only the canoeman himself can know whether or not he's overdoing the heroics and should give heed to warning signals—shortness of breath, unusual pains in the shoulders, neck, or chest. Loads should be moderate, the pace reasonable, and the rest stops frequent. When portaging becomes misery, it's time to stop for a breather, possibly to swap loads with the man under the lighter pack.

Chapter IX

Canoes with Outboard Motors

On Ontario's Lac des Mille Lacs I'd been bucking a sloppy cross-chop in my 18-foot Old Town for better than three hours when I heard an outboard motor overtaking me, at first no more than a dim buzz far astern. Although making good headway, I still had some 11 miles in which to swing my 6-foot maple paddle before reaching my campsite. It was going to be a long haul; to that I'd become reconciled. Soon the purr of the motor was close at hand, then it drew abreast, some 30 yards to my right. It was a 5½-horsepower Johnson, brand-new, pushing a Grumman aluminum canoe, also new, in which sat an Indian. He grinned faintly, something unusual among these people and there was a casual exchange of waves. He surged ahead and disappeared among the islands that lay along my course.

There, I reflected, is a happy Indian. He had probably struggled over many a mile of trapline the previous winter to earn the price of his outfit and now he could travel as swiftly as any white man. I, on the other hand, was happy with relatively primitive equipment. Each of us was seeking a different goal: the Indian, his livelihood probably depending upon efficient travel, needed the best that modern technology offered. By way of contrast, I was escaping from that technology and all of its implications, reverting to the primitive. We'd swapped positions in time, so to speak.

There are those who decry the advent of the outboard motor in the wilderness and justly so. And, but for the foresight of wise men, no area would be sacred, free from the roar of motors and the stench of gasoline. As it is, only a few canoe regions are forbidden to motors, notably Maine's Allagash Wilderness Waterway and the Primitive Area of the Superior-Quetico canoe country. More such areas should be set aside, and probably will be.

But I'm not condemning the gasoline motor. It has its place on many waters, even on a canoe. For extensive travel, for toting heavy loads, for greater speeds in emergencies, for law enforcement, for supplying outlying camps—there are dozens of justifications for the outboard and its tireless muscles. Small motors are highly practical on canoes and their desecration of the wilderness is minimal.

Suitable Canoe Types

While there are square-stern canoes designed for use with outboard motors, the conventional "double-ended" paddling canoe can be fitted with a side-mounted bracket which attaches to the gunwales directly back of the stern seat. Many canoemen prefer this rig. Not a makeshift nor a poor second to the square-stern and motor combination, this is a practical application of power to a paddling craft.

The motor is stationed slightly astern of the helmsman and to his left, so that extending his left arm and hand to the controls is a natural, unstrained position. To make motor adjustments or even minor repairs, he need make only a half-turn in his seat.

With motor mounted on side bracket, steering is done with arm in a natural, unstrained position. Evinrude Motors photo.

By way of contrast, a stern-mounted motor is positioned directly in back of the helmsman so that he must reach backward in an arm-tiring stance, particularly true if he must steer for long distances or in rough

*With motor mounted directly back of the operator, he
must steer with his arm in this rather awkward position.
McCulloch Corporation photo.*

water. Also, in order to make adjustments, he must make a full half-turn
with his body, sometimes disconcerting within the narrow confines of a
canoe's stern seat.

The side-mounted motor has its disadvantages, however. The weight of
the motor, for example, tends to pull the canoe over on its side. With a
light motor this will create only a slight list even when the canoe is
empty, but a heavier engine will capsize the craft unless ballast is
maintained.

By the same token, the square-stern canoe has advantages, notably its
stability when underway in rough seas or at higher speeds. Also, its transom is designed for the powerful thrust of a motor, which is directed along
the full lines of the hull. Steering too is more accurate in tight quarters,
even if somewhat more tiring on the helmsman's arm. All in all, if the canoe
is to be used primarily with a motor, a square-stern type may be preferable. For a combination of paddling and use with a light motor, a "double-
ender" is the better choice.

For those who would like to use an outboard on a conventional
paddling canoe yet fear its slightly increased tendency to capsize when
empty, a pair of outrigger pontoons may be the answer. These are of
polyethylene foam, about 5 feet long, one on each side of the canoe,
attached to cross-arms which are clamped to the gunwales. Although
these weigh only about 8 pounds, the pontoons increase the effective
beam of the canoe to about 50 inches and add more than 100 pounds of
reserve buoyancy.

Outrigger foam pontoons stabilize canoe. Waukegan Outdoor Products Co. photo.

Still another alternative is the sponson canoe. This is a conventional craft except that long, tapered air pockets have been built into its outer sides, just below the gunwale and slightly above the waterline. The square-stern type is extremely stable, though heavy. The double-ender, however, is an abomination when used with paddles. Locating such a canoe may call for shopping in the second-hand market since most companies no longer manufacture them.

The square-stern is more accurately known as the "vee-stern" or "paddling square-stern" and, in many instances, appears to have been a conventional double-ended canoe with about a foot cut from its stern and a flat transom inserted. This is not necessarily so. Most are hulls designed especially for use with a stern transom—somewhat wider in beam, the fullness of the hull carried well forward, and a slight flare of the bow lines. Many are equipped with a sprayrail which casts aside spray when the craft is underway. Extra strength is also built into the hull to withstand the pounding of waves in rough water.

Generally, though, the transom extends to below the waterline, and this presents minor problems when the canoe is being paddled stealthily. Since the lower edge of the transom creates some drag in the water, ripples

Spray rails located just above waterline help keep the canoe dry when under-way. Grumman Co. photo.

develop, and it is nearly impossible to attain absolute quiet. Hence, for wildlife photography or observation, or for hunting, such a craft may prove a handicap. The double-ended canoe can be paddled with a complete absence of sound; the square-stern with deep transom, cannot. To most canoe users this is a relatively minor drawback.

For silent paddling, a more suitable type features a transom extending only to the waterline, where it tapers sharply to form a skeg, or continuation of the keel. This type creates no drag and can be paddled soundlessly. It is also somewhat drier in a heavy following sea.

Another type of square-stern is the so-called "wide-stern" canoe, aptly named since stern width is usually almost equal to the craft's midship beam. This craft more nearly resembles a small boat than a canoe and is also considerably heavier. As car-top craft, it requires two men to load and unload it, and it is difficult to paddle.

Such a canoe has advantages nevertheless. The wide stern permits a full-sized rear seat, where the helmsman can sit to one side for easy steering and motor adjustments. Also, this type has a greater load capacity than the vee-stern craft.

Horsepower Considerations

In choosing an outboard motor for a canoe, bear in mind that a canoe is a displacement craft; that is, it displaces water equal in weight to its own and to its cargo as it moves along. There is an optimum horsepower which can be applied to attain speed; beyond this, the power output gives diminishing returns. And, worse yet, it places undue strain on the hull. For example, attaching a 3-horsepower motor to a 16-foot canoe may prove an excellent combination. Doubling the horsepower, say to 5½, will not double the speed, may make the craft cranky, and most certainly will apply undesirable stress to the hull.

Lest you wonder about the many small boats, often shorter than canoes, that are driven at high speeds by great powerhouses on their transoms, it should be pointed out that these are planing hulls. As power is applied by the motor, the hull rises from the water, changing from a temporary displacement craft into a planing hull which actually skims over the water and not through it. Canoes are not designed to do this. The bow may climb out of water somewhat, but invariably the stern will sink correspondingly. It remains a displacement craft. Trying to drive such a craft at speeds for which it was not designed results only in dangerous strain on the hull and pratICUlarly on the transom.

Manufacturers of canoes generally stipulate the horsepower which their craft will handle efficiently and, although there is no set rule—in laymen's terms, at least—the following are apt guidelines:

Length, in feet	Horsepower
16 and under	Up to 3
17 – 18	3 to 5 or 5½
19 – 20	5½ to 7½

On 22- and 24-foot freighters, with their greater beam and depth plus added structural strength, motors of 25 or more horsepower may be used and are in fact necessary when these great canoes are loaded to capacity.

On Maine's St. John River, rock-strewn as it is, I have used a 24-footer with a 25-horsepower motor. Here, we were faced with the problem of a swift current as well as heavy loads. The craft was not over-powered.

Rough Water and Rapids

Using an outboard-powered canoe in rough lake water involves much the same technique as when paddling. The danger here lies in over-powering the craft at the wrong time. For instance, as the canoe climbs to the crest of a wave, only enough power should be applied to cause the craft to slip gracefully over the top for a gentle downhill plunge into the next trough. Too much power at this point may cause the bow to shoot out into space, then to fall with a heavy slap into the trough, a fall from which it may not recover in time to climb the next wave. There exists added danger of split planking and cracked ribs resulting from the blow to a wooden canoe, along with popped rivets on an aluminum craft, or even a split hull on a Fiberglas canoe. The helmsman traveling in such water should keep one hand on the throttle at all times, applying power when needed for headway, and slowing the canoe to avoid damaging plunges into the troughs.

An outboard-powered canoe can be used in moderate rapids, either upstream or down, and in the hands of a skillful operator can make remarkable time even in a swift current dotted with obstructions. Few canoemen possess this skill, and this is certainly not recommended for novices! However, one has to learn. Before graduating to this phase of canoeing, the canoeman should already be somewhat skilled with a setting pole and be able to "read water."

Some recommend that the motor be locked into a straight-ahead position, at a nominal speed, just enough to make headway. Steering is then accomplished with a pole or with paddles. I suppose, in the hands of a pair of ultra-experts, this technique may be feasible, but it presents far too many hazards for the average learner. Better that steering be done with the motor, possibly assisted by a bowman with pole or paddle and that power be cut back or set ahead according to stream conditions.

For running downstream through rapids with a motor, it has been suggested that the motor be pivoted or geared into full reverse in order to hold back the canoe. This is a "cloud-nine" theory, impractical—in fact ridiculous. I can see no need for power in running rapids. A pole, or paddles, will supply all the speed I can handle in a set of rips and I much prefer one of these to steer by.

My own experience with outboard-powered canoes in rapids has taught me that upstream travel is not only feasible but a time- and muscle-saver, although at the expense of nicked propellers and, in the old days, numerous broken shear pins. Today's rubber clutches have eliminated the latter problem.

Tandem-Rigged Canoes

An ever recurring suggestion in canoeing literature is tandem-rigged canoes for rough-water travel. Two canoes are attached side by side by means of poles extending across their gunwales. The impression is created that tandem canoes solve the rough-water problem. They do not. The waves are just as high and the wind blows just as viciously, whether canoes are handled singly or in bound pairs. So far as rough water is concerned, I would not recommend that canoes be so rigged solely to offset the risks of wildly pitching seas.

In such water, the upwind canoe is in a precarious position. With heavy seas bearing down upon it, it is more or less rigidly held in place by its companion craft and cannot give, or swerve from or into oncoming waves to avoid taking on water. Even with a powerful motor (no more recommended for tandem craft than for single canoes), bringing such a rig about is a slow and cumbersome maneuver.

Although the tandem rig is over-rated in rough water, it has certain applications on calm surfaces. For ferrying heavy or bulky gear across

Tandem-rigged canoes can carry heavy loads safely on calm waters. Canadian Government Travel Bureau photo.

open water, a platform can be rigged between two canoes, to be either paddled or powered by a small motor. In such a case, the motor can be mounted on a canoe bracket or on an improvised transom between the two craft.

Another instance where a tandem rig is justified is during an extensive river cruise which does not involve portages or rapids. Here, supplies can be stored on the platform and covered with a tarp as protection against rain. For such a Tom Sawyer cruise, a small tent may even be set up on the platform, entirely feasible on heavily developed rivers where shore campsites may be at a premium or even completely absent.

During a Minnesota canoe trip I once encountered a young couple with two small children, traveling in two canoes, lashed tandem fashion. The father paddled one craft, the mother the other, with one child riding amidship in each canoe. All four could not have traveled in one canoe nor did the couple feel experienced enough to risk individual canoes with the children. The tandem rig solved their quandary.

During an Okefenokee Swamp canoe trip, my wife and I discovered the advantage of an outboard motor. We wanted to explore as much of this marvelous area as possible but rules forbid overnight camping. This meant traveling into the swamp each morning and returning at evening. With paddles, or a pole, we would have been quite limited. With an outboard motor, however, we were able to make rather extensive daily trips, even at the slow speeds required in swamp travel. Motor travel in such waters requires that the operator keep an eye on the motor's cooling system. Peat moss dissolved in the water tends to clog the water intake, resulting in overheating. When the water-ejecting jet shows no water circulating—it may even shoot a small jet of steam—the motor should be stopped and the intake cleaned. A piece of fine wire will usually accomplish this.

Towing

The canoeman with an outboard-powered canoe may be called upon to tow another, the latter either empty or laden. On quiet waters this presents no problems, but should the lake or river kick up, the inexperienced operator soon finds himself in trouble.

A natural conclusion calls for attaching the tow line to the canoe's towing ring, often attached on the bow deck or, preferably, at the waterline on the cutwater. For towing in quiet water these rings are generally adequate. In heavy seas, where both craft may pitch and toss, the alternately slackening and tightening tow rope may pull out the tow ring. A towing bridle, such as described in Chapter VI, should be devised. The bridle serves to lift the bow, keeping its interior relatively dry and minimizing yawing.

Methods for attaching the tow rope to the towing canoe vary. With a

Towing one or more canoes, even with passengers aboard, is a practical application of power. Passengers should help with steering, however. State of Minnesota photo.

side-bracket-equipped craft, I prefer to tie the line to the gunwale, back of the motor station, thus practically eliminating any interference with the motor. On a square-stern canoe, I usually choose to run the line by the motor and attach it to the gunwale close to the seat.

Duffel may be carried in the towed craft but this should be stowed compactly amidship and lashed in, particularly if the water is choppy. As for passengers, it is feasible for one to ride in the canoe being towed, if the lake's surface is moderately calm. The passenger should station himself at the stern and assist in the steering with his paddle. If two passengers are carried, they can assume normal paddling positions, both of them helping to keep the craft on course. On a straight run, there is little difficulty, but whenever a turn is necessary, the canoe being towed tends to sweep in a wide arc, is suddenly brought up short and pulled sideways. Steering by the passengers can help eliminate this wandering.

In a heavy blow, passengers should not ride in the towed canoe because of the inevitable yawing and pitching which can result in a direct side-pull by the tow line, possibly slopping water aboard or even capsizing.

The outboard-powered canoeman who travels without a tool kit risks having to paddle back to his base. A spark-plug wrench, screwdriver, spark-gap gauge, pliers, and a set of small open-end wrenches, should be included in the kit, along with one or two spare spark plugs. Extra gasoline, mixed with oil to proper proportions, should also be in the craft at all times.

SQUARE-STERN CANOE DIMENSIONS & CAPACITIES

Wood-and-Canvas Canoes

Length	Beam	Depth	Weight	Capacity	Stern Type	Rec-ommended Horsepower
14 feet	34 in.	13 in.	70 lbs.	600 lbs.	Vee	3
15	40	14½	115	900	Wide	7½
15	35	13½	80	650	Vee	3
16	36	13	85	850	Vee	3–5
16	36	14	85	850	Vee	3–5
17	37	14½	95	950	Vee	5
17	45	17	125	1600	Vee	10–15
17	45	17	125	1600	Wide	15–25
18	36	13	90	1000	Vee	5–10
18	38	15	100	1100	Vee	5–10
18	42	14	170	1200	Wide	15–25
18	46	18	135	1800	Vee	25
18	46	18	135	1800	Wide	25
19	51	19	165	2000	Vee	25
19	51	19	165	2000	Wide	25
20	37	13	110	1300	Vee	15
20	52	20	195	3000	Vee	25+
20	52	20	195	3000	Wide	25+
22	39	14	135	1500	Vee	15–25
22	62	24	310	5000	Vee	25+
22	62	24	310	5000	Wide	25+
24	40	14	155	1800	Vee	25
26	40	14	165	2000	Vee	25

Aluminum Canoes

Length	Beam	Depth	Weight	Capacity	Stern Type	Rec-ommended Horsepower
14 feet	38 in.	13 in.	70 lbs.	750 lbs.	Vee	3
15	36	13	61	600	Vee	3
15	36	13	77	650	Vee	3
16	35	13	75	700	Vee	3
16	35	13	80	750	Vee	3
16	37	12	85	700	Vee	3
16	37	13	76	750	Vee	3

16	37½	13½	80	800	Vee	3–5
16	39	14	82	800	Vee	3–5
17	36½	13	85	850	Vee	5
17	36½	14½	105	1000	Wide	7½
19	40	14	116	1300	Vee	7½

Fiberglas Canoes

14½	37	13	75	600	Vee	3
15	36	13	95	650	Vee	3
15	38	15	85	850	Wide	3–5
16	38½	13	105	900	Vee	3–5
16½	34	13	75	700	Vee	3
18	36	13	80	750	Vee	5
18	44	16	135	1000	Vee	7½–10
19½	38	15	95	1000	Vee	7½

Canoe Sailing

Although canoes are used primarily as cruising or white-water craft, a number of owners prefer to sail theirs, an exciting sport. Favorite rigs are the gunter and lateen sails, mounted on a single mast, stepped in a special thwart. Sail area varies between 40 and 75 feet on 15-, 16- and 17-foot canoes, but on larger craft up to 20 feet, sail area may reach 135 feet. Needless to say, the tremendous speeds attained by such rigs call for skilled seamanship!

Some canoe sailors prefer to steer by means of a standard paddle but many canoe manufacturers offer complete rigs which include a tilt-type rudder handled by tiller lines from the cockpit position. Leeboards, attached over the gunwales, prevent undue leeway or side-drift. These are made to tilt upward for beaching or for sailing before the wind.

The American Canoe Association (see Appendix) has set sailing rig standards and rules for competitive events.

Chapter X

Hunting and Fishing From a Canoe

Fishing

FROM THE point of view of the fisherman, probably no watercraft is as versatile as the canoe, whether paddled or motorized. It can slip across deep pools where fishermen in boots or waders cannot tread and, with a little portaging, it turns backwoods ponds into personal fishing waters, even if the shoreline is a tangled mass of alders. It traverses shallows which would ground other craft. With a motor it functions as a powerboat for traveling or trolling, and for still fishing it can be held by the lightest of anchors or even a rock picked up along the shore. Easily loaded or unloaded, it's an ideal car-top craft. For variety of fishing waters, the canoe is at home on a pond, large lake, or river, or winding its way on a rock-littered stream. No sportsman can ask much more of any watercraft.

During canoe trips a trolling line can be let out behind the canoe to supplement camp fare and for sport. Paddling speed is just about right for many lures, ranging from spoons to live bait. One note of caution, however: don't plan to live off the land either partially or wholly even in remote wilderness country. Fish and game have a habit of becoming scarce when most needed! Fish to supplement the larder and for sport but take along enough grub so that you can laugh at unproductive days.

With bait- or spin-casting equipment, or with spinning gear, two anglers can fish from the same canoe with little interference, one with the other. Good technique is to anchor the craft until both men have well covered the water around them. The anchor can then be raised partially, enough to keep it from dragging, while the canoe is moved a short distance to the next station.

Whenever one angler ties into a fish, the other should reel in, cease casting, and haul up the anchor to avoid having the fish tangle the lines

Fishing from a canoe calls for cooperative effort with one angler acting as a "guide" for the other. Province of Quebec photo.

or twist about the anchor rope. He should also act as the "guide," netting or gaffing the fish for his partner.

With fly-casting equipment, canoe fishing technique differs. It is possible for both anglers to cast at once, but because of the lengthy backcasts required, the danger of tangling lines in the air is ever present. Casts can be coordinated, of course, but this requires distracting attention to the partner's activity. Fly fishermen like to concentrate on their own work, not someone else's! My wife and I solve this problem by alternating fishing and paddling in 15-minute sequences. In this way, the angler can cast in nearly all directions and thoroughly cover the water without fear of entanglements. There is one angle at which a cast should never be made however, and that is straight ahead, directly over the bow, due to the danger of the backcast dropping and hooking the paddler. A skilled "guide" handles the canoe so that it turns slowly, allowing the angler to cast in all directions without having to perform body contortions. For example, if the angler is right-handed, the paddler holds the canoe so that the fisherman can cast over his port bow, naturally and easily. For a left-hander, the canoe is held to permit a natural cast over the starboard or right bow. By slowly turning the canoe, the angler can cover the entire area without changing his stance.

The standing position offers distinct advantages to an angler fishing from a canoe but requires skill. Stowe Canoe Co./Orvis Co. photo.

If both anglers are skilled canoemen and their craft is a stable one, possibly a 17-footer or longer, one of them may stand while casting. With a fly rod, standing is a distinct advantage, adding considerably to the length of the cast and to the fisherman's view of the water over which he is fishing. His partner should be solidly ensconced in the stern, steadying the craft with his paddle or pole. Both men standing at once is an invitation to trouble.

In the days when I guided salmon fishermen, I preferred to have them sit on a special canoe seat with backrest, located on the floor of the canoe. This replaced the regular forward seat, which I removed during the fishing season. No matter how unaccustomed to a canoe the angler was, this made for a steady craft. Of course from this low position the length of a cast with a fly rod is limited. One angler whom I guided for several years, and who was unusually adept in a canoe and with a fly rod, often stood just ahead of the bow seat, which I reinstated for him alone. On a few occasions he even stood on the seat, usually on a bright day when the water was clear and the fish spooked easily. From this position he was able to toss off beautiful casts of up to 60 feet with hardly more than a slight teetering of the canoe. He was, of course, a rare combination of canoeman and angler and the sole exception to my rule of "Sit down to cast!"

Holding a canoe for an angler, even in a light breeze, requires some knack. Simply paddling against the current or wind isn't enough to hold it in place. The bow can be gently nudged against a rock, or between two rocks, and the paddle pried into the bottom to hold the craft fairly steady. When there are no convenient rocks, one paddle on each side of the canoe can be driven into the bottom (presuming shallow water, of course) with the shafts held close to the gunwales. Wrapping the arms around these and locking the hands in front so that they pull the shafts against the canoe will then hold the craft against even a fairly stiff breeze.

One of the productive secrets of fishing with a canoe is to propel it slowly, barely edging along while the angler casts. This allows him to cover the water thoroughly. Whenever attractive pools or natural fish hideouts appear, the canoe should be held to permit a few minutes of continuous casting.

A skilled guide keeps the canoe in the shallows, never paddling or poling across deep pools unnecessarily, for this is where fish are likely to be lying. In a winding stream, the inside of a turn will probably include a sandbar or reef and the canoe should be nudged along over this or as close to it as possible, avoiding the deeper water.

In approaching a turn, particularly a sharp one, hold the canoe a few minutes before entering the bend and allow the fisherman to cover the deep water on the outside of the turn and also any pool that may lie above.

Rocks, logs, stumps, fallen trees in a stream and along a lake shore usually harbor fish. Approach these only close enough for the angler to reach them with a reasonable cast. If they prove unproductive at first, move in slightly closer for a better appraisal. You may discover that you're fishing the wrong side of the log! Don't move along to another spot until you've exhausted the possibilities of a catch at the first.

It isn't always possible of course, but in shallow water position the canoe so that the angler, especially if he is standing, doesn't cast a long shadow before him. The canoe's shadow may alarm the fish but this can't always be avoided, despite the ridiculous claim of one canoe manufacturer that his clear Fiberglas craft doesn't cast a shadow!

A clever fishing guide will avoid noise. Whether fish actually hear sounds or feel them as vibrations may be open to some question, but striking the gunwale or hull with the paddle, clanking the setting pole on a rocky bottom or grinding the paddle tip into gravel will alert fish. If they are timid species, such as brown trout or salmon, they may be scared off for some time. Quiet is essential to fishing if not to serenity.

Another factor to consider, especially when fishing downstream—that is, fishing ahead of the canoe being paddled or poled downriver—is the roiling of the water. An alert paddler observes the bottom; if it is muddy, he will avoid stirring it with his paddle or pole for fear of sending ahead a warning in the form of suddenly-beclouded water. Even a relatively unintelligent fish can conclude that trouble is drifting his way!

If a fish is hooked in a pool, allow the canoe to drop slowly downstream, or paddle it upstream a short distance. Playing a fish directly in the pool where it was hooked may well spook any other candidates, whose turn will come later if they're not frightened away.

Occasionally on a stream or river you'll encounter another fisherman, either wading or in a canoe. As in golf, ask permission to "play through." Don't barge across the pool. This is not a legal requirement but a small courtesy to ask and grant. And, once granted permission, don't paddle directly across the pool. The natural course would seem to traverse as far from the angler as possible. This is not correct. If possible, paddle slowly between the angler and the nearest shore point. There are no fish to spook where he is standing. They're in the pool in front of him!

Hunting

Hunting from a canoe requires great skill from the paddler as a canoeman and from the hunter as a marksman. At the outset it should be understood that only one person aboard should hold a loaded gun and this always on safety except when he is about to shoot. What's more, he should never stand to fire. Especially with a high-powered rifle or a shotgun the recoil may throw the shooter off balance with the added possibility of capsizing and, with a semi-automatic gun, the double jeopardy chances of hitting the stern man with a wild second shot.

Ideally, the hunter should be seated just astern of the bow seat on the floor of the canoe, holding his gun in front of him at all times and never turning, nor allowing his eyes to stray from the shoreline. This eliminates absentmindedly turning and pointing the gun dangerously and it also enhances the hunter's chances of seeing game before it sees him.

One valid reason for the hunter's being seated on the bottom of the canoe is that this position is steadiest when sighting. Here, he can adopt the rifleman's sitting position whereas, were he on the bow seat, he'd be compelled to use a seated version of the offhand stance—far less accurate. At best, a moving canoe is an unsteady shooting platform. Solid stance is vital.

The paddler should kneel against the stern seat or, if he's an expert, he may perch more comfortably on the seat. Absolute quiet is a necessity and this calls for the Underwater or so-called Indian stroke, used with great care so that the paddle does not strike the canoe. As already pointed out, this can be critical in an aluminum canoe, whose resonance is akin to that of a kettle drum! The paddler should propel the canoe slowly enough so that its wake is soundless. If there is a slight wind ripple on the water a certain amount of slap-slap from wavelets is inevitable, but these can be minimized by slow travel.

Canoe hunting can involve several species of game. Early in the morning and again at evening, deer and moose will trend to water and may even be encountered wading. Bear spend far more time along riverbanks than some hunters realize. Ducks and other waterfowl can be hunted in marshes by following channels that wind through these. Along streams where overhanging hardwoods are common, hunters will find squirrels and sometimes grouse.

Squirrel hunting, usually done with a .22 rifle or a light shotgun, calls for craning necks and peering into overhead trees that fringe the waterway. Oaks are a favorite of squirrels, which can generally be spotted by movements in the branches. Once the quarry is spotted and the hunter starts to take aim, the paddler must perform the nearly impossible task of keeping the canoe still, no mean trick in a breeze!

I have taken several grouse in this manner, since they like to "bud" (eat buds) in white birch trees which overhang the river near my camp. These are wilderness grouse, relatively tame. My wife and I have on many occasions paddled to a position almost directly under feeding grouse without being noticed. In such cases we're usually observing rather than hunting. Grouse accustomed to being hunted will flush quickly, but when approached with a canoe, they seem unmindful of possible doom.

Deer can be hunted from a canoe quite successfully. Look for them almost anywhere along a wooded stream, at dawn and at twilight, but particularly on sandbars or gradual shoals into which they can wade. Unaccustomed to being approached from the water, deer will often stand for the hunter.

Along the banks of "our river" in Maine, my wife and I have drifted slowly to within easy range of bear, on one occasion approaching to within less than a canoe length. A surprised black bear can be likened only to a 40-mile-per-hour bulldozer. He doesn't seek a pathway to escape. He makes one! It can be exciting.

It's traditional to hunt moose from a canoe; witness the numerous samples of calendar art depicting the lordly moose knee-deep in lily pads as the hunters ease stealthily toward him in a birch-bark canoe! Since most moose hunting is done in areas which require the use of a guide, the hunter has only to follow his advice. He has little need for mine.

"Jump shooting" for waterfowl from a canoe on marshy streams is exciting sport. Here, hunting technique is a little different. The hunter should keep his gun at ready, finger on the safety, poised for a sudden shot. At such close quarters, he may not get a second one.

On some streams, where marsh grass or rushes are quite tall, I have guided hunters for this type of shooting by standing in the stern and poling. This exposed us to the risk of ducks spotting me, but since they usually flush with such a clatter, the hunter was guided by their noise. Also, I could quickly direct the shooter by calling "Right!" or "Left!" If success shines on you, chances are you'll need a pair of hip boots to recover the birds, or a dog accustomed to canoe hunting can perform the chore for you.

Hunting from a canoe need not involve a gun, of course. Two or three evenings a week my wife and I paddle upriver from our camp some two miles and drift back slowly. During our return at twilight, it's an unproductive evening when we do not observe beaver, muskrats, deer and possibly an owl or two, even a bear.

Birdwatching from a canoe can be fascinating, too, especially during early summer mornings when songbirds and their many relatives seem to haunt lakeshores and streambanks. Wildlife photography, of course, presumes skill not only with a camera but with a canoe as well as a knowledge of the habits of wild things.

Chapter XI

Repairs on the Trail, in the Shop

Wood-and-Canvas Canoe Repair

THE LONGEVITY of a wood-and-canvas canoe is only a little short of amazing. For example, an Old Town canoe, serial number 5422 and shipped from the factory in 1907, was still in use as recently as 1968. Old wooden canoes don't die, it seems; they slip into the second-hand market, some worth the asking price, others virtually derelicts.

Determining whether or not a used canoe is worth buying isn't difficult. If there is extensive damage or rot it is usually obvious unless disguised by a heavy coat of paint. The latter should arouse suspicion.

Unlike the woodsman's axe which he claimed he had been using for fifteen years—"It's had two new heads an' seven new handles"—a wooden canoe in need of extensive repair can be a real headache; it may be less expensive in the long run to shop further for a sounder craft.

Rot is the prime enemy. This is most frequent in the peaks, fore and aft, the result of the canoe's having been left bottom-side-up on the bare ground for long periods, thus soaking up moisture. If rot at these points is well underway, so that the planking and the deck have deteriorated, amateur repairs will be difficult. Even factory repairs may prove more expensive than the canoe is worth. Rot also sets in along the gunwale near midship.

Numerous broken ribs will present repair problems. Although two or three of these can be replaced with skillful use of simple hand tools, installing a half-dozen or more new ribs is seldom easy. Cracked or rotted stems (the inside frame members which form the curved ends) may be difficult to detect, since these are not open to view. A knife point will quickly determine their condition, piercing them easily if rot is present.

109

Another sign of defective stems is planking that has worked loose at the ends of the craft. Replacing a stem is a major chore.

Planking that is split slightly here and there, while depreciating the value of the canoe, does not make salvage impossible. Minor splitting, in fact, does not call for replacement. Few indeed are the wooden canoes safely afloat that do not boast a few cracks. However, planking that is broken across the grain, possibly with small sections missing, will require replacement. Splits and small breaks can be disguised with filler and paint but badly damaged planking is impossible to hide. A broken thwart or gunwale, equally obvious, can be replaced with relative ease, however.

It's rare that the canvas on a used wooden canoe is in perfect condition. Generally, this rots in the peaks and along the midship gunwales and there may be breaks below the waterline. Rot is nearly impossible to disguise in the fabric but cuts on the bottom can be well covered with paint. Regardless of the bottom condition, however, the canvas will have to be replaced if rot exists, a lengthy and tedious job in a home workshop but not an impossible one.

Whether or not a used wooden canoe should be purchased depends also upon the buyer's skill with tools and the amount of time he is willing to put into the repair chores. If the hull is generally sound except for minor breaks or easily replaced rotted sections, overhauling such a craft makes a fine winter project for a handyman. At any rate, replacement of ribs or planking will mean a new canvas, since to perform structural repairs it must be removed, or at least rolled back from the end. The paint-stiffened cloth will seldom fit snugly when tacked back into place.

During a recent visit to the Old Town factory, I noted several hulls from which the canvas had been stripped, preparatory to re-canvasing. In most cases there was little rot, few broken ribs or cracked planking. Such hulls are well worthwhile.

The initial step in the overhaul of a canoe in a home workshop is the removal of the outside gunwale followed by the removal of the keel, if there is one, the thwarts, and bang plates. This is a simple chore since all are attached with wood screws. If the canvas is to be replaced it should then be peeled off, and all of the tacks which hold it along the gunwales removed.

When ribs are to be replaced, clinched nails are straightened and driven out through the planking. The rib will then usually slide out or, if balky, can be worked out. Ribs of white cedar ready-bent to shape are available from manufacturers for certain canoes. Straight ribs which can be steamed and bent to fit almost any craft can also be purchased. The new rib is then inserted and clinch nails driven through the planking into it. In order to clinch the nails against the surface of the rib, hold a heavy metal object against the points as they are driven through.

Replacing a section of planking requires much the same procedure.

Care should be taken in straightening the clinched nails in the sound ribs, lest they be damaged in prying up the bent points. Once the nails are driven out, the damaged plank can be lifted off. Planking is also available, usually in red cedar, from canoe manufacturers or possibly a local boat-lumber dealer. It varies in thickness from ⅛- to ⁵⁄₃₂-inch. Old planking should be calipered before ordering, to obtain the same thickness.

Attaching new planking is not difficult. Being thin, it will bend easily to fit the canoe's contours. Nailing to the ribs should be done with rust-proof clinch-type nails. Two persons can perform this task more easily than one. The first drives the nails, the second holds a metal backing such as a hammer head, against the inside of the rib to clinch the nails. These can be headed over after driving but a tighter fastening is obtained by clinching.

Gunwales can be purchased from manufacturers but these may also be made quite easily from local lumber, spruce being ideal. Oak is slightly heavier but more durable. Decks are also available from canoe factories but these too can be made locally of hardwood. The use of C-clamps will aid in the installation of new gunwales, holding them to shape while new screws are attached.

Once structural repairs have been made, the hull should be examined for loose planking and this re-nailed. Planking may also have raised edges, which should be tacked down snugly against the ribs with ⅜-inch or longer copper clinch nails. All nail heads should then be set flush with the planking's surface; otherwise they will wear through the new canvas.

If old interior varnish or paint is to be removed, this should now be done. Most commercial paint or varnish removers are effective in softening the surface. It can then be scraped off easily with a putty knife or the rounded blade of a heavy hunting knife.

Untreated marine canvas is best purchased from a canoe manufacturer or a marine supply house. Canvas weight is designated by number (4, 6, 8 or 10); the higher the number, the lighter the fabric. Most small pleasure canoes, up to 18 feet, are covered with No. 8 or 10 canvas, while craft intended for heavier work, such as freighters, will have a skin of No. 4 or 6 canvas. Lighter canvas is easier to work, of course, and produces a lighter finished craft, also one more susceptible to damage.

Canoe canvas usually comes in 60-inch and 72-inch widths. To determine which you will need, measure around the hull from one gunwale to the other and allow a few inches for handling. As for length, order it 2 to 3 feet longer than the canoe.

Canvas can be applied by one of two methods. The first calls for inverting the canoe on sawhorses and stretching the canvas to fit by hand. This is a tedious process, hard on the knuckles, and unless stretching is done tautly downward and toward the ends, slight bulges in the fabric may result. However, for the amateur workman willing to perform this labor of love, the method is generally satisfactory if he takes care to stretch the fabric well. Should slight bulges occur despite his careful effort, wetting these areas will produce some shrinking, possibly enough to eliminate the bulges.

This inverted-canoe process is started amidship and, here again, is best done by two persons, one working on each side of the canoe. As the canvas is drawn tightly across the hull from gunwale to gunwale, it is tacked along the edge of the planking. These tacks should be so located that they will later be covered by the outside rail or gunwale. The canvas is then stretched and tacked simultaneously on both sides as both men work toward the same end. Skinned knuckles can be prevented by using pliers for pulling the canvas taut.

The second method of re-canvasing provides for forming the canvas into a large envelope, folded lengthwise, the ends nailed together between two sections of strapping. The envelope or pocket of fabric is then suspended from overhead stringers, following which the canoe is lifted, right-side-up into it and pushed downward until the canvas fits snugly as possible. But this alone will not be enough to assure a "bulge-less" fit.

The pocket method for re-can-vasing a canoe, viewed by the author at the Old Town factory. Photo by Katie McMullen.

Two uprights (2 x 4's are ideal) are then inserted, one end resting on a plank placed in the bottom of the canoe and the other wedged against overhead stringers or ceiling joists. These uprights should be long enough so that they will drive the canoe solidly into the canvas pocket. Tacking is then done along the gunwales as described earlier. Tacking over the ends calls for trimming the canvas, allowing for an overlap. When tacking along the gunwales is finished, excess fabric is also trimmed off.

The uprights may then be removed and the canoe inverted for further work. This will include "killing the weave" by applying a filler (also available from canoe manufacturers) to the canvas, thus providing a smooth surface. This should be allowed to dry and harden according to directions; they vary among different fillers but usually require about a week.

The keel, gunwales, seats, or thwarts may then be replaced, following which two thin coats of marine paint are applied to the canvas with a light sanding with fine paper between coats. One or two thin coats of spar or marine varnish follow. Once the varnish has dried on the exterior, the interior of the canoe may be refinished with at least three light coats of varnish or marine-grade paint. The procedure may be reversed, with the interior being done first.

Some may prefer to replace canvas with Fiberglas, it being a tougher fabric. Complete kits are available for recovering canoes and small boats. Fiberglas is easier to stretch than canvas and home workshop applications are usually quite satisfactory. Instructions for applying and finishing the Fiberglas covering accompany kits.

Streamside repairs, following a crunching on a sharp rock, may call for ingenuity. Here there is no lumber yard or canoe dealer to supply parts, and tools are likely to be limited to a knife and an axe. However temporary structural repairs can be made.

Even badly split or broken planking and ribs, while they cannot be replaced, can be reinforced from the inside. These are generally pressed gently back into position. The problem is to hold them in place against water pressure exerted on the hull. There are two means of doing this. The first requires a green stick—maple or ash are excellent but almost any hardwood will do—perhaps 1½ inches in diameter. It is split lengthwise, then bent flat side down into the shape of the rib, pressed into position, and each end securely lashed at both gunwales. Two or more of these may be used. A jury rig at best, it is nevertheless effective.

Another improvised repair is accomplished with a log 3 to 5 inches thick, split lengthwise, its length depending upon the extent of the damage. The split log is placed flat side down over the damaged section, with the ribs and planking pressed back into approximate position. A short upright is then cut and wedged between the improvised floor block and one of the thwarts. If no thwart is located over the damage, a temporary one is lashed to the gunwales. The upright, locked between the thwart and the block, holds the latter snugly into place. Any cut in the canvas should then be repaired.

Probably the easiest repair to accomplish, even in the wilderness, is that of torn canvas. The canoe should be overturned on shore and its fabric dried as much as possible. If the tear is a simple straight cut, not over 3 to 6 inches long, lift the edges so that the interior surroundings will also dry. Cut an oval from a piece of cloth, such as canvas from a repair kit, about 2 inches longer than the tear and about 2 inches wide. Daub one side generously with cement like Ambroid or Duco. With a dull-pointed knife (or very carefully with a sharp-pointed one) spread this oval patch under the cut, cement-side up, using the knife to spread the edges evenly under the canvas. Add a little cement, since fitting the patch may have brushed some off, and close the edges of the cut over the patch. Lay a stone or axe head over this temporarily, to hold the canvas down until the cement sets or becomes tacky enough to hold, a matter of minutes. Now, cut another patch about the same size, daub it with cement, and apply it over the cut. Be sure the edges are well cemented to prevent them from lifting. Allow this to dry and the canoe is ready to resume its journey.

The above suggestions are premised on a repair kit being at hand. Canoe manufacturers supply these, but they can be assembled to include cement, cloth such as No. 10 canvas, unbleached muslin or heavy sheeting, copper tacks, heavy cotton thread, and a needle rugged enough to pierce canvas.

The needle may be needed in the case of an extensive tear, a foot or more long and possibly in the form of a right-angle V. In this case, the interior patch is cut to shape and placed under the canvas, but to hold snugly, the edges of the canvas may have to be stitched together before the outer patch is applied.

Lack of a repair kit in the wilderness doesn't preclude repairs. I once swamped my 18-foot Kennebec in a set of rips which my better judgement had warned me to avoid. The result was a wetting, and a foot-long gash along one chine. Since this was only a one-day trip, I had no repair kit. Despite this, however, I had the canoe back in the water within an hour, following the technique taught me by an older guide. While the canoe was drying on a convenient ledge, I scouted the nearby woods for spruce pitch. This is found on all spruces wherever a break occurs in the bark. I built a small fire, and then tore off part of my shirt-tail to form two 14- by 4-inch ovals. Melting the pitch on my knife blade, I quickly effected the repairs. Back at camp, I applied a coat of paint to the patch and it lasted through the season.

The pitch need not be that of spruce. Pine, balsam fir, or that of any resinous tree will do. When damage to the canvas is light, simply apply the cement of pitch directly over the bruise and allow it to harden.

Aluminum Canoe Repair

Aluminum canoes suffer injuries, too, though far less frequently than their wood-and-canvas brethren. In the case of small dents, leave them until you return home. There, these can be pounded out by holding a small sandbag on the outboard side of the dent and tapping gently on the inboard with a rubber, plastic, or rawhide mallet. Never use a steel hammer; it will only aggravate the damage.

Whenever a dent occurs, large or small, some stretching of the aluminum takes place, so restoration can never be perfect. A slight bulge will remain, inboard or out.

Larger dents require the same treatment but, in some cases, might have to be accomplished on the riverbank if the trip is to continue. Sandbags are not usually at hand in the wilderness nor are rubber mallets but there are alternatives. One man holds the damaged canoe in shallow water, deep enough only to float it with the dented section as low as possible. The second man then stands on the dent and by bobbing up and down drives the dent back into some semblance of its original contour. If the dent is obstinate, he can jump lightly on it. At best this is crude procedure and the canoe will never be the same again, even after finishing touches are applied later with mallet and sandbag. The process should never be tried on dry land or greater damage may result, possibly even a crack or complete break in the aluminum skin.

Small breaks can be patched temporarily with roofing cement, but this is a messy job which will be difficult to clean for a later more permanent repair. A cloth patch may be applied on the outside of the hull, glued over the break with cement or pitch, but even when dry this type of repair is susceptible to peeling.

Welding a break in an aluminum canoe is not usually recommended. The aluminum alloy used in canoes has been heat-treated after forming, and welding will create an annealed, or soft, area with a brittle core at its center. There will be little strength left and the possibility of further cracking.

A break will usually be accompanied by a dent, which should first be pounded back into shape. Repairs are then made with a piece of aluminum fastened over the break with rivets or an epoxy adhesive made for the purpose, obtainable from some aluminum-canoe manufacturers. First, drill a $\frac{1}{16}$-inch hole at each end of the crack. This will relieve stress concentrations and keep the crack from spreading. The aluminum patch is then cut an inch or so oversize and formed to fit the inside hull contour. Some sort of a gasket or sealing compound (stocked by most boat dealers) should be applied under the patch, which is then riveted to the hull. If an epoxy adhesive is used in place of rivets, possibly with small patches, it should be held in place until the adhesive "takes hold."

While dents are common on aluminum canoes, severe damage is rare except among wild-water enthusiasts, especially those competing in racing events during high-water periods. To these canoemen, the risk of damage is trivial compared to the excitement of competing. They expect to, and frequently do, lose a canoe! The average canoeman, however, may never need repairs to his aluminum craft.

Fiberglas Canoe Repair

Much the same is true of Fiberglas canoes, although manufacturers also supply repair kits with full directions for their use. Small breaks can be fixed with these, even along the riverbank. Major breaks are practically impossible to repair in the field, and unless ingenuity can contrive a remedy, it may mean walking out.

However, I know few canoemen of stature who would give up so easily. A few bent bows such as suggested for canvas-canoe salvaging, split cedar strakes for backing and a cotton shirt section well daubed with pitch, can restore a Fiberglas canoe to serviceability, though it might be precarious in rough water.

Ingenuity is commendable but even more so is the presence of a repair kit. Whether for canvas, aluminum, or Fiberglas, this is inexpensive, lightweight, and compact, easily strapped to a thwart or under a seat, or wedged into a forepeak, always ready for use. There's little reason for being without one.

A split paddle shaft can be bound together with a close winding of fishing line, an extra-long shoelace, or adhesive tape stolen from the first-aid kit. Such a repair will probably prove adequate for all but the toughest paddling chore.

A sharp break, one likely to occur in a paddle of spruce or other softwood, is another matter. About the only possible repair consists of a pair of thin splints, split from green maple or other riverside wood. This is then wound as above. It will hardly produce a paddle suitable for white water, but with gentle use, it may get you to a point where a new paddle can be obtained.

A split blade is most likely to occur in a hardwood paddle, resulting from repeated exposure to the hot sun when wet. It's rare that the split results in a complete break, unless pried accidentally against a rock. With care, the blade will probably survive long enough to complete the trip. Repair can then be made by drilling a series of $1/16$-inch holes about ½-inch apart on each side of the split and about ⅜-inch back from the latter. A lacing of fine copper or brass wire, No. 26 or 28, is then wound through the holes. Such a repair will probably outlast the paddle.

Another remedy is to apply a single layer of Fiberglas cloth and epoxy to the blade, adding slight weight but effecting a permanent repair.

Carrying a spare paddle can eliminate having to delay a trip while immediate repairs are made. It will also do away with the possibility of being caught in turbulent water without a much needed blade.

Canoe Storage

Ideally, canoes—whether wood, aluminum, or Fiberglas—are best stored indoors. In the North, winter storage must include protection against heavy snow loads and in woodland areas against falling trees as a result of windstorms or great snowfalls. In building my summer cabin, I provided space between overhead cross-ties for the hanging of our two wooden canoes, a chore requiring only a few minutes' time when we close the camp in the late fall. Thus, the craft are safe from theft, vandalism, snow and windfalls.

During the summer the canoes are left overturned on the ground, near the riverbank. However, at all times short lengths of planking are kept under each peak and under the gunwale closest the ground. This minimizes the absorption of moisture and puts off indefinitely the day when rot may set in.

When indoor space is not available, lengthy storage should be on some sort of a rack, such as a pair of sawhorses, cross-members nailed between trees or cross-arms attached to single uprights. It matters little what form the rack takes so long as it is sturdy. For Fiberglas-canoe storage especially, it should be level, otherwise some warpage might develop in the canoe. Canvas canoes should be protected from the sun. If snowfall is normally heavy in the area, the canoes should be propped by vertical uprights placed along the gunwales and against the interior bottom. This will prevent their being crushed by heavy snow loads.

So far as snow is concerned, an aluminum canoe and most Fiberglas craft can generally be left unpropped. There's no danger of rot, of course, and structurally these will support tremendous amounts of snow. They can, in fact, be buried under huge drifts without damage.

A friend who spends the winter in his cabin discovered another hazard one year, however. He had overturned a new 19-foot aluminum canoe on the shore of the pond in front of his camp, and as the winter progressed he watched a huge drift build up over the craft. When spring approached, and with it occasional warm days, he took to target shooting with his .22 handgun. It was not until late spring that he realized that he'd forgotten about his canoe stored under the drift. He was reminded when he found it peppered with .22 caliber bullet holes! The following year he stored a new canoe in the wood shed!

Chapter XII

Canoeing Safety

NO OTHER CRAFT of its size or draft will survive the mountainous seas or carry the loads capable of being handled by a well designed paddling or square-stern canoe. Given a choice during a severe windstorm, I would rather be caught out in a canoe than in any one of the most modern, high-speed outboard motor boats. Yet canoes continue to become involved in accidents, many of them tragic.

The element of human error is more than a contributory cause; it is, almost invariably, a direct cause. A canoeman who lacks a knowledge of technique, has no understanding of his environment, and who makes improper judgements is dangerous, to himself and to his passengers, It's hardly fair to term the canoe "dangerous." The canoeman, yes; the craft, no.

Basic canoeing techniques have already been described but book knowledge alone makes a poor canoeman. To become an expert takes practice. Canoeing is something that must be learned by doing and necessarily involves progressively more difficult expertise in an increasingly dangerous environment. This is the nature of the beast. Experience, if it is to grow, can't be limited to endless cruising on a mill pond.

While there are certain hard and fast rules, most canoeing safety precautions involve little more than common sense, the most obvious insisting that a canoeman be a strong swimmer. True, many an Ojibway Indian can't swim a stroke—but he was virtually born in a canoe. His skill is inherent, bred in him, so to speak. This is not true of the white man novice. He is starting from scratch. Therefore, complete ease *in* the water is a requisite for skill *on* it. If, due to some circumstance, a non-swimmer must travel in a canoe, he should wear a life jacket from the moment he steps into the craft until he leaves it.

The would-be canoeman should also maintain an objective appraisal of his canoeing ability. To overestimate ability is to invite disaster.

118

Going It Alone

Daily there are canoemen following wilderness canoe trails alone—self-reliant men who cruise for days or even weeks in solitude, contented, at ease, and in absolute safety. These are the experts who are capable of coping with any canoeing situation that might arise.

Solo canoeing by those of novice or intermediate skill should be restricted to sheltered waters and short distances. If he has acquired the basic ability to handle a canoe well enough to be at ease in one, there is no reason why a paddler can't enjoy an hour's cruise along a lakeshore. This is within the scope of his experience. However, to attempt crossing that lake, particularly if it is a large one, becomes foolhardy. Skill should keep pace with risks. As the canoeman's ability increases he may then extend his travel to involve greater distance, running water, and eventually rapids, but only when his skill can match the requirements of such canoeing.

The lone canoeman should recognize risks, readily acknowledge that some water is beyond the scope of his experience. Under no circumstances should he attempt potentially dangerous waters alone. Members of the American White Water Affiliation, who frequently run heavy rapids for sport, live by a safety code which requires no fewer than three canoes in this type of water and these always to remain within close view of each other. If experts insist on this precaution, certainly a beginner or intermediate should not have his pride piqued by limitations.

Rough Water and Wind

Why is it that casual, Sunday-afternoon canoemen invariably head their craft downwind and, as it sails merrily on, exult at how easy it is to paddle a canoe? Suddenly they discover that "the wind has come up." It hasn't, of course; it's blowing no harder than when they started. It simply has a longer sweep and, naturally, the waves have built up. The return trip proves a "harrowing experience," bucking wave and wind. On several occasions I have had to retrieve canoes which were abandoned by such canoemen who chose to walk back to camp. Casual canoemen, then, and novices should paddle *upwind* when out for a short pleasure ride. The return trip can then be made with the help of the wind. The same is true of informal trips on streams; paddle upstream during the first leg of the cruise; then, when muscles are weary, drift back; or paddle with the aid of the current.

Any canoeman who travels on large lakes or some of our huge river impoundments is going to encounter rough water. At times, traversing vast "broads" or open stretches is necessary, but experienced travelers will generally avoid these if possible. It's far more pleasurable to paddle in the lee of a sheltered shore.

Even a vast waterway may be mirror-smooth temporarily. At such times, a canoeman with a knowledge of wind habits, can risk a crossing. Particularly during summer "dog days," large lakes will lie perfectly flat for hours, even days. However, it is also during such weather that thunderstorms may rise, accompanied by winds that will "peel the hide off a bull moose!" An expert recognizes such a storm as it approaches; he can, in fact, anticipate it by observing thunderheads forming in the west and northwest. It is then that he hugs the shoreline. A more thorough discussion of "canoeman's weather" follows in the next chapter.

Swapping Positions

Why it should be necessary for two paddlers to change places in a canoe while afloat has long been far beyond my understanding. During more than forty years of canoeing, I can't recall a single occasion when this was necessary. The American Red Cross Life Saving and Water Rescue Manual describes two methods whereby paddlers can shift end for end although it gives no reason for this. Far better that the Red Cross simply advise: *Never change places in a canoe when afloat.* A canoe is an "ambidextrous" craft; it can be paddled with nearly equal ease from either end. Paddlers simply have to turn at their stations. Trading positions is unnecessary. The risk of an upset by cavorting one over the other amidship can be eliminated by facing about.

Changing places, I suppose, makes an impressive demonstration for proud parents to observe during summer-camp water pageants, along with such stunts as bobbing and tilting, but it has no practical application.

Overloading

Some canoe manufacturers state the capacity of their craft, a few of them realistically, others with a callous disregard for the truth. Generally speaking, when a canoe has less than 6 inches of freeboard amidship, it is overloaded, as already explained in Chapter I. The greater the overloading, the more pronounced the crankiness. Assessing weight doesn't require actual weighing of the load. If the craft sits too low in the water, it is overburdened. Paddlers know their own weight and should know the capacity of their canoe. Deduct one from the other and you have the craft's cargo capacity.

For extended canoe cruises, where heavy loads are almost unavoidable, heft can be cut by using a tent of lightweight fabric; by substituting freeze-dried foods for canned goods; by eliminating equipment that is not absolutely essential. A truism of the canoe trails insists that the more experienced the canoeman, the lighter his load.

Kneeling vs. Sitting

Kneeling and sitting positions have already been compared from the point of view of effectiveness. They should also be compared with safety in mind. That the kneeling stance affords greater stability cannot be doubted. In rough water, whether on a lake or river, only a fool remains perched on his seat. Paddling on the knees lowers the craft's center of gravity; just how much only an engineer or naval architect can determine, but the difference is certainly worthwhile for the sake of stability.

Some experts urge that canoe seats be removed and that paddling *always* be done in the kneeling position. This I refuse to do. When I've battled mountainous waves for an hour or more and my canoe slips into the quiet lee of a headland, or when I've run a bouncing course through a set of rips and the craft slides into foam-flecked but placid waters, it's a welcome relief to aching knees and ankles to be able to relax on the seat! I may even stand for a "seventh-inning stretch!"

Standing in a Canoe

Standard advice, dinned into the mind of the public for generations, is: *Never stand up in a canoe!* Probably no greater fallacy has ever been perpetrated. You can be sure that whenever this counsel is urged upon you its proponent knows little, if anything, about canoes. He is merely repeating an old saw, one that should be set to rest once and for all!

It has already been shown that standing is not only possible and safe but often necessary, as in the case of poling. It is frequently convenient, even advisable, to stand in order to observe obstructions lying ahead along a shallow stream; standing while fishing lends added distance when fly casting; and for sheer pleasure, paddling erect along a quiet shore can be a delight.

Granted it should be done only by a canoeman of some skill, or by a beginner who confines his practice to shallow water. In fact, there is little need for standing in a canoe while in deep water, except to fish, and this by experts only. However, to continue preaching "Never stand up in a canoe" is to malign a fine craft and thousands of adept canoemen!

Cold Water

The springtime running of swollen, turbulent rapids is increasing in popularity, too, the number of competitive events multiplying annually. Winter canoeing is also on the increase, particularly in those latitudes where streams do not freeze over or are frozen over only for short periods, yet where weather may be moderately severe. Apart from the ordinary hazards of spilling, cold water presents subtle but insidious danger. A dunking into 32-degree water will bring complete exhaustion and possibly unconsciousness within 15 minutes, even to the most rugged individual. Death may be a matter only of additional minutes.

When a canoeist is rescued from such immersion, even if he appears to have survived well, he should be stripped of his wet clothing and warmed immediately. The effects of extreme chilling do not cease the moment the victim is removed from the water; they continue for a time afterwards to break down his resistance and erode his stamina. Exposure of this sort may remain dangerous for a half-hour after rescue. It's important that the victim be warmed at once.

Randy Carter, of Warrenton, Virginia, one of the country's leading authorities on white-water canoeing, suggests a warm bath as initial treatment. But at streamside this is likely to be impossible, unless there is a nearby house. In this case, an alternative is for two canoeists to strip and sandwich the victim's body between them, all three wrapped in one or more blankets. Speed is essential.

Spilling in icy waters is a common hazard among Northwoods trappers, particularly those seeking beaver. Breaking through thin ice deep in the wilderness, can be likened to being thrown out of a canoe into a springtime freshet. Woodsmen generally have little help at hand, often working alone in remote areas. Their remedy is a quick fire (a waterproof match container is standard equipment) and exercise to accelerate blood circulation. Not far from my camp, last winter, a beaver trapper who had fallen through thin ice, chose to make a dash to a cabin about a mile away. He died, after reaching its warmth!

Precautions beforehand may eliminate the need for treatment afterward. A "wet suit," for example, will minimize chill, to the extent of nullifying cold water's dangerous effects. Such a suit is usually made of foamed-rubber or plastic encased in a tough outer fabric; it covers the entire body except the head. Despite its foamed-buoyancy, a life jacket should be worn, also a safety helmet for protection against head injuries. The jacket and helmet are year-round precautions in heavy rapids.

A 15- to 20-foot painter of ¼-inch or ⅜-inch rope, should be attached to each end of the canoe when running violent water. This may make it possible to salvage a capsized canoe; more important yet, a spilled canoeman may be able to grasp one of these should the canoe be out of reach.

Spilling in the Rapids

The greatest danger associated with swamping in turbulent rapids is that of being caught by the canoe, now heavily weighted with water, and being crushed against a rock. Don't think of a canoe capsized in rapids as an 80-pound craft whose weight you can ward off. Filled with water it becomes a 1-ton projectile, propelled by a powerful current.

The moment spill occurs, get *upstream* of the canoe, hanging onto it if possible. Should there appear a chance that you can salvage the craft without danger to yourself, try to work it toward shore, bow or stern pointed upstream. Trying to move the craft broadside to the current may be difficult if not impossible and, at best, hazardous to yourself and the canoe.

In extremely cold water or when the canoe seems lodged too solidly to be moved easily, there's no point to further risk in midstream. Save your energy and simply hang on until another craft can reach you or until someone can toss a line from shore. If neither another canoe nor a line is available, you may then work your way ashore, taking advantage of the shelter of rocks or other stream obstructions which deflect the current. In such a predicament, a life jacket and safety helmet prove their value.

In the event that the canoe is free after capsizing, the canoeman should hold on firmly to the upstream end of it, be this stern or bow, and ride the current into quieter water below the rapids where rescue can be effected. Should the downstream prospects appear to include more heavy rapids, possibly dangerous, the only alternatives are to stay put until rescue is made from shore or to make your way there, leaving the canoe to the mercy of the current. It can be retrieved later.

Spilling in a Lake

Capsizing in deep "flat" water, such as on a lake, pond, or quiet stretch of river should immediately bring to mind the oft-repeated and valid advice: "Never leave your canoe!" Canoes, even when fully-awash, will not sink; wooden canoes because of the natural buoyancy of wood, Fiberglas and aluminum because of flotation material or air pockets strategically located in their hulls.

Wood-and-canvas canoes will not right themselves when capsized; they float bottom-side-up. Righting one is easily accomplished by pushing down on one gunwale and slowly rolling the craft until it is upright, though full of water. Even then, it will support the weight of two canoemen, possibly three or four, depending upon its size. With the canoe awash, climbing in is not difficult, though the craft will tend to roll. With the canoemen seated on the bottom, the canoe can then be hand-paddled to shore. If the paddles have been salvaged, so much the better.

Frequently, though, the upset isn't complete. During a lurch, both paddlers may fall out and the canoe will roll to one gunwale, possibly taking on a little water but immediately righting itself. The canoe should be grasped immediately, lest the wind blow it out of reach. The canoemen may then climb in.

To accomplish this, one man holds the bow or stern firmly with both hands, steadying the canoe. The second paddler stations himself at a point about one-third the distance from either end, where he can reach across to the far gunwale. For the moment, however, he places both hands on the near gunwale, his body in a near-horizontal position, approximately at right angles to the canoe. Simultaneously he tightens his grasp on the near gunwale with one hand and gives a powerful kick with both legs, throwing himself upward and into the canoe and reaching for the far gunwale. His body should now rest across both gunwales, or nearly so. Bearing downward on the far gunwale and easing the pressure on the near one, he then pivots or rolls his body into the canoe. With a partner in the water to hold the craft, this is relatively easy.

The second man then climbs in the same way while his partner sits on the bottom of the canoe, one hand on each gunwale to steady the craft.

When alone, climbing back in is a slightly more ticklish operation but the technique is much the same. If some difficulty is encountered, possibly to the point of exhaustion, it is best to remain in the water, hanging onto the canoe and slowly "swimming it ashore."

With a second canoe at hand, the capsized craft can be hauled aboard the rescue canoe in a crosswise position amidship. This is done with the capsized canoe upside down if it is wood-and-canvas. The capsized bow is positioned at right angles to the center of the rescue canoe. Its stern is then pushed down into the water as far as possible, thus raising the bow so that the rescuers can grasp it easily. As it is pulled crosswise over the rescue canoe, the water drains from the capsized craft. It is then rolled to an upright position and slipped back into the water and held while the swimmers climb in.

Emptying a self-righting canoe across a second craft varies slightly from the method used on a canvas canoe. Because a swamped aluminum or Fiberglas canoe has righted itself it is impossible to pull it upside-down across the gunwales of a second canoe. In this case, the spilled canoemen should roll their craft on its side, at the same time pushing the far end deeply into the water to raise the other end. The rescue team can then grasp it, and as they lift it, water runs from the swamped canoe.

Another technique used for emptying a swamped canoe is "shaking out." The canoe is first righted. Then, one end is pushed into the water as deeply as possible to raise the other. This spills much of the water, though enough will remain to make the canoe cranky. The canoeman can then shake this out by grasping one gunwale amidship with both hands, rocking the craft and snapping it to and fro rhythmically. He will receive several gallons of water in the face if he is successful but he'll soon have the canoe floating high and relatively dry. It is, of course, nearly impossible to shake the canoe completely dry. An inch or two of water may remain in the bilge, less if the canoeman has been adept.

Aluminum and Fiberglas canoes will often right themselves so quickly that a canoeman spilled from one of these must grasp his canoe immediately. Otherwise, even a light breeze can blow it out of his reach in a moment or two.

Generally, the dangers of canoeing have been exaggerated considerably. Even though canoes are basically safe craft, good canoeing practices will minimize mishaps further; when these do occur, smooth rescue techniques, though seemingly complicated in print, are easy for strong swimmers who have learned them.

While aimed primarily at white-water enthusiasts, the rules included in the American White Water Affiliation Safety Code may be aptly applied to all canoeists. They are listed here, through the courtesy of the AWA:

BOAT PREPAREDNESS AND EQUIPMENT

1. Never boat alone. The preferred minimum is three craft.
2. Be a competent swimmer with ability to handle yourself underwater.
3. Wear your life jacket wherever upsets may occur. The life jacket must be capable of supporting you face-up if unconscious. A crash helmet is recommended on rivers of Grade IV and over.
4. Have a frank knowledge of your boating ability and don't attempt waters beyond this ability.
5. Know and respect river classifications. (See Chapter VI).
6. Beware of cold water and of weather extremes; dress accordingly. Rubber wet suits or long woolen underwear may be essential for safety as well as comfort.
7. Be suitably prepared and equipped; carry a knife, secure your glasses and equip yourself with such special footgear, skin protection, raincoat, etc., as the situation requires.

8. Be practiced in escape from spray covers, in rescue and self-rescue, and in first-aid.
9. Support your leader and respect his authority.

PERSONAL PREPAREDNESS AND RESPONSIBILITY

1. Test new and unfamiliar equipment before taking hazardous situations.
2. Be sure your craft is in good repair before starting a trip.
3. Have a spare paddle affixed for immediate use.
4. Install flotation devices, securely fixed and designed to displace from the craft as much water as possible. A minimum of 1 cubic foot at each end is recommended.
5. Have bow and stern lines, optional for kayaks, depending on local club regulations. Use ¼-inch or ⅜-inch diameter and 8- to 15-foot long rope. Fasten securely to the boat at one end; other end must release only if tugged. Floats and knots at ends are not recommended.
6. Use spray cover wherever required; cover release must be instant and foolproof.
7. Carry repair kit, flashlight, map, and compass for wilderness trips; survival gear as necessary.

GROUP EQUIPMENT

1. Throwing line, 50- to 100-feet of ¼-inch rope.
2. First-aid kit with fresh and adequate supplies; waterproof matches.

LEADER'S RESPONSIBILITIES

1. He must have full knowledge of the river. He determines the river classification on the spot and adapts plans to suit.
2. He does not allow anyone to participate beyond his proven ability. Exceptions: (a) when the trip is an adequately supported training trip or (b) when difficult stretches can be portaged.
3. He must know what conditions in weather, visibility, and water to expect; he should instruct the group relative to these conditions and must make decisions on the basis of related dangers.
4. His decisions in the interest of safety are final.
5. He designates the necessary support personnel and, if appropriate, the order and spacing of boats.

ON THE RIVER

1. All must know group plans, on-river organization, hazards expected, location of special equipment, signals to be used.
2. Lead boat knows the river, sets the course, is never passed.
3. Rear-guard is equipped and trained in rescue, always in rear.
4. Each boat is responsible for the boat behind; passes on signal, indicates obstacles, sees it through bad spots.
5. Keep party compact. Divide into independent teams if party is too big.

ON LAKE OR OCEAN

1. Do not travel beyond returnable distance from shore.
2. Know the weather. Conditions can change drastically within minutes. Beware of off-shore winds.
3. Secure complete tide information for trips involving tidal currents.
4. Lead, rear-guard, and side-guard boats are strongly recommended to prevent large groups from becoming dangerously spread out.
5. Eskimo roll mastering should be seriously considered by kayakists on tidal or large lake waters. Canoeists should learn to right, empty of water, and board a swamped canoe.

IF YOU SPILL   –

1. Be aware of your responsibility to assist your partner.
2. Hold onto your boat; it has much flotation and is easy for rescuers to spot. Get to the upstream end so boat cannot crush you on rocks. Follow rescuers' instructions.
3. Leave your boat if this improves your safety; your personal safety must come first. If rescue is not imminent and water is numbing cold or worse rapids follow, then strike for the nearest shore.
4. Stay on the upstream side of your boat; otherwise you risk being pinned against obstacles or, in waves, you may swallow water.
5. Be calm but don't be complacent.

IF OTHERS SPILL

1. Go after the boater; rescue his boat only if this can be done safely.

Campsite Comfort and Safety

Naturally, not all precautions to be taken with regard to a canoe trip involve the handling of the craft. The proper choice of a campsite, for example, contributes to comfort, to greater enjoyment of a cruise, and to safety.

The ideal site includes a gradually sloping beach or ledge for easy landing and launching, preferably in a sheltered cove, and with ample room for storing the canoe overnight, bottom-side-up and out of reach of a sudden gust of wind. If wind exposure is unavoidable, some provision should be made for tying down the craft. The tent site itself is best located on a knoll, 10 to 15 feet above the level of the water, exposed to breezes which keep down such pests as black flies, no-see-ums and mosquitoes, yet not in a position to be raked by a storm gale. The choice of a knoll eliminates chances of being washed out by a heavy rain run-off. There should be no unusually tall or dominant trees to invite lightning, nor any with dead limbs which might fall on the camp. Ample firewood should be close at hand along with safe drinking water, although if the latter is lacking, Halazone tablets or a drop or two of iodine per gallon can be used to purify a doubtful supply. A safe fireplace area is required, either solid ledge or mineral soil to prevent the blaze from creeping underground; forest duff, leaves, or other ground debris should be cleared within a radius of at least 5 feet. Trees for shade are desirable during the afternoon, clearings for the warming sunshine in the early morning. A scenic outlook, while not absolutely essential, certainly contributes to soul-deep enjoyment of a wilderness stop-over.

That you will always be able to locate such an idyllic campsite is doubtful. Unless you have a destination in mind, start searching for a camping spot by midafternoon, bearing in mind that traveling too late in the day may result in the last-minute acceptance of a poor site. The perfect campsite isn't always available. The secret to enjoying overnight stops is to settle for as many favorable factors as possible by late afternoon.

Neatness makes for a healthy camp. All rubbish and garbage should be burned and the residue buried. Burying raw food wastes is a futile gesture in the wilds, as well as in areas close to civilization; skunks, raccoons and foxes frequently dig it up during the night or after the campers have left, and litter the site as they feast. Some conservationists today urge that wilderness campers carry out trash that cannot be burned. At campsites of high intensity use, I suppose this must become a logical procedure to prevent them from becoming rubbish dumps.

Sanitary facilities, in the form of a pit, should be set at some distance from the camp, at least 100 feet, and refuse buried after each use. At some canoe campsites, state or federal agencies maintain privies and these should, of course, be used in preference to digging and burying.

Along canoe routes through highly developed regions, it is doubtful that dangerously polluted water can be made safe for drinking, even with tablets or iodine. In such country, it's safest to carry water taken from sources known to be pure, replenishing it en route at various supply stops.

Cooking and eating utensils should be washed immediately after each meal; to allow them to lie about will attract flies. Bits of food left about draw camp pests, including skunks and raccoons.

As for wild animals, there is little to be feared along developed waterways and this is true also of the wilderness, except that the black bear may prove to be a pest. Those that have become semi-tame through frequent visits to heavily used campsites may be more dangerous than their wilder and more timid brethren. In such country, food should never be kept in the tent since bruin may not hesitate to enter, from almost any direction! Food is best kept hung in a tree, high enough overhead so that a visiting bear cannot reach it but far enough down from a limb so that he cannot attain it by climbing.

A bear that brazenly enters an occupied campsite, an invasion more likely to take place at night when occupants are asleep, may not be driven off easily although it may retreat momentarily when shouted at. If the bear refuses to leave, or shuffles to one side to stand his ground, do not try to prod him or to throw stones at him. Remember that he is probably just as worried about you as you are about him. He has come to regard your campsite as his feeding ground, and he hates to leave it. When he realizes that you will not give ground, he'll probably slink off. However, trying to force a bear to leave, or attempting to shoot one with a small-caliber weapon, could well provoke an attack. Stand your ground at a safe distance but don't crowd the issue! Generally, these semi-tame critters are unwelcome guests about which little can be done except to keep foodstuffs out of their reach.

While at a northern Minnesota campsite, my family was once visited by a 300-pound black bear, but so far as we were concerned he was welcome. My wife, two children, and I stood in the doorway of our tent and watched him rummage through our cooking gear, barely 25 feet away, for nearly a half-hour. Never once did he indicate any awareness of our presence. Although armed, I made no move to oust him, and when he finally left, investigation revealed that he had done little damage. This is not always the case. Bear are powerful brutes. A few swipes of a forepaw can ruin a camping outfit; one blow can kill a full grown man. The bear is in charge. Accept that fact.

Summer Camp Canoeing

Canoeing and canoe trips are an inherent part of the programs of most summer camps for boys and girls, at least among those located on or close to a waterway. The American Camping Association* has for many years urged adequate safety measures and the constant upgrading of waterfront activities, particularly canoeing, and is now revising its trip program with an eye to setting up a higher level of qualifications for trip leaders.

Unfortunately, some camps are not members of A.C.A. and their trip programs frequently fail to meet its standards. Even a highly reputable camp sometimes fails to comply fully with prescribed training, safety, and leadership minimums with regard to canoe trips. I suspect that this failure results from ignorance of the true requirements of a fully qualified trip leader or canoeing instructor, rather than from a deliberate attempt to shortchange their youthful charges. Nevertheless, the end result is the same: canoe training prior to actual tripping is woefully inadequate; trip leadership too often is shockingly incompetent.

All too often canoeing instructions are confined to the basics because the instructor lacks the experience for the teaching of more advanced techniques. And frequently even where the instructor may be qualified, no attempt is made to teach canoemanship beyond the level of rudiments.

A typically incomplete program includes the following: before a youngster is permitted to use a canoe alone or allowed to take part in a canoe trip, he must

(1) swim one or two hundred yards with ease;

(2) demonstrate bow and stern strokes, including the Cruising, J, Draw, Sweep, Back strokes;

(3) tip a canoe, right it, empty it, climb in and paddle it back to the dock;

(4) perform the "canoe-over-canoe" rescue;

(5) paddle over a prescribed course, including turns around buoys or maneuvers through a figure 8 course.

The young camper performs all of these on "flat water" and in an empty canoe. On successful completion he earns the title of "canoeman" when, in fact, he is actually still a novice who has mastered only the fundamentals. What's more, he is far from ready for a canoe trip!

Safety should remain the uppermost factor in canoe training, but this is

---

*The American Camping Association, Bradford Woods, Martinsville, Indiana 46151, is the recognized national authority and clearing house for organized summer camps, including those operated privately and by youth agencies.

sometimes overemphasized to the extent that it actually endangers youngsters by cutting short their training. For example, canoeing classes are usually postponed when a stiff wind comes up.

Sound judgement is required, naturally. Gale force winds should keep *all* ashore but when a stiff breeze kicks up a lively chop with waves a foot or so high, those trainees who have advanced to unquestioned competency on flat water ought to be given rough-water training. Up to four canoes can be used, with two paddlers in each. Life jackets should be mandatory and trainees must kneel. The canoes ought to carry cargo amidship—not passengers, but sufficient weight to simulate a camping outfit. If the students are kept reasonably close together along the camp's shoreline, two instructors in another craft need never be more than two to three canoe lengths away. If possible, a power boat hovering around the group will assure the utmost safety, especially if equipped with throw ropes, buoys, and rescue poles.

In this manner, youngsters will get the feel of a canoe on a windswept lake—it won't come as an appalling surprise later during a trip. Also, they will quickly learn that a well handled canoe outfit has little to fear from reasonably rough water.

Where the camp is located on a river or stream, or where such water is easily accessible, classes for advanced youngsters should be held in running water: on flat stretches at first, until they acquire the feel of the current; later in riffles and in small, shallow rapids. At boys' camps where canoeing is a specialty, poling instructions should be included.

With such training as part of their background, there will be no panic or false moves among the young canoemen when they encounter rough water during a subsequent canoe trip. The real risk lies in not providing this advanced instruction.

Naturally, because boys particularly are adventurous and may attempt water beyond their skill, they must be drilled thoroughly in making objective appraisals of water hazards, being made to realize that *some* water conditions keep even the experts ashore.

Understandably, canoeing instructors who can work at this expert level are not always available, especially since most waterfront staff members are college students who, while enthusiastic, simply lack the experience. There are exceptions, of course. Many of today's colleges and universities have outing clubs among whose members are canoeing experts, both men and women, who are active in the increasingly popular sport of running white water. Some of these young canoeists would put a professional Northwoods canoe guide to shame! But, admittedly, the number of such skilled canoeists available for camp work is limited. So camp directors must often settle for less adept college students.

On the camp waterfront itself these young men and women are generally proficient in the basics of canoeing and in water safety. For extended trips, however, where they must take on the responsibility of professional guides, there is reason to doubt their ability to handle the chore.

The fact is that no college student, man or woman, unless raised in a backwoods community can possibly qualify as a guide. Two months per season, over a period of two to three years, simply is not enough time in which to acquire sufficient skill and experience. After all, this is the equivalent of only six months in a professional guide's life! This is also true of adult camp workers, frequently teachers or college instructors, who return year after year to the outdoors to work seasonally among young campers. Unquestionably, some of them attain a high degree of proficiency in the out-of-doors; a few even qualify for a guide's license in some states or provinces; an occasional one is outstanding; but these exceptions are few and far between.

Although a seasonal outdoorsman may have acquired considerable skill in camping and canoeing, he has not had the overall outdoor exposure of the year-round woodsman, who can sniff a storm in a shifting wind, predict the pitch of a river after a rain, find emergency firewood quickly in a downpour, patch a canoe with spruce gum, improvise an axe handle or a tea pail, or outwit a marauding bear.

This isn't to say that *all* canoe trips are well on their way to chaos or tragedy. These are, fortunately, in the minority. I've run into trips made up of well trimmed canoes with bronzed youngsters paddling like voyageurs; attentive counselors slowing the map eaters and prodding the slow pokes; neat, snug camps, safely rigged; campfire food properly prepared. These are trips where fun and discipline go hand in hand.

The difference lies in leadership. Any trip which ventures into a wilderness or semi-wilderness region, whether for an overnight trek or a two-week cruise, should be accompanied by a licensed or otherwise qualified guide who, while the counselors actually operate the trip, makes final decisions as to routes, weather, campsites, and all other matters relating to safety and comfort.

Here, however, the problem of the scarcity of qualified guides arises. In many areas, guiding is a dying profession, particularly that of canoeing guides. Summer camps that seek to employ them simply cannot locate any. The responsibility must then fall on the camp staff, the counselors. And their qualifications if not individually, at least collectively, must match, or closely approach, those of the professional guide.

Where two or three counselors are to lead a canoe trip, among them they should have a sound, workable knowledge of general woodcraft—weather predicting, for example, even if by the simple methods described in Chapter XIII; outdoor cooking so that palatable and nutritious meals are routine, not unusual; skill with map and compass; axemanship, with *one* axe included in the gear, the responsibility of *one* counselor, not to be "loaned" to one of the youngsters; camping ability, beyond the simple rudiments of pitching and ditching a tent, to include the ability to choose a safe campsite; a high degree of skill with canoes, and a *practical* knowledge of first aid.

Skill at building a campfire *under any conditions* is a rare quality among most camp counselors but it should be a prerequisite; a knowledge of firewoods and a knack for finding these quickly are vital. And, most important of all, a sense of responsibility that will preclude any youngster's ever being left alone, no matter what the emergency or reason! Of course, any would-be counselor who has not qualified as an American Red Cross life saver should not be eligible for consideration!

It is doubtful that any one college-age man or woman can qualify fully on *all* of these requirements and what they imply in the way of outdoor skills, but it is possible through careful and thorough investigation, possibly followed by some pre-season training, to enlist three or four counselors, who collectively have all of these attributes. It's a monumental assignment for any camp director, but unless he can call on the services of a professional guide, there is no alternate course.

Chapter XIII

Canoeman's Weather

WHEN A baseball game is rained out, the fans are given rain checks; if high winds come up, the balloon ascension at the county fair is postponed. However, when an unexpected storm overtakes a canoe outfit, it can do little more than run for shelter, usually not without fighting huge waves or getting drenched, often both.

The possibility of bad weather is an inherent risk of canoe travel. The difference between the expert and the amateur is that the latter is caught off-guard and must bear the brunt of the onslaught. The experienced canoeman circumvents the weather because he can usually predict it with uncanny accuracy, even without instruments. He lays his travel plans accordingly.

In a society which plans a picnic according to the TV weatherman's prognosis, this may seem just short of miraculous, certainly not very scientific. However, the war veteran who groans: "It's gonna rain. My old wound aches" is making a prediction founded in scientific fact, as does the woodsman who, glancing up at the sky, proclaims: "It'll be rainin' by mornin'." Such predictions are based on changing atmospheric pressure which is indicated by natural signs.

Rain

Shawnee Indians looked for a "great wind" whenever wild doves perched on low limbs or close to the tree trunks; "great rain" would come if the birds flew low and silently; ravens flying erratically and close to the ground portended a storm. These were not superstitions. The fact is that birds tend to fly low and perch for longer periods when the barometer is dropping. All TV viewers know that a "dropping barometer" means low pressure and, usually, a storm.

134

Before TV, weather watchers relied on weather rhymes such as this:

> When the glass falls low,
> Prepare for a blow;
> When it rises high,
> Let all your kites fly.

The woodsman's ability to foresee weather isn't some form of intuition, nor is it guesswork. Like the Indian before him, he observes and interprets natural signs. No one sign is infallible. Combinations of signs aren't infallible either, but are a fairly accurate portent of what's to come.

One nearly infallible sign, though, is dew—or lack of it. How this works for a wandering canoeman is clearly stated in this old-time weather rhyme:

> When grass is dry at morning light,
> Look for rain before the night;
> When the grass is dry at night,
> Look for rain before the light.

Even if a canoeman cannot find a grassy plot to check, a canoe turned over for the night will serve. If this is dry at dawn, you can look for rain before night. Foul-weather gear should be dug out of the packs and kept ready for use sometime during the day's travels. And if, just before retiring, someone checks the canoes and finds their bottoms dry, slack off the tent guy lines, stash dry kindling under cover, see that the grub supply is in a dry place. Chances are, it will be raining when you awake in the morning.

On the other hand, dew also predicts good weather, explained in this rhyme:

> When the dew is on the grass,
> Rain will never come to pass.

In this case, whether the dew is noted on the canoe at dawn or just before retiring, you can probably count on at least 12 hours of clear weather.

An amateur weatherman need not be a poet, but it helps. Many other weather prognostications were composed in the form of rhymes by old-time woodsmen, farmers, and sailors, all men whose livelihoods were closely dependent upon weather. One such rhyme that is remarkably accurate states:

> Evening red and morning grey,
> Help the traveler on his way;
> Evening grey and morning red,
> Bring down rain upon his head.

Then, there is a briefer version, equally accurate:

Red sky at night, sailor's delight;
Red sky at morning, sailors take warning.

The "red" in both these rhymes refers to the sun rather than to the sky itself. A red sun, peering over the eastern hills, particularly through a haze of gray clouds, should warn a traveling canoe outfit that foul weather can be expected before the day is out. On the other hand, if the setting sun is a brilliant red, dropping into the western horizon as a huge glowing ball of crimson-orange, you can probably plan on good traveling conditions through the next day. However, if the western sky is clothed in a thin, grayish mass of clouds streaked with yellows and greens, a change in weather is due, no matter how red the sun may be—the rhymes do not cover this possibility.

Less reliable but nonetheless a contributory sign of coming rain is the "sun dog" or halo around the sun. This is caused by sunlight streaming through high cirro-stratus clouds which contain ice particles. Though a useful symptom during the summer, the sun dog isn't to be relied upon during the winter.

A "ring around the moon" is a similar sign but there's no truth in the belief that the number of stars within the ring indicate the number of days before rain strikes. Nor is the saying: "The bigger the ring, the bigger the wet" reliable.

Another unreliable belief is one which holds that the "horns" of a partial moon pointing upward "hold water" and, hence, it will not rain, or if the horns point downward "spilling rain," bad weather will follow. However, if the horns, no matter what their position, are unclear or slightly "fuzzy," good weather will continue. If they are sharply defined against the night sky, the chances of rain are good.

In this manner, stars are often deceiving to the unknowing. A clear, summer-night sky, in which "millions" of stars shine brilliantly, does not bode well for tomorrow's weather. Most city residents, if they've failed to tune in their favorite TV weather program, are surprised to find rain falling after a night of bright stars.

Your campfire can predict weather too. If smoke tends to hang low, drift slowly away, or settle into low spots, rain is on the way. Such a day is, of course, without wind and this creates conditions described in still another rhyme:

A stormy day will betide,
Sound traveling far and wide.

On such a day, the distant sound of a dog barking may be heard from a far hillside farm, or the laughter of children at a camp across the lake carries to you distinctly. Possibly, too, there is a lowering canopy of clouds. Rain is coming.

Fog will predict weather, good or bad, as this rhyme indicates:

> Evening fog will not burn soon,
> Morning fog will burn 'fore noon.

Fog which rolls in during the afternoon or evening isn't likely to "burn off" or dispel until the next day, although it does not necessarily point to coming rain. Fog which makes up during the early morning, however, while it may last well past mid-morning, will invariably burn off and reveal a beautifully clear day.

The "fetch of the wind," or its direction, is probably the most reliable of all natural weather signs and there are a number of rhymes which are applicable, one which rarely fails when it states:

> When the wind is in the south,
> The rain is in its mouth.

The scientific basis for this rhyme is obvious. Winds which accompany a low-pressure area circulate it, blowing in a vast counter-clockwise circle, and since storm centers move from west to east, the winds in front of an approaching storm are southerly. A south wind can be deceptive. It usually starts as a gentle breeze, and a warm one at that, thus being doubly deceitful. However, it builds up velocity as the storm center nears. Any canoe outfit which encounters a south wind should be sure to pitch its camp that night on a northerly shore, in the lee. On several occasions I've seen canoe camps flattened by a night storm that started as a friendly afternoon breeze out of the south.

Except in some parts of the Pacific Northwest and in Florida, where local winds make their own rules, a blow out of the east or northeast will bring wet weather, the outlook described in this rhyme:

> When the wind is in the east,
> 'Tis fit for neither man nor beast!

So old are some of these weather rhymes that at least one is still quoted in Elizabethan English:

> When the smoke goes west, gude weather is past,
> When the smoke goes east, gude weather is neist.

The second line refers to smoke being blown in an easterly direction by a west wind, of course—one that clears the air and keeps it so, hence a more recent version of rhyming prediction:

> When the wind is in the west,
> There it is the very best.

Mother Nature sometimes practices deceit. Following a stormy night, a frustrated canoe party may be anxious to get underway at the sight of a bright sun the next morning. Experienced woodsmen and canoe travelers will agree but they'll also insist that the canoe brigade hug a west shore, keeping in the lee of strong westerly or northwesterly winds that will arise. Following any rainstorm, these usually begin to blow about nine o'clock and may reach considerable fury, under a blue sky and flying "puff-ball" clouds.

Shifts in the wind should also be noted. For instance, with a canopy of clouds overhead, shifts from southwest to southeast or from northwest to northeast usually result in squally weather. Even on a clear day, wind fluctuating between southeast and southwest may bring squalls.

According to still another set of rhymes, rainbows can warn or reassure. One reads:

> Rainbow in the morning, shepherds take warning,
> Rainbow at night, shepherd's delight.

Another, making much the same prediction, states the case differently:

> Rainbow to windward, foul fall the day;
> Rainbow to leeward, damp runs away.

Briefly and poetically, these rhymes explain that a rainbow early in the day is the result of sunlight streaming through moisture particles in the western sky, the direction from which storms come. The rainbow, therefore, arches through moisture that's headed your way. On the other hand, an afternoon (the "night" in the rhyme) rainbow is created by late afternoon sun streaming through moisture in the eastern sky, the direction in which all storms move; hence this one has already gone by.

Clouds also contribute to weather lore and they come in for their share of recognition in folk rhymes, such as:

> Mackerel scales and mares' tails
> Make lofty ships carry low sails.

Those who take this rhyming axiom at face value may be led astray since not all "mackerel scales" or "mares' tails" portend bad weather. Certain combinations, however, do.

Mares' tails are cirrus clouds, wispy curls of vapor spiraling upward very high in the sky and traveling at tremendous speeds. An occasional mare's tail here and there on a background of blue sky means nothing more than continued good weather. But let this cirrus formation spread over a large section of the sky in a thin veil of gray and it becomes a threat of rain.

Couple this with the presence of mackerel scales and the threat is doubly certain. Mackerel is a form of cirro-cumulus clouds which colonial mariners thought resembled mackerel scales, certainly an apt description. Modern amateur weathermen often liken them to sand rippled by wavelets on a smooth beach. When a sizeable section of mackerel appears, with a background of spreading mares' tails, the chances of rain within 12 to 24 hours are reasonably certain, hence "tall ships carry low sails." Canoes will wisely do likewise.

Several other cloud formations are forerunners of stormy weather, although none is quite as well known as the mackerel and mares' tails combination. For instance, dark clouds at low altitudes, often with a background of thin, light gray clouds at much greater height, will also bring rain, usually within 12 to 24 hours. Rain clouds are invariably darker and lower than the fair-weather variety.

The colors of clouds, particularly at morning and at evening, are reliable omens. A dull red layer, streaked or overlaid with broad expanses of yellow and orange, will bring rain. These are visible both at sunrise and at sunset and are not to be confused with those described in the rhyme: "Red sky at night, sailor's delight. . . .

Cloud formations are numerous and difficult for laymen to distinguish. The U. S. Weather Bureau recognizes no fewer than thirty-six varieties, all of which indicate coming weather of one sort or another. However, amateur weathermen need not learn to recognize all of them. Close observation of the sky and of the wind, will soon make you aware of the trouble-bearing combinations. Remember that no immediate change will take place until there is a change in the wind, although a Spanish proverb states: "When God wills, it rains with any wind." Despite Spanish opinion, fair-weather winds are invariably out of the southwest, west, and northwest; foul weather is borne on winds from the southeast, east, and northeast.

Without knowing the size of a low-pressure system moving in with its rain nor its speed of eastward travel, it's difficult if not impossible for an amateur weatherman to predict the duration of a storm. However, there's even a rhyme covering this:

> Short notice, soon to pass;
> Long notice, long it will last.

In other words, if a storm has been several days in building up it will probably be a prolonged one, whereas a sudden storm will quickly be on its way.

Thunderstorms

This is typical of the thunderstorm. Without a radio to pick up crackling static, it's difficult to foresee a thunderstorm until its clouds begin to form. These are gigantic, towering formations, often at 20,000 feet, glaring white in the sunlight, edges fringed in gray, and, at their lower levels, overtones of gray or black. Quite often the top of the formation is flat and wider than its base, hence the term "anvil head."

Thunderstorms, like all other weather systems, travel from west to east, and it is possible to determine with a remarkable degree of accuracy whether or not they will strike you. Draw an imaginary east-west line through your position. Any thunderstorm formation astride this line, or slightly north of it, is aimed at you. This can be deceptive, however. A thunderstorm racing at you from the distance may not appear to be very large and you may be led to believe that it will miss you. Bear in mind, however, that it can increase in size as it travels and the forerunner you see may be followed by a much larger turbulence, one that could well cover twice the territory it appeared to encompass on the horizon.

There is little need to flee from thunderstorms which appear well to the south of your east-west base line. This storm will by-pass you, although its fringes may sweep over your position if it is a large one. Any thunderstorm seen to the east has already gone by and is no longer a threat. There is no basis in fact for believing that a storm has "turned around and come back." If you are struck twice in one day by a thunderstorm, this is simply one following another. Once by, thunderstorms continue on their way or dissipate.

There are two dangers connected with thunderstorms to which canoe brigades are susceptible—lightning and wind. Little is known about lightning except that it is caused by a positive charge in the earth joining a negative charge in the atmosphere, after overcoming the insulating resistance of air. These specifics may be of little interest to a canoeman caught out in the open but the results should be. The joining of these two charges causes the earth's positive charge to run up certain objects— buildings, fire towers, tall trees, and other elevated or singly isolated objects, including boats and canoes. The cloud's charge literally comes down to meet that of the earth, and you have lightning. This is oversimplification, but let it suffice to point out that lightning bolts of 100 million volts are possible!

Thunder is the sound created by the explosive expansion of air, heated by the lightning stroke. This can be an aid in determining the distance to an approaching storm and your chances of escaping it. Count the number of seconds between the lightning and the thunder, and divide by five. This will give you the approximate distance in miles. If you're out on a lake when you're estimating this distance, I suggest that you continue paddling while counting!

Needless to say, a canoe on open water, whether it is aluminum, Fiberglas, or wood, is in a dangerous position, a perfect target for lightning. So are dominantly tall trees which might tower over an ill-chosen campsite. Probably one of the most foolhardy ways of seeking shelter would be to lie under your overturned aluminum canoe. Instead, look for thick, even-stand timber, a clump where all of the trees are about the same height. If no shelter whatsoever is available, lie on the ground covered with your raingear.

What are your chances of being struck by lightning? They are slim, indeed. Approximately 600 people are killed annually by lightning and some 1500 are injured. This includes the great many who ignorantly seek the wrong shelter, such as a lone tree on a golf course. With proper precautions, the odds are overwhelmingly in your favor.

Of some interest to canoemen seeking a campsite as a thunderstorm approaches is the fact that oaks are the most frequently struck tree. The American beech is the least susceptible, but nonetheless risky as an umbrella!

Admittedly, lightning is a hazard, but far more to be feared during a thunderstorm is being caught out in its winds. It is the nth degree of foolhardiness for any canoeman to think that his craft can safely outride a severe thunderstorm blow or that from a late start he can outrun one. He may be lucky and escape with nothing more than a drenching but it's like playing Russian roulette with Mother Nature, using her six-shooter! Thunderstorm winds are to feared, unless you are properly sheltered ashore.

During my younger days as a fishing guide, my 16-foot inboard motorboat broke down, with a clogged gas line, in the center of a 6-mile-broad bay of a large northern lake. With one eye on an approaching thunderstorm and the other on the carburetor I worked at a frenzied pace until I realized that I'd already lost the race. Even had I succeeded in time with the repairs, I could not have outrun the winds I saw charging across the lake toward me. With a bait bucket I quickly rigged a sea anchor, attached it to the forward cleat with a double line, and cast it overboard just as the wind struck. With the sea anchor keeping my bow pointed into the wind, I lay down in the bottom and rode out the storm. It's not my intention to attempt this again! Only twice have I known greater fury from storm winds. Once my 36-footer sank at the dock during a hurricane, despite seven new 1-inch lines holding her. The other occasion was during a thunderstorm on a New Hampshire mountain where I manned a forest-fire lookout tower.

Apart from the more obvious and usually more accurate signs conveyed by the clouds and winds, there are numerous folklore symptoms that are not only interesting but occasionally accurate to some degree.

As a storm system approaches, smells become more perceptible. The odor of cooking or a skunk is much sharper and the smell of marshes or swamps is much more vivid. Arthritis sufferers or those having old wounds, injuries, corns, and bunions feel increased twinges of pain.

Sea gulls remain close to shore or perch on pilings; deer and elk leave high ground, seeking the shelter of heavy timber in the low lands; the black-billed cuckoo, sometimes known as the rain crow, emits a throaty croak rarely heard otherwise; cows lie down, all facing the same direction; bits of soot fall from a fireplace chimney apparently without cause; leaves of hardwood trees turn over; dry spruce and pine cones close at least partially.

Whether these are all to be taken seriously depends upon how closely these incidents can be related to an approaching low-pressure system. I suspect, though, that there's more than an iota of truth in each.

One rhyme which isn't always truthful is one that I like because of its optimism. During a soggy night in camp, I repeat it to myself as convincingly as possible—

> Rain before seven,
> Stop before eleven.

Chapter XIV

Planning a Trip

THOREAU, IN his essay *Walden,* wrote of the stumps he had pulled from his garden: ". . . they warmed me twice—once while I was splitting them, and again when they were on the fire. . . ." By the same token, a canoe trip can be enjoyed twice—once in the planning and again when actually underway.

A vital phase of planning involves learning as much as possible about the region you will visit. Advance knowledge will not only help to plot a course affording maximum cruising enjoyment but it may suggest interesting side trips. During the planning of one of our early trips, my wife and I studied an out-of-date map for what historical value it might have. It had little, except that we noted a "fish hatchery" indicated on a remote stream which flowed into a lake we intended to cross. No road was shown leading to the hatchery. Intrigued by such a strange location for a hatchery, we investigated it during our trip, leaving the canoe at the mouth of the stream and hiking to the site. The hatchery, we found, had long been abandoned; the buildings had collapsed, the pools washed out. We wondered about trout which might have escaped from the facility and "gone native." Our guess was correct. We enjoyed some of the best fishing we'd seen in years, catching trout after trout that averaged about one pound each!

The side benefits that may accrue as a result of advance information need not be limited to fishing, of course. Depending upon the part of the country through which you will be canoeing, you may learn of Indian ruins, ghost towns, lumber camps, historical sites, ancient canals, and myriad other attractions which might be overlooked unless prior investigation has been made.

Sources of Information

Learning about a land you've never visited can be fascinating, one discovery leading to another. One way to do this is to build up a file or library of literature on an area of special interest. This can include pamphlets, maps, guides, and directories issued free by state and provincial tourist promotional agencies and state conservation departments. Frequently, these suggest other sources for more detailed information.

Local chambers of commerce are basic sources of data if your trip is to be along developed waterways. Much of their literature refers lavishly to "scenic wonderlands," "lakes teeming with fish," "luxurious accommodations at reasonable prices," "friendly hosts," and such drivel, but, perhaps unintentionally, these publications may disclose more pertinent information—sources of supplies, campsite locations, outfitters, and possibly even canoe routes. Federal agencies offer reams of material including maps, descriptive folders, trip hints, and campsite lists.

Commericial outfitters, too, supply valuable data, generally with a higher regard for facts than most chambers of commerce. Many will send food lists, detailed maps of canoe trails, equipment lists, safety hints, mileage data, hunting and fishing suggestions.

Canoeing associations, local clubs, and outdoors-related groups such as conservation and wilderness-preservation organizations, all issue guidebooks, periodicals and maps or pamphlets of interest to canoemen. Membership in these is usually quite inexpensive and highly rewarding, not only for the great amounts of literature they publish but for the satisfaction that comes from helping to preserve and improve our outdoors environment.

Supplies

Supplies will be discussed in a subsequent chapter, but they too are involved in the planning of a trip. For an extended wilderness cruise you'll have to plan on toting a full load of supplies, the bulk of them probably freeze-dried or dehydrated. It's rare that foodstuffs can be replenished in the back-of-beyond! Planning for supplies to be carried on a river in a settled region isn't as critical but it's important to know the location of supply points and their distance apart.

River Conditions

It's impossible to determine far in advance river conditions which may be encountered, but you can learn something of the seasonal averages— whether a stream is usually canoeable in August, for example. Many smaller rivers are passable only during the early season, when melting snows have swelled their flow, or following heavy rains. Such a stream, attempted at the wrong time, could well leave you stranded with a canoe outfit and not enough water to float it. Local canoeists, too, can indicate a river's status under the International Classification System.

Rivers which are used by timber or pulpwood companies for log drives should be checked to determine the location of the drive during the days you plan to be in the area. Logs are hard on canoes!

In late June of 1966, my wife and I had planned an attempt at poling up Dead River (it's name is a misnomer!) in Maine, starting at its junction with the Kennebec. To our knowledge this had never been accomplished and though we were far from confident of success against this turbulent stream, we did hope to see how much headway could be made with an ash pole. But that year the log drive was a month late, due to a drought at the headwaters. The loggers, unable to maintain a steady flow of high water to carry the logs, closed several upstream dams every night to "build up a head." The next day, although at no special time, these were opened simultaneously. Unaware of this, we spent our first afternoon trying out a new canoe. We were happy with it, until we noticed the water rising rapidly, followed by a heavy rumble from upstream. We shot the canoe ashore, just in time to witness a snarling wall of logs pounding their way downstream by our campsite. Had we been caught a quarter-mile upstream between steep banks that mark this section of the river, it probably would have been our last canoe trip.

Portages, too, should receive advance consideration. Most detailed river maps indicate their length. Overly long portages may force a change of route, but this is better than arriving at the foot of a roaring set of rips around which there's a 5-mile carry!

The possible need for fire or travel permits should be investigated in advance too, since some Canadian provinces and certain states require one or the other if wilderness travel is involved. If hunting or fishing is to be done, licenses will be needed; these can generally be obtained at or near the "jumping-off" place, but it's wise to be sure of this before you go. If you're planning to fish, determine in advance the type of tackle and lures best suited to catch the species you"ll encounter. During my guiding days, I met many an angler who'd brought along nothing but bass plugs for use in trout and salmon waters restricted to fly fishing!

Time and Distance

Most established canoe routes have been appraised as to the time required to cover them, and any attempt at cutting this time during the planning stages may prove disastrous. If a guidebook or local opinion advises a full-day's travel between two certain points, plan on a full day. Getting behind an overly optimistic schedule may prompt you to take foolhardy chances, such as running rapids around which you should carry, or short-cutting across a windswept lake when shore-hugging is indicated. Allow plenty of travel time so that no need for hurrying will arise.

There's no pat formula for the allowance of extra time, such as an occasional day for a lay-over. Repairs to the canoes or equipment may be needed; you may run into some extra good fishing which will warrant more than passing attention; and there's the possibility of being wind-bound. You might simply want to relax in camp for a day. Generally, allowing one day in every five is a suitable ratio, but this is a matter of personal inclination. Some canoemen enjoy a canoe trip most when they're eating up the map; others enjoy dawdling, chasing loons, fishing, or exploring inlets and side streams.

Distances which can be covered in one day vary according to the canoeists' experience and stamina, winds, rapids, and portages. A young couple, capable in a canoe but inexperienced in organizing an outfit, or pitching and breaking camp, may do well if they cover 10 miles in one day; and this is a suitable pace which will allow them to enjoy the trip rather than be slaves to their paddles. Experienced canoe travelers won't wear themselves to a frazzle in covering 20 to 30 miles of lake travel. Head winds may cut this, of course, as tail winds will increase it. River travel is governed by the power of the current. Upstream cruising may be limited to as little as 5 miles—anything less must certainly involve tedious labors which take canoeing out of the fun classification; whereas down-river running may attain 50 miles under favorable conditions. Generally, the best formula in plotting the time element is to allow for minimum distances of travel. Any time that may actually be gained beyond this is frosting on the cake, to be enjoyed as you see fit.

Portages require more time than many canoemen realize, taking into consideration the time required to unload, pack the outfit across, and re-load. Canoe travelers who can cross a 1-mile carry in one hour from unloading to re-loading, are doing well.

It is important to establish a fairly firm itinerary with regard to time as well as route for wilderness travel. Before jumping off on an extended cruise, someone should be told of your plans—where you will be traveling and when you expect to return. Some close relative should be made aware of this, and it is equally important to notify a local ranger, warden, or other official who can reach you in case of emergency or set into motion a search, in the event that you fail to appear at a predetermined time and place.

Here the wisdom of allowing extra time becomes evident. Should you fail to do this and have to lay over for repairs or high winds, with the result that you are a couple days late in "coming out," you may well set into high gear an unnecessary rescue or search operation. On the other hand, should you be in need of help, it will be comforting to know that someone knows where to look for you.

Canoe cruising, whether deep in the wilderness or along settled riverways, is high adventure—exciting, with the unknown around every bend. It can hardly be termed "dangerous," if proper planning has gone into the trip, to be as with Thoreau's stumps, enjoyed twice.

Chapter XV

Trip Equipment

THERE SEEMS to be some misconception regarding the bulk and weight which can be stowed aboard a 17-foot canoe. My summer camp is located along a canoe route of some popularity, so that from my desk I can examine passing craft rather closely. Some canoes look more like ocean freighters carrying a deck load from Rio to Stockholm!

Selecting an outfit for a cruise, whether it be a weekend or a month's trip, should be determined by available space aboard the canoe, the need for a 6-inch freeboard and the possibility of portages. The entire outfit should fit amidship without cluttering the crew's quarters and, preferably, the load should not rise appreciably above the gunwale line. Some compromise and culling is inevitable when gathering gear.

Tents

On portage-free local waters, where travel distances are limited and where two canoes are traveling together, a large tent can be used to shelter four canoemen. However, a balance must be attained among such factors as size, weight, and bulk.

For most canoe trips, the smaller traditional tents are almost mandatory. I say "traditional" because most of today's up-to-date shelters are basically the same tents that were in use 50 to 60 years ago. There are few, if any, truly "new" tents; new fabrics, yes, and updated construction, but no new designs. One has only to refer to Kephart's classic *Camping and Woodcraft** to find the forerunners of almost every "modern" tent. Yet, the book was originally published in 1917!

Most frequently associated with canoe trips is the Explorer tent, of which there are several versions. Most popular is the fully enclosed

---

*Horace Kephart, *Camping and Woodcraft* (New York, The Macmillan Co., 1966), pp. 95–106.

model (Illustration A) with insect-proof door netting and sewed-in floor;

(A) The Laacke Explorer tent is 7' × 8' with a center height of slightly over 6'. It weighs 14¾ lbs. Laacke and Joys photo.

some, too, have a ventilator opening at the peak. A favorite, when insect pests are absent, is a simplified version minus floor and with a fabric door closure which can be tied back in open position. Thus, the open front makes for easy heating with an open fire and seems more like "sleeping out." Most Explorers are equipped with a single interior pole, atop which sets a short horizontal ridge. However, cut-on-the-scene shear poles may be substituted (B).

(B) The author's Explorer tent rigged on shear poles, with his wife, Eleanor, preparing to break camp. Photo by the author.

Probably only one shelter is easier to erect than the Explorer and that is the Miner's tent (C), which requires only staking and the insertion of a single center pole or the hanging of the peak from a tree limb or shear poles. It is available with sewed-in floor and netting front for summer use.

A thoroughly efficient canoe trip tent is one (D) whose lines are closely patterned—whether or not intentionally, I don't know—after the ancient Compac tent which so much impressed Kephart. It is equipped with insect netting and its fabric door may be tied back in open position for the enjoyment of a campfire or for heating.

Another of pyramidal design (E) is distantly related to the Miner's tent

(C) The Stern Wigwam tent, adapted from the Miner's has a 10' × 10' floor area and 7' peak height yet weighs only 10 lbs. Photo by Walter E. Stern, Tentmaker.

(D) The Laacke Cruisemaster, not unlike the Kephart's Compac has a 7' × 7' floor area, 6' height and weighs 11½ lbs. Laacke and Joys photo.

(E) The Point Barrow tent has a 7' × 5' floor space, 5' height and weighs 4¾ lbs. without floor; 7 lbs. with sewed-in ground cloth. Alaska Sleeping Bag Co. photo.

with the addition of low sides and a vertical front opening. This shelter requires only a center pole but guy lines are needed.

Still another combines the lines of the A or Wedge tent with those of the

Miner's to house four persons, even if somewhat compactly. This is a two-piece shelter with a large fly completely overhanging the tent itself (F). Smaller versions (G) are available. These were designed by Gerry

(F) The Gerry Fortnight tent of nylon, with coated nylon fly is 8' × 9' with 6' height, weighing slightly under 9 lbs. Colorado Outdoor Sports Corp. photo.

(G) The Gerry Camponaire tent of nylon has a coated nylon fly, is 6' × 8' with 5' height, weighs under 7 lbs. Colorado Outdoor Sports Corp. photo.

Cunningham, famed Colorado mountaineer whose prototype models were used during the 1953 British ascent of Mt. Everest and the American climb of K-2.

Several popular lightweight shelters, commonly known as "mountain tents" made for climbers and hikers, are well adapted to use by canoeists bent on traveling light. All of these are patterned somewhat after the A or Wedge tent (H).

(H) The Eureka Mountain tent is available in 2-, 3- and 4-man sizes with weight ranging from 8½ to 15 lbs. Eureka Tent and Awning Co. photo.

One tent in this category (I) has its ridge tapering downward toward the rear and is fully enclosed and also has a netting front. Still another is suspended by elastic shock cords on an exterior frame of aluminum designed by the noted Robert L. Blanchard (J).

(I) The Alaska Expedition tent is 8' 10" long, 52" high at the front, 24" at the rear; Width is 58" at front, 24" at rear. It weighs 5¾ lbs. Alaska Sleeping Bag Co. photo.

(J) The Draw-tite Bivouac tent has a 5' × 7' floor area, 3' 10" height and a weight of 9 lbs. Exterior frame is aluminum. Eureka Tent and Awning Co. photo.

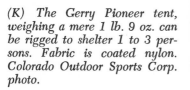

(K) The Gerry Pioneer tent, weighing a mere 1 lb. 9 oz. can be rigged to shelter 1 to 3 persons. Fabric is coated nylon. Colorado Outdoor Sports Corp. photo.

Perhaps the lightest of all tents of this general design is one weighing only 1 pound, 9 ounces (K). It can be pitched to shelter one, two, or three men as a basic minimum tent.

Another mountain-type tent which will help minimize the weight of a canoe trip outfit has openings at both ends, each equipped with netting (L).

(L) The Bishop Pack-lite tent of nylon has netting opening at each end with 5′ × 7′ floor area, 52″ height. Weight is 3 lbs., 8 oz. Bishop's Ultimate Outdoor Equipment Co. photo.

As will be explained later, fully waterproof fabric is not generally used in tents because of the inside condensation of moisture. One lightweight mountain-type tent which has gotten around this problem is made of urethane-coated nylon. Four-foot side vents under canopies and a ridge vent provide ventilation to eliminate this condensation (M).

(M) The Trailwise Vent tent of coated nylon has vents under side canopies and in ridge. Floor is 46″ × 90″ with 40″ peak. Weight is 5 lbs. Trailwise Ski Hut photo.

A tent which appears at first glance to be an ultra-modern design is one with an arched top, adding a touch of glamour to today's tenting (N).

(N) The Avis Mountain tent is suspended on aluminum and Fiberglas frame, has a 7′ × 4′ floor area, 4′ 8″ height. It weighs 13 lbs. Avis Products photo.

However, the basic design harks back more than 50 years to the Ross Alpine tent with its interior curved frame. There the similarity ends. The modern version, designed by Bill Moss, inventor of the famed Pop tent, has a sleeve-fitting exterior frame of aluminum and Fiberglas which keeps the shelter taut without undue strain.

Perhaps the ideal tent from which to enjoy an evening campfire is the Baker (O). Its sloping rear wall reflects heat onto the occupants and its

(O) The Stern Adirondack, a cross between the Whelen and Baker lean-to's has a floor area of 7" × 8¾", front height of 6'. Weight is 9½ lbs. Photo by Walter E. Stern, Tentmaker.

front fabric closure serves as a canopy. Most versions are without floor or insect netting, although these can be added easily.

A series of tents designed by Robert L. Blanchard are well adapted to canoe tripping, particularly the smaller versions. These require no stakes or guy lines and are suspended entirely on an aluminum exterior framework (P). So well suspended are these shelters that they can be picked up and moved without being dismantled.

(P) The Eureka Draw-tite Alpine tents come in five sizes to shelter 1 to 6 persons. Two-man size is 5' × 7' 9" with 48" height. Weight 12½ lbs. Eureka Tent and Awning Co. photo.

(Q) The Bishop Ultimate tent comes in three sizes, 5' × 7', 7' × 9' and 8' × 12'. Weights are 3 lbs., 15 oz., 6 lbs. 3 ozs., and 8 lbs. 13 oz. respectively. Bishop's Ultimate Outdoor Equipment Co. photo.

Similar to these—and also rigged on Blanchard-designed exterior frameworks—is another series (Q) which will house two, four, or six persons, each model with an entry at either end equipped with insect netting.

Although more likely to be found along settled riverways or in

(R) The Thermos Pop tents come in two sizes, 7' and 9' in diameter. Exterior Fiberglas ribs in sleeves provide suspension at 52" and 6' heights respectively. Photo by Thermos Div., King/Seeley Thermos Co.

organized campgrounds, there is a 9-foot domed tent which requires no stakes or guying (R). With a sewed-in floor and netting openings, its dome shape offers more room than most canoe tents. Suspension is by means of exterior Fiberglas rods in sleeves.

The foregoing tents have been cited because they have all or most of the qualities of excellent canoe cruising shelters. All are easily and quickly erected or dismantled; but for one or two, they are lightweight, can be rolled compactly and will withstand the buffeting of high winds.

Most tent manufacturers make one or more tents adapted to canoe cruising. And each varies his Explorer, Wedge, Mountain or Baker from that of his competitor so that the field of choice is wide, especially in view of the varied fabrics available.

Certain models, particularly the mountain tents, are made of "ripstop" nylon, some of this fabric used on ultra-light shelters weighing as little as 1½ ounces per square yard. At first glance, this fabric seems to be the ultimate. However, despite many years of experimenting, the textile industry has not yet come up with an uncoated nylon that will completely shed a heavy shower and, at the same time, allow the passage of interior moisture into the outdoors. However, ingenious tent makers have come up with lightweight nylon tents over which are rigged almost-as-light coated-nylon tarpaulins. With this combination, interior moisture passes out of the tent through the thin nylon fabric and is dissipated in the air under the tarpaulin which, being waterproof, turns away rain. In many cases, the combined weight of tent and tarpaulin is much less than that of shelters made of conventional fabrics.

The most frequently used fabric in canoe cruising tents, however, is poplin. Considerably less costly than nylon, it is a sturdy fabric, windproof, light (about 6 ounces to the square yard usually), and well-adapted to small-tent design. Regrettably some manufacturers are apparently ashamed of their use of this fabric since they invariably dub it with a brand name such as Hilltop Cloth or Wildcat Fabric or some such ridiculous identification. The fact is that poplin is probably the best all-round fabric for canoe tents and, if a point-blank question is required to identify it, don't hesitate to query the dealer or outfitter.

Drill, too is used on many tents suitable for canoe trips but it should have a "dry" finish, as opposed to the more common "wet" or oil finish. Wet-finish drill, while adequate for family camping, where it can be given greater care, isn't likely to stand up as well under the hard usage of canoe cruising. Also, it is considerably heavier than the dry finish drill, which may weigh between 6 and 7 ounces per square yard, as opposed to the 8- to 11-ounce weight of the wet-finish version. Drill tents are the least expensive of canoe trip shelters.

Duck, too, is used on certain models. Army duck, whose fill and warp are doubled and twisted before weaving, is probably the most durable of all tent fabrics but it is heavy, weighing some 10 ounces per square yard. My open Explorer is of this fabric, chosen because of its durability since I use it often as a wrapper for two or more packs while transporting gear in the canoe or over portages. Except for such usages, however, army duck is too heavy for general use among canoe cruisers.

The sewed-in ground cloth, or floor, in most of today's better canoe tents is of vinyl-coated nylon, which is highly durable, completely waterproof and relatively light. The fabric cannot be used for sides and tops of tents, however, because it is waterproof rather than water-repellent. Water-repellent fabrics including cotton textiles, permit the passage of interior moisture into the outer air. Coated nylon does not, so moisture condenses within the interior, and sleepers may awake to find small puddles of water in the tent. As a floor fabric, though, it is excellent.

The romantically inclined may wonder why I have not mentioned such traditional canoe shelters as the tarpaulin draped across the overturned craft, or the lean-to of boughs. Actually, the tarpaulin, whether rigged as a lean-to or strung over the canoe, is a fully adequate shelter except during those months when insect pests such as black flies, mosquitoes, and "no-see-ums" are prevalent. At best, though, it is an improvisation. My dislike for such a rig stems from the inadequate headroom it provides, but it is nonetheless a suitable shelter for those who don't object to its drawbacks.

As for the lean-to of boughs, I suppose every camper should sleep in one at least once during his or her lifetime. Certainly such a night would be a truly close-to-Nature experience but, alas, the days of the bough shelter are numbered. It is an indirect victim of the consequences of the population explosion. If each of us were allowed to cut green growth, we would soon have the woodlands looking as if Paul Bunyan's blue ox, Babe, had been browsing in them. Most states, and the federal government too, forbid the unauthorized cutting of greens on their lands. The owners of the vast tracts of private timberlands also frown on unnecessary cutting, even though most of them welcome outdoor lovers in their woods. In the remote wilderness, no one will miss a couple armloads of boughs when such a shelter is rigged in an emergency, but as a general practice, the bough shelter is going—possibly it's already gone—the way of the ukelele and sofa pillow as standard equipment in a canoe.

Sleeping Gear

A sufficient number of authorities have expounded upon the importance of nighttime comfort during any camping trip and this is especially true of a canoe cruise. A weary paddler makes poor headway against the current or in the face of a wind. Therefore, if financial skimping is necessary in the purchase of equipment, it should *not* be applied to the buying of a sleeping bag. Buy the best you can possibly afford.

There can be no question that a sleeping bag filled with goose down insulation is ideal for a canoe cruise, particularly in the north where even summer nights are cool, sometimes downright cold! Of all the insulating fillers available for sleeping bags, goose down provides the greatest amount of loft or "fluffiness" and this is what provides the insulation. One ounce of high quality down can, in fact, provide some 600 cubic inches of insulation when lofted. Thickness of the insulator is what retains body warmth within the sleeping bag. That's why goose down rates so well.

While goose down-filled bags are designed primarily for hikers and mountain climbers (except for some models made up for use in extremes of weather), they adapt well to canoe trip use. My own Gerry 2-pounder (weight of the filler, not the bag) is hardly larger than a football when stuffed into its waterproof carrying bag yet is amply comfortable down to freezing temperatures.

Susceptibility to cold varies among persons, so that determining the amount of fill is a matter for individuals to decide although so-called "cold-rating charts" issued by manufacturers will be helpful—if they are realistic. On the whole, though, a 1½- to 2-pound (filler) goose down bag will keep most canoeists comfortable during the summer months in the United States and in lower Canada. For exposure to more rigorous climates or seasons, 2 to 3 pounds may be required.

It should be pointed out that the amount of down in a sleeping bag is not the sole determinant of comfort. For instance, 1 pound of high grade down which will loft or "fluff out" fully is far superior to 1 or 2 pounds of cheap reprocessed down or combinations of down and feathers, which will loft poorly. In no other item of camping equipment is quality so important. Also affecting comfort is the manner in which the down is distributed and the bag is sewn. Overlapping tubes or sections of down within the bag, for example, will prevent body warmth from escaping through thin spots. Unfortunately, the quality of down isn't visible, and often it's difficult to determine the type of construction without help from an expert. There remains only to purchase a down sleeping bag from a well known maker and to pay a realistic price. A $40 down sleeping bag will invariably prove a disappointment; one costing twice that amount will guarantee absolute comfort for canoe cruising. By "shopping around," you may reach a compromise between these two price levels, but buy cautiously!

Most lightweight goose down bags, and these are made primarily for climbers and hikers, are the "Mummy" type. These are tapered bags, as

Down-filled, mummy-type sleeping bag. Colorado Outdoor Sports Corp. photo.

the name implies, and some campers find them constricting. However, they are the most compact for stuffing into a pack and one soon gets used to the restrictive confinement. For those who prefer, though, there are full-size rectangular bags available.

Where economy dictates, sleeping bags filled with polyester fiber are quite adequate for canoe trips, although they are bulkier than goose down bags. A 3-pound polyester bag, for example, takes up to four to five

Down-filled rectangular sleeping bag. Colorado Outdoor Sports Corp. photo.

times the space of a down bag of similar weight. However, the cost of polyester bags is only about one-quarter to one-fifth that of down sleepers.

For average summer use, a 3-pound polyester bag will provide ample comfort, although a person susceptible to cold (often the case with women) may find a 4-pounder necessary. Buying a quality polyester bag is easier than buying a down bag since specific brand names indicate suitable polyester, these including the well-known Dacron 88, Kodel or Vycron. Lacking a known brand-name, seek the words "polyester fiberfill" and be sure that it is not reprocessed or otherwise "restored." No other man-made or synthetic filler is as efficient as virgin polyester fiber-fill.

Bargain sleeping bags, made for the mass market and sold usually in discount or cut-rate stores, often include a rubberized or plastic bottom, touted as a "built-in ground cloth." These should be shunned, since such fabric is completely waterproof and restrains body moisture from escaping, the sleeper awakening in a damp, clammy sleeping bag.

A rugged zipper, preferably No. 7, running entirely down one side and across the bottom, is an indication of an adequate product, as is a "weatherstrip" fold in the fabric which insulates the bag along the zipper. Another asset, offered usually at a slight increase in cost, is a removable liner of sheeting, flannel, or even wool blanketing for added warmth. This eliminates the necessity for frequent washing or dry-cleaning of the entire bag. Only the liner needs this attention.

Because of their weight and bulk, folding cots are not practical on canoe trips. An air mattress of rubberized fabric substitutes. Plastic air mattresses, though very inexpensive, do not stand up under repeated use. For those who must keep an outfit to the barest minimum weight, mattresses can be inflated by mouth but this is a tedious chore. Small hand-operated pumps are handy.

In recent years, foam mattresses have come into popularity. They are somewhat less expensive than air mattresses but are quite bulky, since of course they cannot be "deflated" but are rolled compactly—a feat tantamount to extracting a tooth from a wildcat! Foam mattresses are remarkably comfortable. For minimum comfort, bulk can be cut by using a hiker's mattress, which is only three-quarter length and slightly over an inch thick, sufficient to smooth over some of Mother Earth's gouging knuckles.

Young canoeists often prefer to omit all mattresses, and I suppose to a young frame this need not be torture. During the first twenty years that I enjoyed canoe trips and worked as a guide, I chose to sleep directly on a simple ground cloth, minus padding. It did little to improve either my character or my bone structure. For those who prefer it, roughing it may not cut into canoe trip pleasures but, to those unaccustomed to such Spartan enjoyment, a mattress of some sort is highly recommended!

The bough bed is pretty much in the same predicament as the bough shelter, frowned upon in most areas. In certain backcountry regions, some canoemen still make them, but they must spend miserable nights. Usually, bough beds which I have found abandoned at far-flung campsites, were inadequate to support the weight of a fat squirrel! Amateurs at bough-bed building fail to realize that a depth of 12 to 18 inches of boughs is required and, those placed on the bottom half should be at least 1 inch thick at the butt. The top layers are thinner for a smooth, cushioned effect. Few of today's campers build such beds!

Not only is indiscriminate cutting of boughs to be discouraged in this day of vast inroads into our natural resources, but the labor involved

The author ready for a portage, with a Duluth pack riding atop his packbasket. Photo by Eleanor Riviere.

should be considered. The average non-professional woodsman will require more than an hour to cut enough boughs and to place them properly for comfort. Inflating an air mattress or unrolling one of the foam type may not be quite as "woodsy," but it can be accomplished in 10 minutes or less and the time saved applied to enjoying other phases of an overnight stop at streamside.

Admittedly as an afterthought, it should be pointed out that the bottom of a down sleeping bag loses much of its loft, and therefore its insulating value, once the sleeper lies on it. Body heat then escapes and chill sets in. Some type of pad, whether foam or air, not only contributes to comfort but provides insulation replacement. Polyester bags, too, suffer somewhat from this compression but not to the extent of down.

Packs

Some years ago I took a Maine packbasket on a Minnesota canoe trip. It was a handsome basket made for me by an Indian and I used it many years. To my surprise, Minnesota canoemen directed endless ribbing at my "clothes basket" and refused to concede that it might be a suitable rig on canoe trails. The only pack, they insisted, was the Duluth, also known as the Northwestern or Poirier. This is, in effect, a large square pocket of canvas, sewn flat with bellows at the side, and equipped with shoulder straps and a tumpline. Its advantages were quickly apparent to me. I returned with one to Maine, where canoemen allowed that it was a "nice pack" but "couldn't hold a candle to a packbasket." Lo, the geographical point of view!

State-of-Mainers and Minnesotans would do well to examine each other's gear, including packs. I found that the Duluth is marvelous for stuffing; there's always room for one more item, but if it is hard or has sharp edges or corners it should be placed on the outboard side of the bag, not against the side that rides next to the carrier's backbone!

Duluth packs are usually made of 15-ounce canvas with a large overlapping cover held closed by three leather straps and buckles. Most Duluth packs are also equipped with a tumpline, a notable invention for those accustomed to it, but a torture device for novices. Most popular are the No. 2 bag, 24 by 28 inches and the No. 3, 28 by 30 inches.

Despite my appreciation for the Duluth pack's virtues, I have not given up my packbasket; I have, in fact, four of them on hand. These are hand woven of ash strips and equipped with a shoulder harness. A waterproof case, fully enclosing the basket, is available. Sizes have never been accurately standardized, baskets being rated according to the "pecks" they will hold. A two-peck basket is about 15 inches tall; a three-peck unit, 18 inches. I'm not sure how many pecks my favorite holds, but since it is 24 inches high, my claim that it is the biggest packbasket in Maine has never been disputed. Made more than twenty-five years ago, it is still in good condition although used extensively over the years.

The prime advantage of a packbasket is the protection it affords breakable or fragile items such as cameras, binoculars, or even eggs! Also, it's easy to find items within one rather than having to probe blindly as in a fabric pack. A basket used during one or two trips soon forms itself to fit the carrier's back and becomes remarkably comfortable to tote. New baskets should be given a coat or two of spar varnish to protect them.

The duffel bag, far from being outdated, is still a fine pack for canoe trips and is available from some of the better outfitters. Equipped with either a top- or side-opening, modern versions have a zipper closure. Practically all gear can be packed in one of these but they are most aptly suited to hold clothing and miscellaneous personal items.

For canoemen who may encounter turbulent white water during the course of a trip, some sort of waterproof bag is necessary to insure a quick change into dry clothing. Such bags, although not common, are available, in sizes up to 20 by 16 by 12 inches, from outfitters who specialize in white-water equipment. Most of these, I believe, are government surplus items.

On some trips, I have wrapped sleeping bags in my Explorer tent to form a rather bulky but not particularly heavy pack. For such an approach to packing, an adjustable pack harness is sold, designed to fit a pack of almost any size or shape.

Until recent years, camping literature touted the tumpline, with justification. However, few of today's generation have ever seen one. It consists simply of a 5- to 6-foot length of leather strapping, webbing or even rope, equipped at its middle with a broad band which fits just back of the forehead. The ends are attached to the pack so that the brunt of the load is carried by the neck. Once accustomed to this technique, the carrier can tote tremendous loads, whether bulky or unusually weighty. Unless the carrier has had some experience with it, though, the tumpline is a torturous device. When it is combined with shoulder straps, however, the weight is alternated between or shared by the neck and the shoulders. At any rate, the tumpline will "out-tote" any set of shoulder straps.

Another container seen on some northern canoe routes is the canoe box, also known as a tote box, grub box, or even canoe pannier. This is little more than a wooden container, usually housing the cooking gear and grub, fitted with shoulder straps for portaging. Usually these are home-made and often feature a rounded bottom, to fit the contour of the canoe. Tent designer Gerry Cunningham recently came up with a commercial version, 8 by 17 by 28 inches, weighing slightly under 6 pounds with packstrap.

Some western outfitters can supply collapsible panniers which, although designed for use on pack horses, are adaptable to canoes. However, they lack a carrying harness.

Clothing

So-called sports clothing marketed today is better designed for the patio or golf course than for canoe cruising. Being fashionable *and* comfortable in a canoe borders on the impossible. High fashion, particularly women's, is simply not practical. Out-of-place garb—occasionally seen on canoe trips—also fails to do the job. A ten-gallon hat, for example, is an encumbrance on a windswept lake unless held down by a Teddy Roosevelt chin strap. Then, I've seen bush jackets that may cloak their wearers in glamor but certainly add little to ease of paddling!

Clothing worn on a canoe trip should protect the wearer from sun, wind, and rain or, in the case of winter canoeing, against cold water and biting wintry air. For a summer weekend excursion, all members of the family can probably get along with odds and ends of informal clothing providing it performs the above functions. For a lengthy cruise, however, the choice should be more discriminating.

At first appraisal, footwear may seem unimportant. However, low-cut moccasins or shoepacs of good leather will curl comfortably with the feet as they shift with the various kneeling or sitting positions for paddling. The softer the uppers, the better. If rocky portages are anticipated, the Maine Guide shoe is ideal—a moccasin with ankle-height uppers. Heavy leather boots, however glamorous they may appear on a Hollywood lumberjack, are too heavy and stiff.

Several solutions, including silicone, are on the market for treating leather and I suppose these are adequate, but I have as yet to find a boot dressing that compares with neat's-foot oil, available from some cobblers, shoe dealers, and outfitters. This is best applied with a discarded toothbrush, which is then used to work the oil into the seams. Repeated applications should be made, preferably when the leather has been warmed to at least comfortable room temperature. This will not only waterproof the leather but make it soft and pliable. Don't be disheartened if the attractive artificial color of the leather turns to an ugly, uneven black. That's a sign of properly treated leather.

Tennis shoes or sneakers are an inexpensive compromise, especially for youngsters or women, and quite adequate for most canoe trips, although they provide little foot protection on a rocky portage.

During warm weather, cotton trousers or ladies' slacks are suitable; blue jeans, while not stylish, are an excellent choice. Avoid the tight-fitting western style, however. These will bind miserably during long hours of paddling.

For cool weather, wool trousers, or slacks for the ladies, are a good choice, the weight depending upon the anticipated weather. There's no reason why shorts cannot be worn in appropriate weather.

Drip-dry shirts and blouses are a godsend during the mild seasons but these should be supplemented with flannel or wool shirts for cooler days and chilly evenings in camp. A windproof jacket, lightweight and of tightly-woven fabric, such as those worn by climbers and skiers, completes the protection against chill.

Going into the summer woods without a hat verges on madness—and may even lead to it. Any canoeman who has ever made a lengthy portage hatless and had one or two deer flies attach themselves to him knows the torture to which I refer. Flying insects on portage trails may be impossible to get rid of and, while insect repellent may protect other parts of the body, they can't be prevented from buzzing above the hairline! A hat is the only protection against these, as it is against rain and the hot sun.

The battered felt hat is the traditional head gear of the oldtime canoe cruiser and it is still a good choice. With the crown punched up and the brim turned down, it sheds rain like a tent. However, it is not imperative that the tradition be observed. Lighter hats of poplin or cotton suede, such as worn by sport fishermen, serve well. Some of the more reasonable wide-brimmed western styles shade the eyes nicely against the glare of the sun.

Women will find that the flimsy plastic scarf-like headgear they have adopted to protect their hair against wind and rain is inadequate for lengthy exposure to an occasional downpour. They would do well to adopt men's fashions.

For a prolonged rainy spell, it's difficult to improve on the protection afforded by a fishing shirt of neoprene-coated nylon. This is almost ankle-length and looks not unlike a man's old-fashioned night shirt with a hood. However, it isn't the easiest garment to don or remove and, worse yet, it is badly ventilated so that perspiration, unable to escape, may prove as objectionable as rain. Much the same is true of the so-called Navy storm suit. Both of these may also prove dangerous in case of capsize since they encumber a swimmer seriously. Probably the best choice is a poncho which, when you're seated or kneeling in a canoe, covers the entire body except the wrists and forearms, yet is amply ventilated.

While not actually wearing apparel, sun glasses are vital, particularly for lake travel, where the sun's reflection on waves can be dazzling and eventually painful. Cheap glasses should be avoided in favor of scientifically ground lenses such as Cool-Ray, Ray-Ban, or Polaroid. Not only are these better protection but they allow you to examine clearly the stream bottom as you float by, a fascinating diversion on quiet waterways.

Vital Miscellany

Apart from the canoe and paddles, it's a toss-up as to which is more important to a canoe trip, a 100-foot length of ¼-inch rope, or a sharp axe. I would hate to do without either! Dozens of uses are found for the rope: tying gear into the canoe, guying the tent against a stiff blow, rigging a clothes line, lining the craft through turbulent pitch, hanging food supplies out of reach of hungry critters, tying packs for portaging and emergency towing—to name only a few.

Given a choice between the rope or an axe, I'd probably choose the latter, but I'm an advocate of the 3-pound pole axe with a 28-inch handle, not a hatchet, as suggested by so many who have never had to cut wood for a livelihood. The hatchet is lighter and more compact, they insist, and I agree providing you have a pet beaver at each campsite to help you produce firewood. The hatchet, being a one-hand tool, requires longer hours at the wood pile; its short handle places the user in jeopardy—he's too close to his work; and because of its lightness, it is less efficient than a full axe. It must be *driven* into the log; an axe head is merely *dropped*. For a compromise, the Hudson's Bay axe, usually with a 2-pound head and a 24-inch handle will perform most wood-cutting chores. No matter what the choice, the blade should be kept sharp. A dull edge makes for more work and is dangerous since it is prone to glancing. A sharp bit bites in where it is directed.

Next in order of importance is a knife, either a sturdy folding jackknife or one of the sheath type. Jackknives are generally of reasonable size and, if of good quality, more than adequate for most camp work. Sheath knives are more popular, being considered more "woodsy." Beware, however, of the giant 6- to 8-inch blades, which are so often purchased by those who know no better. Better suited as bayonets on a Marine's rifle, they are awkward to use. A narrow, 4-inch blade of good steel will do all the work for which any camp knife may be called upon. My own, which I have carried for more than twenty years, has gutted numberless deer and several bear, cleaned countless fish, whittled pot hooks and fire cranes, repaired my canvas canoe several times, and performed hundreds of other unrecorded chores. Its blade is only 2⅞ inches long and only $\frac{7}{16}$-inch at its widest point. It has failed me only once—when I tried to skin out a South Dakota buffalo!

A waterproof matchbox is another canoe cruise requisite, an item to be accorded utmost reverence, its contents never to be used sacrilegiously for lighting a pipe or cigarette. I have no objection to smoking but a pocket supply of matches should be used for this, lest the matchbox be found empty when needed urgently. Such match safes are for emergencies only!

A first-aid kit should be included, of course, its contents depending upon the length of the trip and the remoteness of the area being cruised. Ready-assembled kits are sold in drug stores and by some outfitters and these may be added to with items suggested by the family doctor. Be sure to include a supply of any special medications some member of the party may require regularly or in an emergency.

Maps and a compass, the latter if travel is in a wilderness area, are absolute necessities and are discussed in a later chapter.

Don't overlook insect repellents during summer cruises: 6-12, Off, or Cutter, the latter a new cold-creamlike lotion whose consistency and pleasant odor may appeal to women. We have found all three effective during the height of the black fly season in northern woods. Repellent should be applied sparingly, not only to assure that the supply will last, but also because it is not necessary for it to drip from the skin to be efficient.

Other items to be included are toilet kits for men and women, soap, towels, toilet tissue, flashlights or lantern with batteries or fuel, needles and thread for clothing repairs, and a canoe repair kit. Personal preference may dictate the addition of other items such as binoculars, cameras, nature or field guides, all—as pointed out earlier—with an eye on the scales!

Firearms are rarely needed on a canoe trip, unless of course hunting is the prime object. "Protection"—or a presumed need for it—is all too often nothing more than justification of romantic nonsense. Canoeists have nothing to fear along canoe routes. And there's always the possibility of violating a local law by the possession of a gun. Admittedly, it's fun to "plink" or punch holes in a target or tin can but local laws should be checked first. Handguns, for example, are barred in Canada, and within our own states it's impossible to travel with firearms in possession without violating a gun law somewhere.

Canoe Trip Cooking

The canoe trip menu which traditionally, and monotonously, featured beans, bannock, and bacon has—happily for today's camper—been relegated to a page in Northwoods history. Imaginative use of modern freeze-dried and dehydrated foods, along with the many supermarket ingredients adapted to packing, now provides camp fare that is not only nutritious but tasty.

Utensils have been updated, too. Reflector ovens of aluminum now fold compactly. Nesting cook kits are equally compact and lightweight. Campstoves, where these are necessary, are practically foolproof. It remains only for at least one member of the canoe brigade to possess or develop skill as an outdoor chef.

To attempt a just treatment of outdoor cooking in the limited space provided by one chapter in a book such as this would be to render the subject a heinous injustice. It deserves a book of its own. To that end, I suggest that the reader refer to the *Outdoorsman's Cook Book*, by Arthur H. Carhart, *Camping and Outdoor Cooking*, by Rae Oetting and Mabel

Otis Robinson or to my own *Family Camper's Cookbook* (see Bibliography).

EQUIPMENT LIST

Basic Items

Canoe(s)
Paddles (including one spare for each canoe)
Life preserver cushions (jackets for dangerous water)
Tent(s)
Canoe repair kit
100 ft. ¼-inch manila rope, or similar
Sleeping bag(s)
Air or foam mattresses
Axe; file or whetstone
Cooking and eating utensils
Food supply
First-aid kit
Insect repellent
Gas or propane stove (where open fires not permitted)
Flashlight or lantern
Fuel for stove and lantern
Spare mantles for lantern
Spare batteries for flashlight
Spare bulb for flashlight
Candles (for ultra-light outfit omitting lantern or flashlight)
Packs—Duluth, basket, or duffel
Maps and compass
Hunting, fishing, travel, or fire permits (where applicable)
Emergency waterproof match supply

Optional Items

Tarpaulin (coated nylon preferable)
Canoe pole
Folding buck saw
Spare axe handle
Air mattress pump
Folding shovel
Carrying yoke
Safety helmets (for dangerous rapids)
Tumpline
Pack harness
Gun(s) where permitted
Small coil stovepipe wire

Personal Items

Underwear
Trousers or slacks

Shorts
Lightweight shirt or blouse (wash and wear)
Heavy shirt or sweater
Hat
Bathing suit
Pajamas
Poncho, or other rain gear
Socks (three or four pair for extended trip)
Handkerchiefs
Toilet kit (toothbrush, paste, comb, shaving equipment, etc.)
Toilet tissue
Towel(s), washcloth(s), soap
Knife
Pocket compass
Pipe(s), tobacco, cigarettes
Waterproof match safe
Sewing kit
Sun glasses

Optional Personal Items

Camera, film, accessories
Binoculars
Small notebook or diary, pencil
Field guides (mammals, birds, flowers, insects, etc.)
Fishing tackle
Other hobby or special interest equipment

Special Equipment for Outboard Motor Travel

Motor
Gasoline and oil
Lower housing lubricant (if for extended trip)
Spare spark plug(s)
Plug wrench
Spark-gap gauge
Pliers
Screwdriver
Adjustable crescent wrench
Shear and cotter pins
Friction tape
Spare propeller and nut
Safety chain

Naturally, not *all* of the items in the foregoing lists are essential to *all* canoe trips. All items of practical use during *some* cruises have been included in a sort of master list from which a more pertinent list can be made up to suit your particular needs.

Chapter XVI

Finding Your Way

THE OUTDOORSMAN who boasts that he has never been lost is either by-passing fact or else he has not wandered in the out-of-doors long enough for the law of averages to catch up with him. Like the Maine guide who once admitted to me: "I've never been lost but I was a mite turned around once or twice," few experienced woodsmen can honestly claim that they have never spent at least a few anxious hours searching for a misplaced trail!

Canoemen are less likely than woodsmen to get "turned around"; after all, it's difficult to stray from a stream in a canoe. However, paddlers have been known to turn upstream into the wrong tributary, to miss a portage, to overshoot a take-out point, or even to wonder "which way is north?" while crossing a large lake.

Map Reading

To a canoeist, the ability to read a map accurately is probably more important than the knack for using a compass skillfully. Few maps are drawn with canoeing in mind. Noteworthy exceptions are those published by the W. A. Fisher Co. of Virginia, Minnesota, describing canoe routes in the Superior-Quetico boundary waters of northern Minnesota and southern Ontario. These are specifically detailed for canoeists, showing routes, portages, rapids, and campsites. Otherwise, good canoe maps are scarce—practically nonexistent, in fact.

Those issued by the U. S. Forest Service, portraying the various national forests, are generally excellent travel and camping guides for land-bound users. Riverways, however, lack detail. The same is true of National Park Service maps, except in those instances where an established canoe trail runs through or within a national park or forest.

Timber companies frequently issue "sportsman's maps" but primarily for hunters, fishermen, and automobile campers. County maps and those published by the various state conservation departments, unless drawn specifically to describe a limited number of regular canoe routes, generally show little more than access points and major landmarks, omitting rapids, portages, and danger spots. Rarely do they include contours or elevations, much less river gradients.

Even the maps of the U. S. Geological Service are usually minus data essential to canoe travel. Rapids on major rivers are indicated, but those occurring on relatively minor but canoeable streams cannot be included because of the small scale. Maps of the Canadian Department of Mines and Technical Surveys, like those of the U. S. Geological Survey, are marvelously accurate as to lake outline and stream courses, but they, too, are inadequate concerning rapids. In fact, many pitches which were included on earlier editions, are being deleted from current maps.

Fortunately, an ever increasing number of canoe trip guidebooks is appearing (see Appendix and Bibliography), and these include either maps with pertinent data or text describing the location and difficulty rating of many rapids. Nevertheless, guidebooks fall far short of covering all of North America's waterways. A canoeman must make do with what is available—maps of the U. S. Geological Survey, the U. S. Army Corps of Engineers, and in Canada those of the Department of Mines and Technical Surveys. And despite their inadequacies, maps remain nearly indispensable to canoe trips. True, downriver paddlers may have to locate dangerous pitches by listening for them, or find portages by peering along the shoreline, but features are shown that are of more than passing interest.

Rivers, lakes, and streams are of course indicated. Roads may lead to access points; bridges, islands, phone and power lines, ranger stations and fire towers provide accurate reference points; campsites, picnic grounds, springs indicate possible stop-over areas; tributaries, marshes, beaver ponds are side trips; towns, villages, and trading posts are supply stations; canyons, cliffs, rock slides warn of danger.

Other map features may prove helpful—foot and riding trails, railroads, airports, and landing strips (these in an emergency), tunnels, fords (indicating shallows), lumber camps, trappers' cabins, parks, and recreation areas. Even a distant mountain peak may provide a bearing by which to steer a course.

To be of utmost value on an extended canoe cruise, though, a map must also include the date of survey or revision, a scale, compass declination, and contour intervals.

The date is vital. Stream flow and lake outlines change little from year to year, but a dam may have been built, or one washed out; a ranger station abandoned and a new one opened elsewhere; a backwoods access road closed to traffic. Obviously, the more recent the map, the greater the accuracy. Regrettably, many quadrangles of the U. S. Geological Survey are sadly out of date, with revisions more likely to cover population centers and areas of economic importance than the isolated regions frequented by canoe travelers.

Scale

Scale expresses the distance and size relationship between map features and those same features on the actual terrain. Geological Survey maps utilize several scales, depending upon the region shown and the general demand for maps in that region. Large-scale quadrangles, such as the 7½-minute series, are generally scaled 1:24,000 or 1/24,000. The numerator (1) indicates distance on the map, 1 inch; the larger number (24,000) represents the number of inches on terrain. Thus, one inch on the map is equal to 24,000 inches, or 2,000 feet, on the earth's surface. This is considered a large scale and is used on maps of highly developed sections or rural areas where a special need for detail exists. The larger the scale, the more details that can be included.

Most Geological Survey maps of eastern sections, especially among the older editions, are of medium scale—1/62,500 or 1 inch to slightly less than 1 mile. For all practical purposes, these are generally referred to as "one inch to the mile" quadrangles. There is less detail than on maps of larger scale, naturally, but these maps are usually adequate for canoe travel. Still smaller scales are used on maps of the West and Southwest where vast distances and sparse populations do not warrant the detail of the compacted eastern regions. The scale here is usually 1/250,000 or 1 inch to slightly less than 4 miles. U. S. Army Corps of Engineers charts of major waterways and parts of their tributaries have scales as large as 1 inch to 1,000 feet; other charts and maps issued by this agency correspond roughly in scale to those of the U. S. Geological Survey.

Much the same ratio of scaling exists on maps of the Canadian National Topographic System, published by the Department of Mines and Technical Surveys. Maps of compacted areas use a scale of 1/126,720 or 1 inch to roughly 1⅔ miles. Maps scaled 1/250,000 or 1/253,440 or 1 inch to slightly more than 3 miles are also issued, some of these covering canoe routes in the northern wilderness. Still another series of maps which cover most of Canada is scaled 1 inch to 8 miles.

Scale, of course, is necessary in estimating a day's canoe travel. Air line distance can, naturally, be figured accurately, but on streams that wind and twist greatly, it produces little more than an educated guess. For more accuracy a map measurer may be used. This is an inexpensive instrument with a small wheel which is run along the proposed route on the map. This wheel activates a needle or pointer on a small dial where actual mileage is indicated. Some such instruments have a multiple dial for use on several maps with varying scales.

Declination

Declination can be described as the directional difference between true north and magnetic north. True north is the "North Pole" or the geographical "top" of the earth. Magnetic north is not a specific, pinpointed "pole" but rather a somewhat broad region located roughly at 75 degrees north latitude, 101 degrees west longitude (as of 1960—it moves slightly each year) in the vicinity of the southern end of Bathurst Island in the Canadian Arctic Sea.

That the compass needle does *not* point to a "magnetic pole" has been established. Observations from various parts of the continent show that straight lines drawn along the direction pointed out by compass needles, *do not converge* at the so-called magnetic pole but, instead, criss-cross each other over a wide area. In fact in some sections of the United States the compass fails to point to a specific magnetic pole by as much as 10 degrees. The compass needle is not controlled by the magnetic pole, nor by any other specific spot on the earth, but rather by the sum total of magnetism over all parts of the earth.*

The only constancy of the compass needle is that, in the eastern part of this country, it points *west* of true north by 25 degrees or more; in the Pacific Northwest, it points *east* of the North Pole by at least 20 degrees. This is declination, inconsistent but reliable enough in the United States and parts of Canada for directional findings. However, as one approaches the "magnetic pole" area in the Canadian Arctic, the more erratic the compass needle becomes, so much so that it is of little value to canoe travelers on the Canadian Barrens! Here, navigation is usually done by celestial observations, noting the sun by day, the stars by night.

An isogonic chart of the United States illustrates another phenomenon. Along a line running through parts of Georgia, Tennessee, Kentucky, Ohio, Indiana, Michigan, and lower Ontario, the compass needle happens to point to true north!

Nearly all maps of areas where declination exists include a declination symbol, usually in the form of an offset V. One leg of the V is vertical and points to true north and is so marked. The other leg indicates the direction in which the compass needle points, in that region. Between the two legs, on some maps, will be stated the number of degrees of deviation.

This symbol helps users to "orient" the map. This is done by placing the compass on it, on a flat, level surface. When the needle stops wavering

---

*For a detailed explanation of the compass and the magnetic pole phenomenon, see U.S. Coast and Geodetic Survey, *Magnetic Poles and the Compass* (Serial 726, second edition; Washington, D.C.: U.S. Government Printing Office, 1962, 10 cents).

and points firmly in one direction, the map is then turned until the magnetic leg of the declination symbol is parallel to the compass needle. The map is thus oriented or in proper relation to the geographic and man-made features around it.

Contour Lines

Contour lines give maps a third dimension so that mountains, hills, and valleys are clearly defined, hence the term "topographical." Contour lines are imaginary, of course; you'll find no sign of them on actual terrain. They serve as a constant reference to altitude and, naturally, one never crosses another. If you could walk a contour line for its entire length, you would remain constantly at the same altitude. The "contour interval," too, will be indicated on the map. This is the *vertical* distance between lines, usually 20 feet on Geological Survey quadrangles of the 15-minute series with a scale of 1/62,500. Thus, by walking—or paddling—from one contour line to another, you would descend or climb 20 feet.

When contour lines run closely together so that they nearly blend, the terrain will be very steep. Should contour lines cross a stream in this manner, you can probably expect a violent pitch, possibly a waterfall. On the other hand, if the lines are widely spaced where they cross a waterway, chances are you will find relatively quiet water. This is not an infallible sign, though. With contour lines a mile apart, for example, the stream in that section will have an *average* gradient of 20 feet to the mile. This may be gradual or it may comprise a single, wildly tossing 20-foot drop where a portage will be necessary. Contour lines help to determine the general nature of a stream, but they are not necessarily detailed pictures of rapids or smooth stretches.

Compasses

Companion to a map, of course, is a good compass. Some are simply glass-enclosed dials with the cardinal points, N, E, S and W printed on the perimeter. One outfitter boasts that his compass of this type is not "all cluttered with figures" to puzzle its user. This is nonsense. For finding your way across a 40-acre woodlot, such a compass is adequate but for extensive travel it will be found wanting.

A more suitable instrument has a circular scale of degrees along its outer rim, starting with zero at north and running clockwise 360 degrees back to north. A still better compass, especially helpful in figuring declination and orienting a map, has a second set of 360 degrees, this one running counter-clockwise.

This type of compass simplifies the taking of a bearing. First orienting the map, place the compass so that the needle's pivot point rests on your location on the map. Next, draw an imaginary line from the pivot to your objective on the map. Where the line crosses the outer rim of the compass is your bearing. In other words, if the line crosses over the figure 80, your bearing is 80 degrees from north.

Some canoemen traveling on waterways where a compass bearing is vital—across a large lake, for example—tape the compass to a thwart in front of the helmsman so that at a glance, and with a twist of his paddle, he can keep the craft on course. This works well on smooth water but is of little value when the canoe is tossed by rough seas.

A better system is to pick out a distant landmark that coincides with your bearing, for example a mountain top, a tall tree, or a dip in a far ridge. The canoeman can thus avoid crossing large open water, taking a more protected course along a shoreline but with his goal still in view.

Incidentally, the so-called emergency "Watch Method," whereby the shadow of a matchstick cast across the face of a pocket watch supposedly points to South, is unreliable and can, in fact, lead the user far off course.*

Maps are subject to much abuse during extended trips, particularly from rain and spray. For protection, glue them to chart cloth. To prevent wear along the folds, cut them, possibly along the lines of latitude and longitude, with a ¼-inch margin between sections, folding them along the cloth margin. Thus, a map can be opened to the section being used and, by slipping it into a transparent plastic bag or map case, it can be preserved from undue wear or wetting. Some wilderness canoemen strap the map to the exterior of a pack so that it is constantly visible.

Map sources are listed in the Appendix.

---

*Two authorities have pointed this out: Harold Gatty, the noted aerial navigator in his book *Nature Is Your Guide* (New York: E.P. Dutton Co., 1958); and Robert Owendoff in his article "How to Get Lost in One Simple Lesson," *Izaak Walton League Magazine,* January 1963.

Chapter XVII

Canoe Country

TRADITIONALLY, Minnesota and Maine have been considered the "canoe country" of the United States; and for the ultimate in a canoe cruise, the goal has always been the vast Canadian river systems.

These limitations are unrealistic. There *are* other unspoiled canoe waters. What's more, only a small percentage of canoe owners will ever run the Allagash, prowl the Superior-Quetico boundary waters or run the Albany down to Hudson's Bay. Closer-to-home waters comprise "canoe country," too. In fact, any body of water that will float a laden canoe, whether it be for 2 miles or 2000, offers canoeing possibilities.

Scenic environment, of course, enhances the experience. It may require some diligent searching, but even in this day of sprawling housing developments, measured in acres, idyllic settings for canoeing are still to be found along hundreds of our waterways. Some of these may be preserved in public recreation areas, others will be adjacent to the green fields of farming areas or in airport-size shopping centers, and concrete and brick industrial complexes commercially-operated forests. In highly developed regions one of nature's last strongholds is the streambanks, where little bits of wilderness can still be found almost within sight of great cities and their suburban octopus-like tentacles.

Canoeing adventure is where you find it, and there's nothing quite so enchanting as urging a canoe around the bend in a strange stream, be it in farm country or deep in the wilderness. Exploring coves, inlets, and side streams, north or south, is fascinating. Passing the time of day with a Hudson's Bay post factor may seem romantic, but a Missouri farmer's hospitality may prove as warm and interesting. When it comes to running rapids, it matters only slightly that an exciting pitch may be located within sight of an expressway bridge; the thrill of bounding among rocks on frothy waves is still there. So much the better, of course, if the environment is primeval, but there is still adventure to be found on developed waterways.

This chapter is not intended to be a guidebook. Naturally, it's impossible to describe all canoeable waters in the United States and Canada, even in brief detail. I merely suggest canoeing possibilities on flowing water that is close to home for many thousands of actual and would-be canoemen. This chapter merely points the way and urges: "Go try 'em!" Local guidebooks and other sources of information, suggested in the text and listed in the Appendix, should be consulted for river details. A number of clubs are mentioned in this chapter, but since their officers may change from year to year, it is impractical to list them and their addresses. Current local club officials may be contacted by obtaining their names and addresses from Bart Hauthaway, Executive Secretary, American White Water Affiliation, 640 Boston Post Road, Weston, Mass. 02193.

United States

Alabama

Information regarding canoeing in Alabama is not easily obtained. Tourist promotional literature barely mentions the subject and, despite several efforts, I could uncover no publications on canoeing. Yet, Alabama has numerous canoeing streams which I observed during a recent trip through the northern end of the state.

In addition, there are the Chattahoochee and Black Warrior Rivers. These are not wilderness waters; in fact, they have been developed by the U.S. Army Corps of Engineers and there is barge traffic on them. However, they have otherwise been left pretty much in their natural state. The lower reaches have numerous campsites, swimming areas and public landings.

Alaska

Many of Alaska's rivers are navigable by canoe but a lack of access and exit routes, the vastness of the area and the wilderness nature of the riverways prescribe that a canoe trip must almost take on the proportions of a major expedition.

On the Kenai Peninsula, however, there is the established 120-mile Swan Lake Canoe Route connecting some fifty-five lakes within the Kenai National Moose Range, operated by the U.S. Fish and Wildlife Service. Eventually this canoe route will encompass 260 miles of riverway and connect some 130 lakes. The placid Swanson River offers a leisurely 45 mile trip from the Swan Lake Canoe Route to Cook Inlet.

Portages on the Swan Lake Canoe Route are generally short, the longest about a half-mile. The lakes are small; rough water a rarity. Information is obtained from the Refuge Manager, Kenai National Moose Range, Box 500, Kenai, Alaska 99611.

The Gulkana Float Trip which runs from the vicinity of Paxson Lake to Sourdough, accessible at either end by car from the Richardson Highway northeast of Anchorage, is an interesting 25-mile (approximately) run in moose country. The trip also parallels a caribou migration route. Information is obtainable from the Bureau of Land Management, P. O. Box 2511, Juneau, Alaska 99801.

Arizona

Stream canoeing in Arizona is rather limited but there are three trip possibilities, one being the Colorado River below Parker Dam, providing over 100 miles of relatively easy water with only a few portages around dams.

Another is the Verde River, flowing southward through central Arizona and offering a wilderness trip starting in the vicinity of Camp Verde or Clarkdale and terminating at Horseshoe, northeast of Phoenix. Access points along this route are few, however.

A pleasant run is possible too on the Salt River, putting in at Salt River bridge on Highway 60 in east-central Arizona, and running down to Roosevelt Lake.

Both the Salt and Verde rivers have stretches of fast water but none is considered dangerous, at least to canoeists of moderate skill.

Float trips are possible on the Colorado River between Lake Powell and Lake Mead, but these are for daring experts using special equipment. Permission is required from the National Park Service for any run through Grand Canyon National Park.

Arkansas

The free flowing rivers of Arkansas are fast attaining the fame of Maine and Minnesota waterways. In the Ozark Mountains, for example, a favorite among advanced canoemen is the Mulberry River in Franklin County, flowing through the wildest and steepest portions of the Boston Mountains. The average float is 30 miles and the river is at its best pitch from mid-April through May, sometimes into June, and also in October if rainfall is adequate.

Big Piney Creek, in Johnson and Pope counties, is a moderately fast stream with the best floating from Ft. Douglas to Long Pool Campground, a two-day jaunt. Canoeing is possible all the way to the Dardanelle Reservoir although the river grows "tame."

The Buffalo River, the "Gem of the Ozarks" among canoeists, flows from west to east across Newton, Searcy, Marion, and Baxter counties. A beautifully scenic river, it is best floated from April through June, with the section from Mt. Hershey to Buffalo State Park navigable through July. Below this point, to White River, canoeing is enjoyed year-round.

The Eleven Point River, is threatened at this writing by a dam proposed for a Dalton site. In the meantime, the best float in Arkansas on this stream is from the Missouri line at Narrows Aquatic Farm to a short distance below Dalton, an easy two-day trip.

The King's River float is best from Trigger Gap to the Berryville bridge in Carroll County while the Spring River and its south fork are ideal canoeing waters, especially in the vicinity of Cherokee Village. Other popular Ozark streams include the War Eagle, Illinois Bayou, Richland Creek and Strawberry River.

The much impounded Ouachita River, in Arkansas' Ouachita Mountains, still has fine canoeing with moderate rapids above Lake Ouachita. It is also canoeable from Pine Ridge, Oden, Pencil Bluff and Mt. Ida. The U.S. Forest Service maintains float camps at Rocky Shoals and River Bluff.

As this is written, construction is underway for a dam that will flood most of the Caddo River canoeing waters except for the section between Glenwood and the iron bridge below Amity.

The Little Missouri River, above Greeson Reservoir, is considered "wild and woolly" and is not for amateurs especially during April and May. During the summer it is too low for canoeing. Below Greeson Dam, the river consists of flat water.

The Saline River, below Benton and in the area of Haskell and Traskwood, is considered interesting canoeing, especially near Boy Scout Camp Quapaw. There are no public facilities, however.

The White River is a beautiful, bluff-lined stream, but its level fluctuates considerably as water is withheld or released at Bull Shoals dam. It is popular late in the summer when other streams are too low for canoeing. A favorite float starts on the Buffalo River and enters the White near Buffalo City, then continues down to Norfolk or Sylacore.

Among the organized canoe groups active in this area is the Ozark Wilderness Waterways Club.

California

In California there is far more interest in canoeing than one might suppose; many groups there are affiliated with the American White Water Affiliation, including Boy Scout Troop No. 708 in Whittier, Explorer Post No. 55X in Temple City, the Feather River Kayak Club in Marysville, Gahonga's Elite in Santa Barbara, the Haystackers Whitewater Club in Los Angeles, the Sierra Club in San Francisco, Sacramento, Berkeley, and Hayward, and the Southern California Canoe Association, with headquarters in Santa Monica. Contact with any of these groups, through the American White Water Affiliation, will undoubtedly lead to fine canoeing experiences.

Other groups which will undoubtedly prove equally helpful are affiliates of the American Canoe Association (Doris C. Cousins, Sec., 400 Eastern Street, New Haven, Conn.). These are The Golden Gate Canoe Club, San Bruno; Lera Canoe Club, Los Altos Hills; The River Touring Section of the Sierra Club, Mother Lode Chapter, Carmichael; and the Sierra Club, River Touring Section, Sunnyvale.

That California has ample canoeing waters is evidenced by the following listing of rivers and streams, with many more which must go unlisted for lack of space!

The Trinity River from Willow Creek to Hoopa is a high Class I or low Class II stream with a put-in below Willow Creek bridge and several take-out points 5 to 8 miles downstream. In the Big Bar area, the Trinity becomes a Class III or IV river, which must be scouted before running. Access points are numerous since a road parallels it. From Douglas City to Junction City, the river reverts to Class I or low Class II, running through a roadless region. The Trinity is a year-round canoe water, its flow regulated by Trinity Reservoir, Lake Clair Engle.

The Main Fork of the Eel River, between Dos Rios and Alder Point, is a two- to three-day run through wilderness country for experienced canoemen only, since it consists entirely of Class II and III water. From the Hearst Ranch to Dos Rios, about a two-day run, is another difficult wilderness stretch, Class III most of the way.

An easy Class I run is the Lower Navarro River where it parallels Highway 128, with many access points available.

The Russian River, from a point below Squaw Brook to Cloverdale averages Class II to III and should be scouted closely since its water level varies. From Cloverdale to its mouth at Jenner, the Russian is generally Class I. The Eel, Navarro, and the Russian are best run from February to May.

The Sacramento River, between Redding and Red Bluff, a two-day trip, is primarily high Class I water while from Red Bluff to Sacramento it is all easy Class I with numerous access points. This river is canoeable year-round with optimum flow of water during the summer.

The North Fork of the Feather River between Queen Lily Campground and Belden is Class III or IV, with the upper sections definitely Class IV. As an indication of the type of water found here, this is the stretch on which the National Kayak championships are held!

The Feather River, from the Great Western dam below Oroville to the Gridley Road, about a five-hour trip, is high Class I or low Class II. From the Gridley Road to Yuba City, a long day's paddle, Class I water can be expected, while the section from Yuba City to Verona, which can be broken up into two one-day trips, is easy Class I.

The Middle Fork of the American River from the washed-out Forest Hill Greenwood bridge to Murderer's Bar is a variable Class II and III run. The take-out point should be well scouted in advance since Murderer's Bar is well named!

Between Highway 49 and Folsom Lake, the North Fork of the American River is a Class II run, followed by 2 to 4 miles of flat-water paddling on the lake. Take-out point is at Rattlesnake Bar.

The American River's South Fork from Coloma to Lotus is rated II and III with one well-named set of rapids known as "Old Scary." Above Coloma there is Class IV water, for experts only. Class IV water exists much of the way too, from Lotus to the south arm of Folsom Lake.

The Bear River from Highway 65 to the confluence with the Feather River is an easy Class I trip, but it is navigable only between February and May. There are several access points on local roads.

The Consumnes River from Bridgehouse to Sloughhouse is a brushy Class I stream. From Highway 99 to Thornton is easy Class I water.

Class II and III water is prevalent on the Mokelumne River from the power-house above Highway 49 to the highway itself and should be scouted. From Clements to Highway 99 (Interstate 5), the Mokelumne is entirely Class I, while from Woodbridge to Thornton, a long day's run, more Class I water is found.

The King's River, below Pine Flat Reservoir to Highway 180, consists of Class I or low Class II water, good training for beginners with some experience. They should scout carefully, however.

There are many other California rivers which are "runable" depending upon the degree of skill attained by a canoeman. Most of these should be scouted carefully, or information obtained locally, before running. In northern California these include the Klamath, Redwood Creek, the South Fork of the Eel, the Mad and the Mattole.

In central California, the San Joaquin River from George Hatfield State Park to the Delta is all Class I water, as are the lower reaches of the Stanislaus, Tuolumne, and Merced.

Colorado

Viewing Colorado's canoeing rivers one gets the impression that they consist of one great Class III and IV rapids. Turbulence is typical.

The Animas River, for example, has an average gradient of 80 feet per mile for some 25 miles below Silverton, an old mining town in southeastern Colorado. This is a run for experts only, when the pitch is right and in decked craft.

"Wild-water" competitions are held on the Arkansas River near Salida at 7,000 feet through a 20-mile stretch of frothing rapids.

However, there *is* water for beginners. The Colorado Academy in Denver and the Colorado Rocky Mountain School at Carbondale sponsor competitions and training at the novice and intermediate levels. Another exciting competition is the Crystal River Slalom held near Carbondale.

Two important groups in the state are the Colorado White Water Association, with headquarters in Denver, and FibArk Boat Races, Inc., of Salida. There are probably more white-water sportsmen per capita in Salida than in any other town or city in the U.S.!

Connecticut

There is only one dam on the Connecticut River below the Massachusetts line, this one at Enfield. From here to Saybrook Point, on salt water, it is 68 miles, including about four miles of easy rapids below Enfield. Downstream of Middletown there are campgrounds at Dart Island and Hurd state parks.

The Hockanum River is canoeable for some 11 miles from Talcottville to the Connecticut at Hartford, if one doesn't mind portaging around numerous dams.

About 80 miles of varied canoeing are available on the Farmington River, ranging from placid waters to wild pitches. The rougher stretches of this stream are scenes of thrilling competitive events, with most of the canoeable waters lying between Otis and the river's confluence with the Connecticut.

The Scantic River's 20 miles between North Somers and its mouth at the Connecticut, offer generally easy paddling through much pleasant country. There are a few dams requiring portages.

Canoeing on the Housatonic River within Connecticut (it rises in Massachusetts) is best from Falls Village downstream 19 miles to Kent, plus 17 miles more to New Milford with a dam and canal at Bull's Bridge.

There are numerous other small rivers in the state which are canoeable in sections, because of numerous dams. The spring run-off creates white-water possibilities on streams which are too low for canoeing during the summer.

The most reliable source of information is the *A.M.C. New England Canoeing Guide* published by the Appalachian Mountain Club (see Bibliography).

Three active canoeing groups in the state are the Connecticut Chapter of the Appalachian Mountain Club, the Waterford Canoe Club of Waterford, both associated with the American White Water Affiliation; and the Columbia Canoe Club of Columbia, a member of the American Canoe Association.

Delaware

Delaware has little water suitable for extended canoe trips but there are slalom and white-water possibilities on the Christina River during the early season, usually in April. The Christina flows northeast from Sunset Lake to Wilmington.

Other streams and rivers on which canoeing is possible, although sometimes limited, include the Appoquinimink River, Blackbird Creek, Little Duck Creek, all crossed by Highway 13; Cedar Creek, the Murderkill, Broadkill, Indian, and Nanticoke rivers.

While no river detail is included, a map issued by the State Development Board (see Appendix) includes access points, highway crossings, state parks and their camping areas, as well as tidal marshes.

Florida

Although little known as a canoeing state, Florida has marvelous flat-water streams for leisurely trips, some over relatively long distances through wilderness-like country.

The famed Suwanee River, which rises in Georgia's Okefenokee Swamp, is navigable all the way to the Gulf of Mexico, a distance of some 210 miles. There are several highway access points.

The Shoal and Blackwater rivers in Santa Rosa and Okaloosa counties of northwest Florida, offer 80 to 100 miles of wilderness-like canoeing on their way to the Gulf.

The Chipola River is canoeable from the state line in Jackson County to Dead Lakes, a distance of about 100 miles interspersed with occasional mild rapids and a number of highway crossings.

The Apalachicola River, also in northwest Florida, is a large stream from Jim Woodruff Dam to Apalachicola with over 100 miles of canoeing possibilities. There are wild stretches along this route although there is also some barge traffic.

Some 80 miles of paddling are possible on the Ochlockonee River from the Jackson Bluff dam near Tallahassee to the Gulf. This is a wilderness-type river with several boat landings.

The headwaters of the St. John River in southern Florida are an attractive canoeway, although the lower river may find canoeists dodging power boats.

The Santa Fe and the Ichetucknee rivers of northeast Florida are spring-fed, clear and generally beautiful canoe routes. They are tributaries to the Suwanee.

Another beautiful stream, slow-moving and sub-tropical, is the Oklawaha River in the central part of the state, along with the Withlacoochee. The annual Citrus County Canoe Race is held on the Withlacoochee at Inverness.

Other Florida rivers which might bear investigating by inquisitive canoe explorers are the Peace, Myaka, Blue Run, Weeki Wachee, Silver, Kissimee, Wakulla, and the St. Mary's.

Georgia

Georgia canoeing waters are relatively little known beyond its borders and information is difficult to obtain. In fact, it wasn't until a recent trip through the state that I was able to learn anything at all about its waters. I found that Boy Scout and Explorer Scout cruises are often made on the Savannah River below Augusta but I learned little else until I entered Okefenokee Swamp. Here, I realized, are fascinating canoe waters. No rapids, of course, but mile upon mile of twisting and turning "boat trails," well marked and easy to follow, though vast "prairies" and moss-hung cypress jungle.

Operated by the U.S. Fish and Wildlife Service as the Okefenokee National Wildlife Refuge, the great swamp is fast reverting to the primeval wonder that it was before loggers devastated sections of it.

The area manager loaned my wife and me a Grumman aluminum canoe and for three days we prowled solitary waterways surrounded by wildlife. Incidentally, alligators pose no threat to canoeists. They are timid and slither away quickly. The only drawback to exploring by canoe is that overnight stays in the swamp are not permitted.

Access to the swamp and refuge is possible only from three points: Folkston, which we chose, Waycross, and Stephen Foster State Park. A detailed map of the area is available (see Appendix).

Organized canoeing in Georgia is represented by the Georgia Canoeing Association with headquarters in Marietta.

Idaho

One has to be cautious in evaluating Idaho rivers. Readers may be thinking in terms of canoes while Idahoans are more likely to have in mind the rubber rafts with which they shoot tumultuous water within steep-walled canyons. Some of these trips—sections of them, at least—may be possible for decked canoes or kayaks but they should be chosen only after seeking knowledgeable local information. Many of Idaho's rivers traverse inaccessible wilderness where even a minor accident takes on serious proportions.

Some of the state's rivers, considered "slow," "safe," or "average" for rubber-raft floats and which might be suitable for fast-water canoeing include:

seven miles of the Buffalo above its mouth, best run between June and October;

the North Fork of the Clearwater for 80 miles between Larson and Elk creeks, in July and August;

parts of the Middle Fork of the Salmon for 125 miles between Dagger Falls and its mouth, classified as "fast-average" and, therefore, for experts in canoes between July and October;

the St. Joe, between Avery and St. Joe City, a relatively leisurely 36-mile trip during June and July;

the Selway, a remote "fast" river for 45 miles between Moose Creek and Selway Falls which experts might be able to handle during July and August;

five miles of the Snake between Big Springs and Mack's Inn, a "slow-safe" trip from June to October;

the Lower Snake, from Pittsburg Landing to Lewiston, a distance of 80 miles best run during the summer;

the South Fork of the Snake, between Palisades Dam and Heise, 35 miles of "slow-safe" running;

the Priest, for 35 miles from Priest Lake to the mouth, rated "fair" from July to September.

The sections of the Snake mentioned above should not be confused with the famed Hell's Canyon section of the river, which includes 75 miles rated as "dangerous" between Oxbow and Pittsburg Landing.

Other Idaho rivers with canoeing possibilities are the Teton, Bear, Boise, Payette, Salmon, Clearwater, and the Kootenai; all however, including stretches of white water which canoeists must portage.

It should be remembered that the foregoing ratings are slanted toward rubber-raft boating. Open canoes may be out of the question, possibly even decked canoes and kayaks. Before attempting any Idaho river without prior knowledge of its gradient, a check should be made with the Fish and Game Department, or with the U.S. Forest Service, the latter if the run is through a national forest.

Illinois

Illinois streams may generally lack exciting pitches, but because of this they are ideal waters for beginners and those who most enjoy leisurely tripping. Among the canoeable waters—a few only after a substantial rain—are the scenic (despite its name) Big Muddy south of Murphysboro, the cliff-lined Cache, the Des Plaines (unfortunately polluted) and the Embarras with its 130 miles of navigable water.

The Fox River, located in one of the most heavily populated areas, is canoeable from the Wisconsin line for a downstream distance of 95 miles.

The Green River, characterized by high banks, has access points at Highways 26, 88, 92, 78 and 82.

The Illinois River is "big water," formed by the junction of the Des Plaines and the Kankakee and flowing some 272 miles through central Illinois to empty into the Mississippi at Grafton. Several dams and locks, plus commercial navigation, may depreciate this river in the eyes of some canoemen.

The Illinois-Michigan Canal, with little current most of its length, is easy paddling for 20 miles east of Morris to a point 5 miles west of that town.

The Illinois-Mississippi Feeder Canal, some 29 miles long, is ideal beginner's water, considered the safest in Illinois.

The Kankakee River, some 55 miles of which is in Illinois, is most scenic upstream of Momence, a secluded, swampy area rich in wildlife. Below Momence, however, motorboat traffic may be heavy.

The Iroquois River is a placid, remote prairie stream, running approximately 36 miles between Watseka and Kankakee with little evidence of pollution.

Between Cooks Mills and Shelbyville, the Kaskaskia River is canoeable during the spring and early summer months, with numerous access points and campsites. Brush piles and log jams are also plentiful, however.

Shoal Creek is canoeable for about 57 miles in Bond and Clinton counties; an isolated stream ideal for canoes except for occasional brush piles and tree tops dropped into the water during logging operations.

The least spoiled of all Illinois rivers is the Mackinaw, with the most favorable canoeing section found below Mackinaw on Rt. 9, for a distance of 60 miles to the Illinois River. The river is clear of obstructions and deep enough for paddling most of the year.

The Pecatonica River, originating in Wisconsin, flows for 76 miles through Illinois. Although attractive in many ways, it has few access points and no campsites as such. Landowners, however, usually grant permission to camp, making possible a four-day trip.

The Rock River, 150 miles long in Illinois, is open to canoeing all year but is badly polluted and runs mostly through highly developed areas. The Saline below Equality is an easy cruise, campsites are plentiful and, since it is remote, much wildlife can be observed. The Middle Fork of the South Vermillion River is canoeable from Potomac to its junction with the Salt Fork. The latter, except in dry periods, provides about 25 miles of canoeing from Rt. 49 to Danville. The first stream in Illinois to be dedicated as a canoe trail is the Sangamon River. Upstream of the bridge below Argenta, however, it is frequently obstructed by brush and fences. The best starting point is the Lincoln Trail Homestead State Park in Macon County, which makes possible 93 miles of paddling to Beardstown.

The Spoon River, for 120 miles from Elmore to its mouth at Havana, is in a primitive region to be enjoyed by those who prefer to rough it. The Vermillion River, flowing through Livingston and La Salle counties, is a wild stream, isolated except for the towns of Pontiac and Streator and has some sections of white water.

Some 25 miles of fine flat-water canoeing are possible on the Little Wabash River between Carmi and New Haven, with camping areas in scenic spots.

Canoeing groups located in Illinois include the Lincoln Park Boat Club of Chicago, an affiliate of the American Canoe Association; and the American Indian Center Canoe Club; American Youth Hostels, Inc.; Prairie Club Canoeists, and the University of Chicago Outing Club, all of Chicago and members of the American White Water Affiliation.

Indiana

Indiana is another state which has recognized canoeing as a sport by establishing canoe trails. These include the Blue River for 45 miles between Freeport and Columbus and for 55 miles between Fredericksburg and the Ohio River.

Then there is the Eel River's 50 miles of canoe water running from South Whitley to Logansport, also 50 miles more between Reelsville and Worthington. The Fawn River, from Crooked Creek at Snow Lake to the Michigan state line, offers 20 miles of paddling.

Between Kankakee State Park Game Preserve and the Illinois state line there are 55 miles of paddling on the Kankakee River. A 60-mile cruise is possible, with only one portage, on the Mississinewa River from Eaton to Peru while the Muscatatuck River, from a point north of Austin to Sparksville, has 30 miles of canoe water.

The Pigeon River, starting at the dam at Mongo and running to the Michigan state line, includes 20 miles of canoeing, but there are four portages. Also with four portages within 35 miles is the St. Joseph River, between Bristol and the Michigan line. From Darlington to Montezuma a 45-mile trip is possible, with four portages, on Sugar Creek. The Tippecanoe River has only two portages within the 75 miles that lie between Rochester and Lafayette.

Indiana's longest canoe trip is on the famed Wabash, from Bluffton to the Ohio River, a distance of 360 miles with only three portages. Another lengthy cruise is possible from Columbus to Mt. Carmel, Ill., on the East Fork of the White River, a distance of 175 miles. A 210-mile trip is possible on the West Fork of the White, with six portages between Anderson and Mt. Carmel, Ill. The Whitewater River has only one portage along its 55 mile course from Connorsville to the Ohio.

The Sugar Creek Canoe Race is usually held during mid- or late April at Crawfordsville.

Indiana groups active in canoeing are the Western Canoe Union of Craw-fordsville, associated with the American Canoe Association; the Kekionga Voyageurs of Fort Wayne; and the Indiana Canoe Racing Council, also of Crawfordsville, both of which are allied with the American White Water Affili-ation.

Iowa

More than a dozen specific canoe routes have been established on Iowa rivers and streams. One of these is the Boone River trip from Webster City to the Des Moines River, a distance of about 23 miles, with a 4.8 feet per mile gradient, indicating some mild rapids. While the Des Moines River meanders through some 500 miles of Iowa countryside, a favorite trip on its waters is but 11 miles long, between Kalo and Lehigh.

Most canoeists running the Iowa River put in below the dam at Iowa Falls for the 25-mile trip to Eldora, although the river is navigable all the way to Albion, an additional 25 miles. There are a few riffles and the current is gen-erally somewhat fast, though hardly dangerous.

The Little Sioux River between Linn Grove and Cherokee suggests 35 miles of paddling in a slow current. There are no dams or rapids but high banks make camping difficult.

In central Iowa, the Raccoon River runs some 46 miles from Jefferson to Adel, mostly through timbered country unhampered by dams. The first 20 miles has a swift current and the water is clear. The trip can be extended 36 miles to the Des Moines River.

Running through a narrow valley closed in by high hills and steep cliffs is the Volga River, comparatively little used. For those who like to explore, it's ideal, especially in the 17-mile section between Osborne and Garber. The trip can be continued about 13 miles from Garber to Millville on the Turkey River.

The Upper Iowa River is considered one of the most beautiful streams in the Midwest and a favorite canoe trip includes the 24-mile section between Lime Springs and Kendallville. The stream is at its best early in the season but is navigable all year with occasional wading during dry spells. From Ken-dallville to Decorah, a distance of about 30 miles, parts of the river are walled in by 400-foot cliffs, but it remains navigable with some riffles but no heavy rapids.

The Shell Rock River, which rises at Albert Lea Lake in Minnesota, flows some 100 miles southward to Nora Springs and includes riffles, swift currents, respectable rapids, to say nothing of 69 barbed-wire fences crossing the stream! The fences, however, can be negotiated.

The Turkey River, although 135 miles long, offers its best canoeing waters within the 34-mile stretch between Elgin and Garber. Except for a dam at Elkader, about halfway, there are no obstructions to the fairly strong current.

Running about 41 miles from Otranto to Charles City, the Red Cedar River trip is without sizable rapids but there are two dams and a low footbridge around which short carries must be made. Much of the distance is through heavy timber.

"Wapsi" for short, the Wapsipinicon River provides an interesting stretch of canoeing for about 50 miles between Independence in Buchanan County and Stone City in Jones County.

The most turbulent of Iowa rivers is the Yellow, with a gradient varying from 6 to 25 feet per mile. Rapids are numerous though not rated as dangerous. There are no dams.

An interesting note regarding the many wire fences that cross Iowa streams, often to the disgust of canoeists, is that the stream bed of a "non-meandered" river is privately owned. Owners of these who keep cattle are *required* by law to fence across streams to keep animals within bounds. The stream bed on meandered rivers, on the other hand, is owned by the state, even if adjacent property is private. These may not be fenced.

Kansas

Another delightful surprise with regard to canoeing in the Plains states is the revelation that Wichita, Kansas, High School is the only one in the state, possibly in the nation, that offers an accredited course in canoeing!

Most Kansas rivers can be navigated by canoe at some time or other during the season, but among the more attractive trips are the following:

Shoal Creek in the extreme southeast, for a distance of 6 miles with good rapids but no serious danger points;

Spring River, also in the southeast, with 15 miles of canoeable water which can be floated into Missouri and Oklahoma;

The Verdigris River, for 75 miles south of Toronto Reservoir; a few old mill dams must be portaged but there are no dangerous sections;

From John Redmond Reservoir, 100 miles southward, the Neosho River offers varied water, including several rapids of easy-to-moderate difficulty and a few mill dams requiring carries;

The Fall River, for 60 miles below Fall River Reservoir, includes many rapids, though none dangerous; a few abandoned dams must be portaged.

Other canoeing possibilities in Kansas are the Caney River, south of Howard; the Elk River above Elk River Reservoir; the Walnut River in Kansas and Oklahoma, from Winfield, Kansas, southward; and the Kaw River from Manhattan to Kansas City. All of these entail running some rapids, though none is considered difficult.

An active canoeing group in Kansas is the Prairie Voyogeurs Canoe Club of Wichita, associated with the American White Water Affiliation.

Kentucky

Bowling Green is the site of the famed 21-mile Barren River Canoe Marathon, usually held in April and co-sponsored by the University of Kentucky Cooperative Extension Service and the Kentucky Rivers Canoe Club.

The Barren River is a beautiful canoe stream located in the Pennyrille area of rolling hills. Water levels are fairly constant, being controlled by the Barren River Reservoir.

Kentucky also shares further canoeing fame with Tennessee in the running of the annual Angel Falls (Tenn.)—Devil's Jump (Ky.) race on the Big South Fork of the Cumberland River, the race course crossing the state line between Tennessee and Kentucky.

Other than these two events, however, canoeing gets little attention in state promotional literature. That Kentucky has some of the country's finest canoe streams is beyond doubt. It remains only for promotional officials to make them known beyond their borders.

Louisiana

"The launching of canoes in Louisiana is akin to the subject 'how high is up'!" This is the comment of one state official regarding canoeing in that state. In view of Louisiana's thousands of waterways, fresh water and brackish, the claim is certainly valid. However, little, if any, specific information is available beyond a list of launching ramps available from the Wild Life and Fisheries Commission, 400 Royal St., New Orleans 70130.

Maine

Maine's waters are varied—placid streams, large lakes, rapids, up to Class VI, beaver flowages, often all included in one trip. The Maine Forest Service maintains over 200 campsites, most of them along canoe routes. The common belief that a guide is *required* for wilderness trips is incorrect. A guide is *recommended* to novices for back-of-beyond cruises, but knowledgeable canoemen can make any of Maine's established trips on their own. Campfire permits are not required if you camp on designated campsites marked by signs. Building a fire elsewhere is illegal. Incidentally, in Maine, a portage is a "carry."

Maine's most challenging trip is the St. John River from Northwest Carry at Moosehead Lake, or from St. John Pond, to Fort Kent, a distance of 201 miles best run during the early season, since a dry summer may find the St. John much like the upper Missouri—a mile wide and an inch deep!

Most famous of the Pine Tree State's trips, of course, is the Allagash, recently designated by the state as a Wilderness Waterway with special regulations, copies of which are available from the State Park and Recreation Commission, Augusta 04330. The original Allagash trip started at Northeast Carry at Moosehead Lake and traversed a variety of waters, including large lakes, before terminating at Fort Kent, where the Allagash blends with the St. John. More recently, however, canoeists have tended to originate the trip at Telos Lake, just west of Baxter State Park, shortening the distance to under 100 miles.

The Fish River Chain of Lakes trip runs from St. Agathe to Fort Kent, a distance of 52 to 93 miles depending upon put-in. This is a flexible trip which can be adjusted to suit a time schedule.

The Allagash Lake trip, not to be confused with the Allagash River trip, may be started at Northeast Carry on Moosehead or at the Chesuncook Lake dam. It covers close to 100 miles of wilderness and logging country.

The East Branch of the Penobscot is considered a "sporty" trip, and for this run the recommendation that a guide be hired isn't to be shrugged off lightly by novices. Experts will have no trouble, however. This trip, too, starts at Northeast Carry or at Chesuncook, and runs to Grindstone, 118 miles of water that ranges from docile to turbulent.

Also an exciting trip is the West Branch of the Penobscot. Depending upon put-in and take-out—there is some choice of these—it covers 32 to 78 miles, starting at the Big Eddy and running to Millinocket Landing or Norcross.

One of the state's more leisurely, and one of its shortest, trips is on the Fish River between Patten and Island Falls, a distance of 12 miles. This is through relatively "civilized" country with no portages.

Also in a developed section, is the Molunkus Stream trip from Sherman Mills to Macwahoc, a distance of 28 miles with three carries.

Baskahegan Stream and the Mattawamkeag River combine in a 40- to 46-mile cruise starting at Baskahegan Lake and terminating at Mattawamkeag. There are four carries and though the trip is short it is considered difficult.

The East Grand Lake and St. Croix River trip covers 95 miles between Orient and Calais, including six portages. The trip may be extended into salt water to Perry, Lubec, or Jonesport, but this entails open water travel—for experts only.

Although the Penobscot River has been badly polluted, recent efforts to clean it up have encouraged the return of Atlantic salmon runs, and greater canoeing activity. With the water level at the right pitch, canoe travel is possible from Wytopitlock to Bangor, a total of 82 miles. However, between Wytopitlock and Mattawamkeag the river is dangerous at high water, and during a dry spell much dragging and carrying may be necessary. The best section of the trip is from Mattawamkeag down the Mattawamkeag River to the Penobscot, thence down to Bangor.

The Union River and Great Pond trip, from Amherst to Brandy Pond, covers 36 miles of wild country, while the somewhat lengthier Union River trip, from Amherst to Bluehill Bay on salt water, ends near Bar Harbor in Maine's famed coastal resort area.

The Attean Lake trip, a favorite of the writer many years ago, is actually a combination of river and lake travel in a circuitous route covering between 30 and 40 miles of wild country. The trip may be started at Big Wood Lake near Jackman, or at Holeb Pond on the Canadian Pacific Railroad right-of-way.

The Moose River trip also starts at Jackman, for a 29-mile run to Rockwood on Moosehead Lake, through wilderness much of the way, including two large lakes and much swift water.

The Moosehead Lake trip is all flat water (if the wind isn't blowing!) and consists of following the lake's 200-mile shoreline from Greenville and return.

The 125-mile long Kennebec River trip starts at The Forks—the junction of the Kennebec and Dead Rivers—and continues to Bath on tidal water. There are ten dams requiring portages. The upper section is in relatively wild country, but the river gradually emerges into developed regions and eventually passes into Merrymeeting Bay, noted for its wildfowl population.

While only 7 miles long and ideal for a day's paddling and dawdling, the Chain of Ponds trip is within some of Maine's most scenic country. Chain of Ponds lies near the Canadian border in northwestern Maine with Highway 27 paralleling the lake and access at both ends.

The Flagstaff Lake and Dead River cruise is also through charming country, combining lake and river travel for a distance of 16 miles to Long Falls dam. With a carry around the latter, the trip may be continued another 6 miles to Grand Falls with two short portages. Grand Falls is spectacular and worth a visit. The river below Grand Falls has many section-rated Class IV and V and should be attempted only by experts in decked canoes and equipped with life jackets and helmets. Between Grand Falls and The Forks, the trip's terminus, the country is extremely isolated. Rescue would be difficult.

Another flat-water trip is the Rangeley Lakes cruise, with few carries, many campsites and attractive scenery. The most frequent starting point is Haines'

Landing on Mooselookmeguntic Lake at Oquossoc with most groups ending their trip at South Arm on Lower Richardson Lake. However, several combinations are possible, including a long carry (5 miles!) around Rapid River, where the 1941 National White Water Championships were held, into Umbagog Lake. Travel then is possible upstream into the Magalloway River, followed by another long carry into Aziscoos Lake and, eventually, into Parmachenee Lake. The basic Rangeley trip, covers about 20 miles from Haines Landing to South Arm but can be extended to well over 100 by the exploration of numerous bays and feeder streams.

The Androscoggin River trip, 114 miles long, originates in New Hampshire at 13-Mile Woods and terminates at Merrymeeting Bay in Maine, near Bath. Rapids above Berlin, N.H. are classified II and III and are the scene of annual canoe races. Below Berlin, the river is relatively quiet in most sections but gradually grows more polluted by the time it re-enters Maine. There are dams in the many communities through which the river runs and, generally, it is unattractive to canoeists. I know of no one who has bothered to complete the trip to salt water.

Except that it is only 32 miles long, the Belgrade Lakes trip is similar to the Moosehead trip in that it is all flat water. A circuitous cruise, it can be started and terminated at either East Pond or Oakland. This is developed country but nonetheless attractive.

One of the most attractive yet easy trips in Maine is on the Saco River, starting at North Lovell and terminating at Biddeford, some 84 miles. However, since there are numerous access points, trips of any length can be made. Much of the course is through hardwood growth; the river has a clean, sandy bottom with many swimming spots and sand bars. The river is currently under study by the state with an eye to its increased recreational possibilities and is, without doubt, the best in Maine for novices.

Another attractive and easy trip is on the Ossipee River, originating at Effingham Falls, N.H., and running 49 miles to Biddeford, Maine. There are shoals and a few dams, with many access points.

The Crooked River and Sebago Lake trip covers 65 miles starting at Sebago Basin and traveling northward to Harrison and return. This is a highly developed resort section, however, and much powerboat traffic may be encountered.

The Grand Lake-Machias River trip is a wilderness route, 75 miles long, running from Princeton to Whitneyville, a combination of lake and river travel with several rapids varying from Class I to V and, naturally, several carries. The course permits several side trips, particularly among the lakes north of Highway 9.

Maine, like Minnesota, has an infinite number of canoe trip waters, with hundreds of short, one-day excursions possible along with the numerous one- and two-week cruise possibilities. State literature covering the more popular routes is not as detailed as it might be, however, nor does it cover any of the smaller streams which are canoeable. All in all, the best source of information is the *A.M.C. New England Canoeing Guide* (see Bibliography).

Maryland

Maryland boasts several fine canoeing streams although some of them may be at their best during the spring run-off or following a substantial rain. These vary greatly, from relatively easy trips which beginners can handle under supervision of skilled canoemen to wild pitches which will cause the experts to pale!

These are so well detailed in two small, but accurate guidebooks that there is little point in describing them here beyond listing them briefly as "teasers." Further investigation is recommended in the pages of *Blue Ridge Voyages,* Vols. I and II, by H. Roger Corbett, Jr., and Louis J. Matacia, Jr. (see Bibliography).

Whether a canoeman wants a leisurely afternoon on the water or wild-water excitement, one or more of the following Maryland streams will supply it:

Upper Antietam Creek for some 10 miles between Funkstown (near Hagerstown) and the mill dam on Rt. 68;

Antietam Creek, from Rt. 68 to a point upstream of the town of Antietam, with 12 miles of fast water suitable as a beginner's practice course;

The Potomac River, starting at Harper's Ferry (actual starting point is upstream at dam No. 3), and running somewhat under 6 miles to Knoxsville, presenting white-water thrills for canoemen of intermediate or better skill;

From Great Falls downstream to the Brookmount dam, the Potomac affords 8 miles of wild-water canoeing, up to Class V—for experts and those familiar with this stretch of the river. This run is well detailed in Randy Carter's *Canoeing White Water* (see Bibliography).

Catoctin Creek, some 45 miles northwest of Washington, D.C., maintains enough headway for about 10 miles to be an interesting river on which beginners can whet their wild-water appetites. Like so many streams in this part of the country, the Catoctin affords only early-season runs.

Marked by easy-to-run riffles, the Monocacy River, between Highways 355 and 28, is another beginner's workshop area, also best run early in the season.

Several canoeing groups are active in Maryland, among them the Canoe Cruisers Association of Greenbelt, a group-member of the American Canoe Association.

Maryland groups which are associated with the American White Water Affiliation are Explorer Post No. 757, Brookeville; Mariner Girl Scout Ship No. 1000, Kensington; and the Monocacy Canoe Club, Walkersville.

A nearby group, connected with the American Canoe Association, is the Potomac Boat Club of Washington, D.C.

Massachusetts

Massachusetts boasts several beautiful waterways ranging from placid flowage to rip-snorting pitches. But many of its rivers and streams are badly polluted, a situation certainly not confined to the Bay State. There are also many dams, sometimes several in one town or city. However between dams are sections which permit leisurely paddling without the need for lengthy portages. At the same time, there is no dearth of challenging pitches for the expert, at least during the early season when melting snows have swollen the streams.

The following list is by no means a complete compilation of Massachusetts canoeing waters. For this, one should consult the *A.M.C. New England Canoeing Guide* (see Bibliography).

Among the rivers affording flat water in an attractive surrounding is the Housatonic between Stockbridge and Falls Village, Conn. There are occasional dams and some rapids.

The Connecticut River, bisecting Massachusetts north-to-south, is canoeable for its first 10 miles below the state's northern border. During high water, the section near the mouth of the Millers River may be dangerous to all but experts, while the 32-mile segment from the mouth of the Deerfield River to Holyoke is generally easy paddling.

The North Branch of the Westfield River, between West Cummington and the Swift River confluence, is one long set of rapids, though not dangerous except to absolute novices, being rated as Class II rips. If water is above normal, however, there may be hazards.

Swift River, from its junction with the North Branch of the Westfield River to the Knightsville flood control dam, is also rough water, parts of which are Class IV. At the West Chesterfield gorge a portage is necessary, except at low water.

Swift currents and some riffles, none dangerous, are common on the Ware River, between Ware and Three Rivers.

Between East Brookfield and West Warren, the Quaboag River offers some 17 miles of flat-water canoeing, interspersed with occasional easy rapids and several carries around dams. From West Warren to Blanchardville, a distance of 8 miles, runs some of the sportiest white water in Massachusetts, strictly for canoemen who can negotiate rapids up to Class IV. This stretch has been the scene of competitions held by the Eastern Division of the American Canoe Association.

The Millers River upstream of South Royalston affords several miles of easy paddling, as it does between Athol and Erving. Between South Royalston and Athol, however, there are continuous rapids, and from Erving to Millers Falls, heavy white water is preponderant.

The Shawsheen River, for 15 miles between Bedford and Ballardville, provides a variety of paddling through much smooth water and occasional rapids.

On the Concord River, you can follow Henry David Thoreau's route to the Merrimack with only one carry, at Billerica. The Concord is also the scene of certain American Canoe Association events.

Interesting paddling through marshes is possible along the Sudbury River, from Saxonville to Concord, a distance of about 17 miles.

Between West Townsend and West Groton, the Squannacook River maintains a steady current, best enjoyed at high water. There are some portages and part of the course is through a swamp.

Despite numerous dams to be portaged, there are attractive possibilities on the Blackstone River, between Fisherville and Woonsocket, R.I., some 18 miles apart.

The Taunton River boasts an 11-mile stretch between Monponset Pond and Madfield River, flowing alternatingly among marshes, meadows, and cranberry bogs, a pleasant trip.

The Charles River area bordering on Cambridge and Boston is famed for small boating and may even prove a bit crowded when the weather is good. However, the section between the Rt. 27 bridge on the Sherborn-Medfield line, and the Natick dam, some 9 miles long, is attractive considering its close proximity to metropolitan Boston.

The Appalachian Mountain Club, with headquarters in Boston, is active in Massachusetts canoeing. Two other groups, members of the American White Water Affiliation, include the Kayak and Canoe Club of Boston and the Cochituate Canoe Club of Cochituate. The latter group often runs a spectacular saltwater tidal race which never lacks for water, being refilled twice a day by the Atlantic Ocean!

Michigan

Michigan's established canoe routes run the gamut from placid to turbulent and they traverse all types of country, wilderness and settled. In fact, the state probably has more designated canoe trails than any other, which may come as a surprise to State-of-Mainers and Minnesotans!

So numerous are they that it is impossible to include much detail regarding them in this chapter. They are listed briefly for quick reference. More detail can be obtained from a Conservation Department booklet (see Appendix).

Black River, Gogebic County, 30 miles. A wild river for experts only.

Presque Isle River, Gogebic County, 93 miles, four to six days' travel time, for experts only.

Ontonagon River, Ontonagon, Gogebic, and Houghton counties; West Branch, 40 miles, three days; South Branch, 65 miles, five days; Middle Branch, 75 miles, five days; Middle Branch, from Agate, 50 miles, three days; East Branch, 60 miles, two days.

Otter River, Houghton County, Nisula to Portage Lake.

Cisco Chain, Gogebic County, 15 lakes connected by channels.

Sturgeon River, Houghton; several portages along upper end; placid waters lower section.

Net River, Iron County, 24 miles, two days.

Paint River, Iron County, 45 miles, three days to one week.

Fence River, Iron County, 16 miles, one to two days.

Michigamme River, Marquette and Iron counties; 20 miles in Marquette, 30 miles in Iron; one week.

Brule River, Iron County, 47 miles, two to three days; famous trout stream.

Menominee River, Dickinson and Menominee counties; 35 miles in Dickinson, 75 in Menominee; one to two weeks.

Escanaba River, Dickinson, Marquette, and Delta counties; eight to fourteen days.

Au Train Waters, Alger County, 17 miles, two days.

Whitefish River, Delta County, 12 miles, one day.

Sturgeon River, Delta County, 15 miles, one day.

Indian River, Schoolcraft County, 25 miles, one to two days. No fast water.

Manistique River, Schoolcraft County, 90 miles, four days.

West Branch Manistique River, 50 miles, two days.

Fox River, Schoolcraft County, 15 to 20 miles, one to three days.

Sucker River, Alger County, 17 miles, one day.

Two Hearted River, Luce County, 25 miles, two to three days; for experts only.

Tahquamenon River, Luce and Chippewa counties; 45 miles in Luce, 18 miles in Chippewa; one to two weeks. Considered an easy trip except that black flies are vicious during June and early July.

Waiska River, Chippewa County, seven miles; placid canoeing.

St. Mary's River, Chippewa County, 40 miles, three days; busy route for freighters which, with possible high winds, may present some hazards.

Carp River, Mackinac County, 12 miles, one day.

Indian Lakes Route, Emmet and Cheboygan counties, 45 miles, three days; boat traffic extremely heavy during July and August along Indian River section.

Black River, Cheboygan County, 45 miles, three to four days; difficult trip due to log jams and swift water below dams.

Ocqueeoc River, Presque Isle County, 30 miles, two to three days; fast stream, best run during late May or early June.

Thunder Bay River, Montmorency and Alpena counties, 33 miles in Montmorency, three to five days; 50 miles in Alpena, five to seven days.

Jordan River, Antrim and Charlevoix counties, 15 miles, one day; no portages and one of the most scenic rivers in Michigan.

Intermediate Chain of Lakes, Antrim County, 60 miles, four days. These are big lakes, so beware of high winds.

Boardman River, Grand Traverse County, 40 miles, two to five days; famous brown trout stream.

Betsie River, Benzie and Manistee counties, 44 miles, two to four days.

Big Manistee River, Crawford, Missaukee, Kalkaska, Wexford, and Manistee counties, 215 miles, at least 10 days.

Bear Creek, Manistee County, 40 miles, one to two days.

Pine River, Wexford, Lake, and Manistee counties, 70 miles, three to four days; not recommended for novices due to swift water, rapids and sharp turns.

Little Manistee River, Lake, Mason, and Manistee counties, 85 to 100 miles, three to five days.

Big Sable River, Mason County, two days.

Pere Marquette River, Lake and Mason counties, 100 miles, four to seven days; a tricky but interesting trip!

White River, Oceana and Muskegon counties, 60 miles, two days; mostly through swampland.

Muskegon River, Roscommon, Clare, Mecosta, Newaygo, and Muskegon counties, 227 miles, one to two weeks.

Au Sable River, Crawford, Oscoda, and Iosco counties; Grayling to Mio, 75 miles, three to five days; Grayling to Lake Huron, 180 miles, 10 to 15 days.

Rifle River, Ogemaw, and Arenac counties, 90 miles, five to six days.

Tittabawassee River, Gladwin County, 30 miles, one to two days; quiet waters in a wilderness area.

Pine River, Isabella, Montcalm, Gratiot, and Midland counties, 110 miles, four to seven days; shallow and weedy during summer.

Bad River, Saginaw County, 12 to 14 miles, one day. Runs through wildlife preserve.

Cass River, Tuscola and Saginaw counties, 65 miles, two to three days.

Shiawassee River, Shiawassee and Saginaw counties, 65 miles, two to four days; placid waters flowing through farming country.

Maple River, Shiawassee, Clinton, Gratiot, and Ionia counties, 60 miles, four to five days; runs through game management area.

Grand River, Jackson, Ingham, Eaton, Clinton, Ionia, Kent, and Ottawa counties, 185 miles, 10 days.

Thornapple River, Eaton, Barry, and Kent counties, 45 miles, one to two days.

Kalamazoo River, Calhoun, Kalamazoo, and Allegan counties, 75 to 80 miles, four to six days; difficult when water is low.

Black River, Van Buren County, 8 miles, one day; this is a lazy stream.

Paw Paw River, Van Buren and Berrien counties, 40 miles, two days.

St. Joseph River, St. Joseph County, 60 miles, two to four days.

Raisin River, Lenawee County, 42 miles; through farm lands with many access points.

Minnesota

With more than 15,000 miles of streams and rivers, plus some 10,000 lakes, the majority concentrated in the upper third of the state, the canoe trip possibilities of Minnesota are practically infinite. In the famed Boundary Waters Canoe Area, for example, a canoeist can paddle all summer, rarely retracing or even crossing his own trail. Few regions in the world have as many lakes so conveniently linked by navigable thoroughfares or short portages.

Practically any combination of routes and mileage is possible in planning a Minnesota canoe trip. Some indication of the vastness of this canoe empire is the size of the Superior National Forest, encompassing some 2,000,000 acres, of which 1,036,000 are in the restricted canoe area where power boats are banned. Abutting this maze of water routes, across the Canadian border, lies Quetico Provincial Park, 1,750 square miles of waterways similarly set aside for canoeing and wilderness camping. These Canadian waters open into the even more infinite canoe country of central and upper Ontario. A lifetime of paddling could not cover all of these canoeing waters!

Many of the Minnesota routes, however, have found greater favor than others. Among these is the International Boundary Route covering 235 miles and including 9 miles of portaging. This trip starts at Grand Portage at Pigeon River and extends westward to International Falls on Rainy Lake. At least three weeks should be allowed, although side trips could well extend this cruise into an all-summer excursion.

The Clearwater-Bearskin Loop, starting near the Gunflint Trail in northeastern Minnesota, is a 38-mile route involving 5 miles of portages and three days' travel. (Portage figures include the overall carrying distance and usually entail several carries.)

Also starting from the Gunflint Trail, the Poplar-Brule Loop is a 47-mile circuitous route, conveniently covered in one week and returning to the starting point.

The Little Saganaga Route, however, is a one-way trip of some 25 miles, with 4 miles of portages. It too originates on the Gunflint Trail, returning to it several miles west of the starting point. Three days are recommended for this cruise.

Still another route originating on the Gunflint Trail is the Sea Gull-Red Rock trip. This one, however, starts at the trail's western terminus, Sea Gull Lake, and provides 23 miles of travel with a half-mile portage, before returning to Sea Gull Lake via Sea Gull River.

The Sawbill Loop, starting at Sawbill Lake on the Sawbill Trail, includes 62 miles of cruising waters and 5 miles of portaging. The trip crosses the Laurentian divide from one side of which waters flow into Lake Superior, while from the other they flow westward and northward. Six days are suggested for this trip.

The Kawishiwi Loop leaves the Fernberg Road near Ely and winds through 83 miles of cruising territory with somewhat over 9 miles of portaging required. The suggested time for the trip is ten to eleven days. I have fond memories of the Kawishiwi including the visit to our campsite by the biggest black bear I have ever seen.

The Fernberg Road near Ely is also the starting point of the Kekekabic

Loop, a 49-mile trip with over 4½ miles of portages. This is usually a six-day trip but, like so many in Minnesota, can be extended almost as long as time permits.

The North-South Kawishiwi Rivers Loop can originate at any one of several points east of Ely and covers 30 miles of paddling with a mere 2 miles of carrying. The entire trip can be graciously accomplished in three days.

Winton and Basswood, like Ely, have a magical ring in the ears of Minnesota canoe enthusiasts. Originating at Winton and terminating at Basswood Lake astride the Canadian border, the Winton-Basswood Route offers alternate routes; one has a half-mile portage; for the other, with its much longer carry, outfitters will lug your outfit if you prefer. In the heart of the canoe country, it is a short, one-day, 13-mile jaunt.

The Stuart and Moose Rivers Loop originates at Burntside Lake, west of Ely and Winton, and provides nine or more days of cruising over a circuitous route covering 57 miles, 11 of which must be under a portage yoke. The route crosses the Ely-Buyck road at two points where take-out and put-in are also possible.

Another circuit route is the Vermillion and Little Indian Sioux Rivers Loop, with a good balance between river and lake travel for 116 miles, starting at the southeast end of Vermillion Lake and returning to this point. Portages cover 7½ miles.

Unique services are available to canoeists at such jumping-off places as Ely, Winton, Tofte, and Grand Marais, where dozens of outfitters supply complete outfits. Most, too, will supply individual items of gear on a rental basis and nearly all operate retail stores where equipment is sold. Nearly all will arrange to tote an outfit to its starting point, arrange for trucks on some lengthy portages and pick up canoeists at the end of their trip. Some maintain canoe bases and even overnight accommodations at trip-starting points. All in all, probably no canoe area in the world is as well set up to cater to canoe parties.

Along some of the more popular established routes, a number of the campsites are suffering from overuse, with firewood becoming scarce in the immediate vicinity. Regrettably, too, "civilization" encroaches in the form of unkempt campsites, despite the pleas of outfitters and the U.S. Forest Service that canoeists leave their overnight stops unsullied.

While Minnesota is best known for its Superior National Forest canoeing country and its Boundary Waters Canoe Area within the forest, several other sections of the state offer excellent canoe trips in more developed regions. Trips are possible, for instance, on the Mississippi River, from a point north of Minneapolis to Lake Winnibigoshish and on such rivers as the Rum, Red River of the North, Minnesota, Whitewater, Root, Bigfork, and Littlefork.

A leisurely and scenic trip is the 78-mile run down the St. Croix River between Minnesota and Wisconsin, from Riverside, Wis., to St. Croix Falls, a few miles above Interstate State Park at Taylors Falls. With carries, the trip may be continued southward, on somewhat more congested waters, to Osceola, Marine, Stillwater, Bayport, or Hudson.

In the central part of the state, too, is the Crow Wing River Canoe Trail, a 75-mile downstream jaunt through relatively developed country and part of it through the Huntersville State Forest. The trip has numerous access points. The full trip starts near Menahga and terminates at Syaples.

Organized canoeing in the state is represented by the Minnesota Canoe Association of Minneapolis, associated with the American White Water Affiliation.

Mississippi

There seems to be little enthusiasm for canoeing in Mississippi, although in the DeSoto National Forest the U.S. Forest Service maintains two float-trip routes, one on Beaverdam Creek and the other on Black Creek.

The Black Creek trip starts at Big Creek in Forrest County and terminates at the Old Alexander bridge, north of Rt. 26, east of Wiggins, a distance of 42 miles over a wide, meandering stream dotted with sandbars.

The Beaverdam Creek cruise originates at Spring Branch, just off Rt. 308 and also terminates at the Old Alexander bridge, a total distance of 27 miles. Beaverdam Creek is narrow and winding, often completely arched by overhanging trees.

Access points are clearly marked on both routes, campsites are plentiful and the currents lazy.

Missouri

Missouri is the country of gentle rivers, most of its streams rating Class I or II although, at high water, experts are delighted to find sections qualifying for Class III, IV and sometimes V. There are well over 2000 miles of canoeable water, a great many of the streams spring-fed and noted for their numerous sandbars which afford fine campsites. Some alertness to rising water should be maintained as an upstream storm may raise the water level and wash out a sandbar campsite.

A highly detailed and accurate guidebook is available—*Missouri Ozark Waterways*, by Oz Hawksley and published by the Missouri Conservation Department (see Bibliography). The following suggested trips are described briefly, due to their great number, but before actually tackling any of them, the canoeman should consult Dr. Hawksley's book. It is indispensable!

One of the most famous rivers is the Current, canoeable year-round downstream of Welch Spring, 140 miles to the Arkansas state line. Access points are fairly numerous.

The Jack's Fork River, navigable from Highway Y to the Current River at Jack's Fork, offers 45 miles of paddling, with several access areas. The first 25 miles are confined within steep hills where a sudden rise of water might endanger a streamside camp.

As famous as the Jack's Fork and the Current, is the Eleven Point River, affording nearly 50 miles of canoeing from Highway 99 to the Stubblefield Ferry. The Eleven Point is noted for its Greer Spring, second largest in the state.

The Black River has highway access points on each of its three branches, with a possible run of more than 85 miles to Poplar Bluffs.

The St. Francis tumbles over boulders during much of its course and is, therefore, an expert's run, particularly at high water, when some sections may even prove dangerous. Upstream access point is at Highway H, some three miles below Farmington and take-out is possible at Highway 67 at Greenville.

Two side trips on this watershed are possible, one on the Little St. Francis for a distance of 15 miles, and the other a 17-mile run on Big Creek. The Little

St. Francis put-in is at Highway 72 near Frederickstown, while access to the Big Creek run is via Highway 49 bridge near Sabula.

The Flat Creek trip, a year-round favorite, puts in at Jenkins and takes out at Highway 173, 24 miles downstream.

Early in the season, Beaver Creek offers better than 40 miles of canoeing, starting at Highway 76, some 8 miles southwest of Ava, and terminating at' the Kissee Miles access below Rt. 160. In dry weather, the section above Bradleyville may be too low for canoes, thus cutting the trip to about 17 miles.

The upper reaches of the North Fork of the White River run through the Mark Twain National Forest to Norfolk Lake, affording a 48-mile run. Easiest upstream access is between highways HH and E.

Bryant Creek, also flowing into Norfolk Lake, is canoeable for 40 miles from Highway 14 to the Corps of Engineers campground at Tecumseh.

The Spring River trip, close to 63 miles long, originates via Highway V near Mt. Vernon and ends at Highway P, 2 miles from Belleville. There are at least 8 highway access points en route.

Somewhat trickier than most Ozark streams, Center Creek provides exciting canoeing from a point 3 miles south of Carthage to Belleville. Overhanging trees and bridges present some hazards at high water.

Like Center Creek, Shoal Creek is livelier than most, offering 40 miles of fast canoeing from Ritchey to Schermerhorn Park near Galena, Kansas.

Elk River and its tributary, Big Sugar Creek, combine to provide a 46-mile trip from Rt. 90 to the bridge on Highway 43. It may be continued into Lake of the Cherokees in Oklahoma.

Indian Creek is a high-water stream for some 28 miles between Highway D near Boulder City and its junction with the Elk River.

Having first paddled a canoe on New Hampshire's Merrimack River (at the age of 12, I used to "borrow" it without my parents' knowledge!), I've always felt an affinity for Missouri's similarly named Meramec. I'm further drawn to this river because it is the site of the National Poling Championships and I much prefer poling to paddling! At any rate, most trips on the Meramec start at Meramec Spring and terminate 94 miles downstream at Meramec State Park. The trip may be continued down to the Mississippi, a total distance of 190 miles, but the lower section of the river is unattractive, having been highly developed.

Huzzah Creek, a tributary of the Meramec, is canoeable for nearly 23 miles below Davisville. Courtois Creek, also a Meramec branch, includes 22 miles of navigable water between Palmer and its junction with the Meramec.

The winding Bourbeause River, covers about 100 miles within 27 as the blue heron flies, all of it canoeable. A slow-flowing stream, it has more than a dozen access points, the furthest one upstream at Highway 19.

Still another tributary of the Meramec, the Big River affords 84 miles of paddling, including a traverse of Washington State Park. Access points are numerous, starting at a point north of Bonne Terre.

The Gasconade River trip is more than 250 miles long, starting at the Woods Fork of the Gasconade near Hartville and running to the Missouri River at Gasconade. Above Competition, the water may be quite low during the summer.

Little Piney Creek, a branch of the Gasconade, offers an additional 18 miles of canoeing water downstream of Yancy Mills.

A 77-mile trip is possible on the Big Piney River, running through unspoiled country between high bluffs, its starting point being the Dog's Bluff access point on Highway 17, its ending at the junction with the Gasconade. At Mile 46 is the last take-out spot before entering Fort Leonard Wood Military Reservation which may not be crossed without a permit, even by canoe.

The Sac River, a slow-moving stream, with access at Dadeville, provides 97 miles of cruising before it enters the Osage below Highway 92. Access points are numerous.

A Sac tributary, Turnback Creek affords an additional 16 miles below Highway K.

The Little Sac River, with a put-in site near Aldrich, runs 25 miles to the Sac. Cedar Creek, with access at the Ivy bridge on Highway K, is canoeable for 18 miles before it, too, enters the Sac.

The Pomme de Terre, despite the building of the dam which created Pomme de Terre Reservoir, still provides 23 miles of canoeing, upstream of the lake. Put-in is at Sunset Bridge, southeast of Bolivar. With a 17-mile automobile carry via Highways 83 and V, an additional 38 miles is possible to Fairfield. The trip may also be continued into Lake of the Ozarks.

With many access points available, canoemen can travel on the Niangua River from Highway 32 near Buffalo to Lake of the Ozarks.

The Moreau River trip originates at Rockhouse Bridge, a few miles south of McGirk on Highway 50 and ends at the Missouri River, more than 60 miles downstream.

Other worthwhile, though shorter, trips are possible on Naubleau Creek, near Gerster, 20 miles; the Little Niangua River, 35 miles, starting at Highway 54; Grand Auglaize Creek, 14 miles, beginning about one mile above Highway A on the West Auglaize; Tavern Creek, 34 miles, starting near Iberia; and Maries River, 28 miles, with put-in between Freeburg and Koelstown.

With such a variety of canoeing waters at hand, it's not surprising that several organized canoe groups flourish in Missouri. These, all associated with the American White Water Affiliation, include American Youth Hostels, Inc., St. Louis; the Central Missouri State College Outing Club at Warrensburg; the Meramec River Patrol of Florrisant; the Meramec River Canoe Club of Maplewood; and the Ozark Wilderness Waters Club.

Montana

Montana residents, like those of Idaho, often look at their rivers from the deck of a rubber raft or from the cockpit of a kayak. To quote one state official ". . . canoeing is not a major activity . . ."

However, this does not necessarily eliminate the sport. In southwest Montana, sections of the Big Hole River below Divide Dam are canoeable, as are parts of the Madison River above Ennis, although the area below Ennis Lake dam through Beartrap Canyon is extremely dangerous.

The Yellowstone River is floatable for its entire length, but the section between Yellowstone National Park and Emigrant is considered hazardous also. Between Livingston and Billings, there are few danger spots. Canoemen interested in the Yellowstone should obtain a copy of the booklet *Floating, Fishing and Historical Guide to Yellowstone State Waterway* (see Appendix).

In western Montana, sections of the Clark Fork River offer extensive canoeing possibilities.

The Main Flathead River above Flathead Lake in northwest Montana, and a part of the state's Recreational Waterway System, is not hazardous and there are numerous public approaches between Columbia Falls and Flathead Lake.

In this part of the state the Swan River is a well behaved stream, although downed timber and log jams may force occasional portages.

The Marias River in central Montana, between Tiber dam and the river's junction with the Missouri near Loma, has many access areas; the Dearborn River, although it may be quite low during the summer, can be floated from Highway 287 to the Missouri.

Another float is possible starting at the Fish and Game Department access point near Fort Logan on the Smith River to a point just below Hound Creek between Cascade and Eden.

For a big-water trip, consider the Missouri River between Fort Benton and Fred Robinson Bridge, a distance of 160 miles. This is "the last of the wild Missouri," still much unchanged since the white man first saw it.

Many of the waterways suggested above consist of flat water, but Montana's rivers can range from placid to boiling, and wind can also create serious hazards on larger rivers.

Although aimed primarily at rubber-raft and kayak floats, the booklet *Montana Boating, Floating* (see Appendix) may prove helpful in planning a trip.

Nebraska

That Nebraska offers extensive canoeing may come as a surprise to many. Its Republican River, for example, provides a safe 120-mile trip from McCook to the lower end of Harlan Reservoir.

Other trips are possible, with few if any rapids, on the North, Middle, and South Loup rivers, and the Loup tributary, the Calamus River, which runs through the sand hills country. The Middle Loup trip requires some five to six days for the run to its junction with the Platte.

The Little Blue, in the southeastern part of the state, affords an easy beginner's trip.

Further north, the Elkhorn provides three to five days of downstream cruising, mostly over lazy waters.

The Niobrara, while gentle most of its length, injects wild-water canoeing into a trip for some 20 miles in the vicinity of its junction with Plum Creek. This is water for experts. Below Plum Creek, to Lewis and Clark Lake, the river is docile.

The Snake is generally considered "for experts only."

During dry periods, most of Nebraska's rivers may drop to a point where long portages or wading may be necessary. Local conservation officers can generally advise of water levels.

New Hampshire

The canoeing waters of northern New Hampshire can generally be considered seasonal because of low water levels in the summer; also they are apt to be boulder-strewn, with steep gradients, but they traverse beautiful country. Waters in central New Hampshire are more moderate while those in the south include much flat water.

The Merrimack is the state's largest river, formed at Franklin by the junction of the Pemigewasset and the Winnepesaukee rivers. It is canoeable for its entire length over smooth water, except for minor rips in its upper reaches and two tricky sets of rapids, one at Manchester and the other at Goff's Falls. There are numerous dams to be portaged, also. Above Manchester the river is generally pleasant, but pollution detracts from its beauty as it flows southward into Massachusetts.

The Souhegan, between Greenville and Wilton, is largely for experts. Below the latter, the flow alternates between moderate to heavy rapids and flat water, to the Merrimack about 20 miles away.

The upper waters of the Suncook are for white-water experts only, but below North Chichester to the Merrimack, some 15 miles, it is largely smooth flowing.

For about 25 miles below Peterborough on the Contoocook River, a series of dams provides flat-water canoeing and, of course, portages. Between Hillsboro and Henniker are 8 miles of Class IV and V rapids, no place for a beginner! Below Henniker for 25 miles to Penacook, the take-out point, easy paddling prevails.

The Pemigewasset is primarily a mountain stream, although skilled canoemen can handle it for about 25 miles between North Woodstock and Plymouth, except for a bad drop at Livermore Falls, some five miles below Campton. The Plymouth to Bristol section is easy paddling for about 17 miles. Below Bristol are severe rapids.

For canoeing on small rivers, with gentle to moderate rapids and much flat water, the coastal plain includes the Cocheco, Bellamy, Lamprey, and Exeter.

The Saco River below North Conway can be interesting to a canoeman of moderate skill, for it includes a variety of flat water and sharp though not dangerous rapids. Below Conway, crossing into Maine, the run is pleasant over a sandy bottom with some riffles.

New Hampshire's Connecticut River watershed provides for white-water action, as well as some smooth-water canoeing. The Ashuelot's upper reaches in the Surry area are rough-and-tumble; below Keene it is generally easy going, while below Ashuelot the river becomes violent.

A short stretch of about 5 miles on the Ammonoosuc River near Bretton Woods is pleasant easy paddling until the impassable Lower Ammonoosuc Falls are reached. The rest of the river is frequently interspersed with heavy rapids during its 40-mile dash to the Connecticut.

Although there is fine fast-water canoeing in New Hampshire on the Androscoggin River, this has been described in the Maine section, since it forms a part of an established Maine trip. The Connecticut River, which New Hampshire shares with Vermont as a boundary, is described in the Vermont listing.

All in all, New Hampshire's rivers tend to offer high-water sport for experts only, but there are numerous stretches of smooth water if one seeks them out. For this, the *A.M.C. New England Canoeing Guide* is indispensable (see Bibliography).

The Ledyard Canoe Club of Hanover, connected with both the American Canoe Association and the American White Water Affiliation, is New Hampshire's most active canoeing group. Its membership includes some of the country's best white-water canoemen.

New Jersey

Most of New Jersey's canoe runs are relatively short, and except for the Delaware River, generally one-day trips.

The Hackensack River, for instance, is canoeable from New Bridge to Newark Bay, about 20 miles, although the lower segment of the trip is through rather ugly industrial complexes. The upper portion, between West Nyack and Harrington Park, is an exciting white-water run during the spring run-off.

In the Passaic River, when the water level is up there are about 35 miles of canoe cruising between Millington and Singac.

Also requiring high water, the Ramapo River includes some white water and much smooth paddling for about 20 miles from Suffern to its juncture with the Passaic.

Still another high-water run is the 8-mile stretch of the Wanaque River from the village of Wanake to the Pequannock River.

One of the most attractive rivers in New Jersey is the Millstone, with 8 miles of paddling water between Cranbury and Princeton. From the latter, it is about 15 miles more to Bound Brook, where the Millstone joins the Raritan. A few miles down the Raritan at New Brunswick, there is a carry into the Delaware and Raritan Canal, making possible a 12-mile return run to Princeton.

The South Branch of the Raritan, from Flemington Junction to Somerville, is a beautiful 16-mile run as late as July. The trip can be continued down the Raritan through Bound Brook to Perth Amboy.

For about 10 miles in the vicinity of Whitehouse, the North Branch of the Raritan is cruisable at high water, while the Rancocas River is excellent canoeing water for some 25 miles from Brown's Mills to the North Branch of Rancocas Creek.

Running through wild pinelands, the Wading River provides 25 miles of cruising from Chatsworth to Great Bay. The Great Egg River, starting at Braddock, is canoeable for some 35 miles to tidewater at Great Egg Bay.

The Delaware River, which New Jersey shares with Pennsylvania, is a well known cruising stream, offering some 130 miles of varying water from Port Jervis, N.Y., to Camden. An additional 50 miles can be added to the trip by starting upstream at Hancock, N.Y. The run is through scenic country with ample campsites. There are shallows and rapids, too, with caution the keynote at Foul Rift near Belvidere and at Wells Falls near Lambertville. A carry is necessary at Trenton if the trip is to be continued to Camden. If a portage into the Delaware and Raritan Canal can be arranged at Trenton, the trip may be shifted to Carnegie Lake at Princeton.

Other canoeing suggestions are included in the fine volume *Exploring the Little Rivers of New Jersey,* by James and Margaret Cawley (see Bibliography).

Several groups active in canoeing have headquarters in New Jersey and are members of the American White Water Affiliation. These are: Adventure Unlimited, Belvidere; the New York Chapter of the Appalachian Mountain Club, Florham Park; the National Council of the Boy Scouts of America, New Brunswick; Camp No-Be-Bo-Sco of the Boy Scouts of America, Riveredge; the Kayak and Canoe Club of New York, East Brunswick; and the Murray Hill Canoe Club, Freehold.

New Mexico

Although justly regarded as an arid state, New Mexico provides some 100 miles of canoeable waters, but they may offer sport on a seasonal basis and may involve much rough water plus numerous portages. Among riverways where canoeing is possible, at least in some sections, are the Canadian, Rio Grande, San Juan, and the Gila rivers.

The upper stretches of the Rio Grande should be regarded as hazardous during the high-water period of June, July, and August. An outstanding authority on the Rio Grande, both in New Mexico and in Texas is Bob Burleson, current president of the Texas Explorers Club (see Appendix).

Other experts on these waters are members of the Albuquerque Whitewater Club of Albuquerque, also associated with the American White Water Affiliation.

New York

The variety of canoeing waters in New York rivals those of Maine and Minnesota, may even exceed them! State officials are to be complimented for their interest in canoeing as a sport, evidenced by the establishment of regular canoe routes and the publication of information concerning them.

Among river runners at least, New York's most famed waterway is the 7-mile stretch of the upper Hudson River near North Creek, where the annual Hudson River White Water Derby is held, usually in May. This should be ample description of its waters!

The Delaware River, between Hancock and Port Jervis, takes a kindlier attitude toward canoeists, at least during part of the 70-mile run. There are some 30 rapids, varying from Class I to III, but there are also long sections of smooth paddling. This is, however, somewhat of a seasonal stream, best run between ice-out and early June. A substantial rain will also bring the water up to canoeing levels.

Perhaps the best guide to this run is a 1960 folder entitled *The Delaware River*, published by the American Canoe Association. Parts may be out of date, but if a copy can be found it should certainly prove helpful.

Still another publication important to New York canoeists is a reprint from *The American Canoeist*, July, 1963, also a publication of the American Canoe Association. Entitled "Canoeing Across Central New York" and written by Harold Rodman and John Garrow with the aid of the Ka-Na-Wa-Ke Canoe Club of Syracuse, it details many of that state's favorite canoe routes. These include:

Genegantslet Creek, ideal for novices, and running from Smithville Flats to its confluence with the Chenango River near Highway 12. This is a 12-mile run, usually navigable only during March and April.

Tioughnioga River, also a beginner's run from Cortland to Chenango Forks, a distance of 36 miles.

Another novice stream is the Otselic River from Highway 80 at Otselic to Cincinnatus, a 22-mile trip. The run can be lengthened to 46 miles by continuing to Whitney Point. Portages will be encountered and barbed-wire crossings may occur frequently.

From Malloryville to Varna on Fall Creek a 15-mile run is possible, but there are sections definitely not for beginners, especially between Etna and Varna.

Fish Creek, starting at the public access area 2 miles south of Camden, provides placid waters through a scenic region. Below the dam at McConnellsville are tricky sections.

A 70-mile run is possible on the Chenango River from Earlville to Chenango Forks, a relatively easy trip with some moderate rapids.

For white-water thrills (experts only!) Limestone Creek provides rough-and-tumble water between Manlius and Fayetteville during the spring run-off.

Another early-season run is possible on the Little Salmon River from Highway 11, 2 miles above Hastings to Lake Ontario, about 14 miles.

East of Syracuse, the Erie Canal offers interesting canoeing for about 8 miles between DeWitt and Kirkville. The New York State Barge Canal, starting from Jack's Reef on Rt. 31, provides some 36 miles of paddling, via Cross Lake, and Baldwinsville to Oneida Lake at Brewerton.

Another useful reprint is one entitled "Canoe Trips," by A. T. Shorey, originally published in the *New York State Conservationist* and briefly detailing several trips which are safe, even for family groups. No rip-roaring rapids will be encountered on any of the following:

The Upper Mohawk River, starting at Westernville on Highway 46, provides some 5 miles of steady but gentle current to Rome.

Cayuta Lake, starting near the junction of Highways 22 and 28 at Forestport, through the canal feeder to Boonville, providing 7 miles of gentle current.

Black Creek, from a point east of Highway 8 near Gray, features a swift but safe current most of the way to Hinckley Reservoir, a distance of 6 miles.

An easy trip is provided too via the Kunjamuk, leaving Moffit Beach State Campsite on Lake Sacandaga, then through the inlet to Lake Pleasant, east to the Sacandaga River outlet, then branching upstream into the Kunjamuk to Elm Lake. An occasional short portage is necessary.

The Unadilla River is a stillwater route for several miles near Highway 413.

The West Branch of the Sacandaga, from Arietta to Shaker Place, provides 10 miles of flat-water canoeing through attractive meadows.

For a weekend cruise, the route from Oswegatchie Inlet to Cranberry Lake has the atmosphere of a northwoods trip, including beaver dams. Access is from Highway 3, about 5 miles west of Wanakena.

A quiet stream for easy paddling is the Indian River, from Eel Weir campsite near highway 87 in the Ogdensburg area, into Black Lake, then into Indian River itself, for an upstream leg to Antwerp on Highway 11.

Canoe trips in the Adirondack region offer a variety of routes, plus side trips. Total distances, except for the 37-mile trip from Old Forge to Blue Mountain Lake, vary only slightly. Assuming a start from Old Forge, Tupper Lake is 83 miles away; Saranac Inn, 75; Ampersand Dock, 79; and Saranac Lake Village, 86.

Probably no publication so well details a canoe area as *Adirondack Canoe Routes,* by William G. Howard, M.F., published by the New York State Conservation Department as Recreational Circular No. 7 (see Appendix).

One of the itineraries suggests a leisurely six-day cruise as follows:

First day: Old Forge to Eighth Lake Campsite. Distance—18 miles, including 1.7 of carry.

Second Day: Eighth Lake Campsite to Blue Mountain Lake. Distance—19 miles, including 2 miles of carry; or Eighth Lake Campsite to Forked Lake dam (outlet). Distance—17 miles including 1.7 miles of carry.

Third day: Forked Lake dam to Lost Channel lean-to on Raquette River below Long Lake. Distance—17 miles, including 2.1 miles of carry.

Fourth day: Foot of Long Lake at Lost Channel to Axton. Distance—13.25 miles, including 1.25 miles of carry.

Fifth day: Axton to Tromblee Clearing lean-to. Distance—8 miles.

Sixth day: Tromblee Clearing lean-to to upper lake. Distance—10 miles; no carry.

Alternate Route:
Fifth day: Axton through Upper Saranac Lake to Fish Creek Pond campsite. Distance—12 miles, including 1.3 miles of carry.
Alternate Route:
Fifth day: Axton to Ampersand Dock boat livery at east end of Lower Saranac Lake. Distance—16.25 miles, including 1.5 miles of carry.
Alternate Route:
Fifth day: Axton to Toms Rock lean-to in Lower Saranac. Distance—14.25 miles, including 1.5 miles of carry.
Sixth day: Toms Rock lean-to to Saranac Lake village via Saranac River. Distance—10 miles.
It can be seen, then, that canoe trips in the Adirondacks can be varied to a considerable extent, much like canoe routes in Minnesota. The wealth of information contained in *Adirondack Canoe Routes* should make it easy for any canoeman to plan a trip to his liking!
Canoe groups active in New York State include: the Cornell Outing Club, Ithaca; the Genessee Downriver Paddlers, Wellsville; the Ka Na Wa Ke Canoe Club, Marietta; the Niagara Frontier Sons of Ahab, West Valley; and the Oneonta State College Outing Club. All are connected with the American White Water Affiliation.

North Carolina

The mountains of western North Carolina precipitate some of the country's finest white-water flowage. While some of these streams are of moderate gradient with low-hazard rapids, nearly all also include Class III, IV, and V pitches and are, hence, for experts. Intermediate paddlers—and novices, too—by choosing carefully among the Class I and II segments, can also enjoy some of these sporty streams.
Some prior knowledge of these rivers is necessary before any attempt at running is made. On-the-scene scouting in advance is wise. As a preliminary, however, there is no substitute for a canoeman's acquainting himself with *Canoeing White Water* by Randy Carter, who overlooked no minute detail in describing these waters (See Bibliography).
My one trip to this area having come at the wrong time of the year, when water level was unusually low, I have never had the opportunity to run any of the rivers described in Randy's book. I did, however, examine some of them, and even at low water I could well imagine the challenge they present when "the pitch is right!"
Some of the rivers and streams in this area that will attract white-water canoemen are:
The French Broad, with some 85 miles of Class I and II water, but with an additional 40 miles which encompasses pitches rated at IV, V, and even VI;
The Green, mostly Class II, with at least one Class III dip;
The Little Tennessee, Class II to V;
The Nantahala, Class IV to V;
The Ocanaluftee, Class III to IV;
The Pigeon, Class II to IV;
The Raven Fork, Class III to V;
The Toxaway, Class II to IV;
The Tuckseigee, with some 22 miles of moderate water and a 7-mile segment rated III to IV.

Since Randy Carter's book is concerned primarily with rapids-running, it does not cover the relatively placid coastal streams and rivers. Most of these offer flat-water canoeing above tidewater, including the Waccamaw, the Norfolk between locks, the South, the Cape Fear, the Neuse, and the Roanoke. Many tributaries to these afford varied canoeing, too.

North Dakota

With so many large reservoirs impounding some of its larger rivers, North Dakota's water sports are strongly powerboat-oriented. Nevertheless, there are almost innumerable canoeing opportunities on its many prairie streams, at least during the early season.

One trip which affords fascinating travel is the 130-mile run on the Little Missouri River between the South and North units of the Theodore Roosevelt National Memorial Park in the western Badlands. Low water, however, can be a problem during a dry period.

Canoemen who like to prowl brush-lined streams and don't mind carrying over blowdowns or other obstructions, should investigate the Mouse River. It flows into North Dakota from Canada and back out again in the north central region. Total stream length is 170 miles.

The James River is picturesque, with headwaters in the eastern part of the state and flowing straight south into South Dakota to join the Missouri. Total length is 125 miles, but it too has numerous obstacles of brush, fallen timber, and several small dams.

The Red River, forming the state's eastern boundary, has many canoeable segments along its 250-mile length, but here too there are problems with debris, some pollution, and agricultural fences.

Developed specifically as a canoe trail is a 4-mile section of waterways connecting lakes in the Wakopa Game Management Area in the Turtle Mountains of north-central North Dakota, near Dunseith and St. John. This is an unspoiled area and there are excellent campsites.

Ohio

Ohio, like Illinois and Indiana, is not generally thought of as "canoe country"; at least, not until recently. With increasing interest in the sport, however, the state has established a series of canoe routes and published information on these (see Appendix). Although hardly a wilderness region, many of these canoe trails cross or border on state parks and relatively primitive wildlife areas.

One of these is the Little Miami River trip from Clinton to Cincinnati, a distance of 95 miles, running through the Spring Valley Wildlife Area and Fort Ancient State Park. There are several short portages.

The Great Miami River trip runs 140 miles from Indian Lake, north of De-Graff, to the Ohio River below Hamilton. As with the Little Miami, this trip affords many access points so that any section is accessible for short cruises.

The state's longest canoe trip involves 162 miles of travel over three rivers, the Muskingum, Walhonding, and the Mohican. The starting point is Mohican State Forest on the Clear Fork of the Mohican which flows into the Walhonding, this in turn emptying into the Muskingum. Terminal point for the trip is Marietta, although there are numerous access areas along the route so that the trip may be shortened. Dams and locks occur frequently on the Muskingum.

The Cuyahoga River trip, some 56 miles long, includes rapids in the section between Burton, the starting point, and Hiram. Inexperienced canoeists may prefer to launch at the latter since there is quiet water thereafter. As boating is not permitted on Lake Rockwell, the Akron water supply, a portage is necessary here. The final 10 miles to Lake Erie penetrate rather hideous industrial sections so that most canoeists prefer to take out at Granger Road in Cuyahoga County.

The Maumee River trip originates on the Auglaize River, 15 miles above the Defiance power dam. The Miami and Erie Canal, with its restored locks, bypasses the dam and re-enters the Maumee at Florida, 1 mile below. Total distance is 81 miles with a 4-mile portage necessary between Missionary Island and the trip's terminus, the city of Maumee.

The Sandusky River trip runs through farm lands and picturesque rolling country, its entire length through rural areas except for the cities of Tiffin and Fremont. Put-in is at Upper Sandusky with take-out at Sandusky Bay or upstream at Fremont.

Ohio's laws regarding riparian rights are briefly and clearly explained in the booklet *Ohio Canoe Adventures* (see Appendix). The law is even more lucidly detailed in an article appearing in the May, 1963, issue of the *Ohio Conservation Bulletin*.

American Youth Hostels, Inc., of Columbus, is an active member of the American White Water Affiliation.

Oklahoma

While Oklahoma has numerous streams and rivers suitable for canoeing, at least during the early season when water levels are up, little specific information is available. Nearly all of the major waterways in the eastern third of the state have been, are being or will be impounded by the U.S. Army Corps of Engineers, to whom the sight of running water is a challenge—not to run it, but to dam it!

However, much of the upper and middle segments of the Cimarron, Canadian, Washita, and Red Rivers, along with their almost numberless tributaries, still flow freely.

Oregon

Although there are many smaller streams affording leisurely canoeing, Oregon's rivers are generally tumultuous, with a few exceptions.

The Willamette River, for example, is easy to navigate from Armitage State Park near Eugene to Portland, a distance of 120 miles. Near Oregon City, though, there is a waterfall which must be portaged.

The famed Columbia, from Umatilla to Astoria, a run of 295 miles, is certainly navigable, but canoemen will encounter three hydroelectric dams necessitating portages. Too, this is large, open water, exposed at times to heavy winds. The Columbia is a "civilized" river, with highways and railroads encroaching on both banks most of the way.

The John Day River, running 157 miles from Service Creek to its mouth at the Columbia, is best run in November and again in March, April, or May.

During the summer, low water raises many obstacles. The river has many long pools with small rapids between them. One mile below Clarno is a dangerous pitch, and some 8 miles upstream of the mouth are falls requiring a portage. Rattlesnakes are common along the shore.

From Rome to Owyhee Lake, the Owyhee River comprises some 53 miles of difficult-to-run water, even at its best during March, April, and May. Rattlers lie along the shore here, too.

The Rogue River appeals to experts and novices alike. From Grave Creek to Agness (river mile 27), the run is strictly for experienced white-water rivermen. From Agness to the mouth is a pleasant, easy trip.

From Barton to its mouth, a distance of about 17 miles, the Clackamas River has some white water but is generally not a difficult run. Water levels in the winter are likely to be high and somewhat low in summer.

The Deschutes River is for the daring only and for those willing to portage around its treacherous chutes and rapids. It should be left strictly alone by all but experts.

Pennsylvania

An oversight of Pennsylvania promotional agencies is their failure to provide information for canoeists. For fishermen and powerboaters there is a wealth of data—charts, booklets, maps, but for the canoeman, nary a word! This, despite the fact that the state boasts some of the finest white-water runs in the country. For details on Pennsylvania streams and rivers, one must turn to the privately published *Appalachian Water* by Walter Frederick Burmeister (see Bibliography), a work of infinite detail and thorough description. Regrettably, it is now out of print and one must seek a copy from the library or from a canoeing friend. However it is obtained, a copy of Volume I (it is published in two volumes) is a must for Pennsylvania river running.

An excellent map of the state's waterways is available from the state university (see Appendix). The chart is huge, almost 3 by 5 feet, and includes every permanent stream in the state. Due to the intricacy and number of these waterways, however, there is little detail.

One of the best known of Pennsylvania's rivers (among canoeists, at least) is the Youghiogheny in Fayette County, abutting the West Virginia and Maryland state lines. This is not a stream for the novice, although the first 11 miles below Confluence to Ohiopyle is rated Class II. Here, supervised beginners and intermediates may acquire experience safely. Below Ohiopyle for about 7 miles, river ratings climb to Class IV and V, while from Stewarton to Connellsville, a distance of about 12 miles, Class III water prevails. For canoeists who can handle it, the Youghiogheny can be run all summer long, since its level is controlled for the benefit of traffic farther downstream.

Dropping only about 700 feet between Eldred and Pittsburgh, a distance of more than 300 miles, the Allegheny River is considered an excellent training ground for beginners. With its gradient rarely exceeding 2.5 feet per mile, no section is rated more dangerous than Class I. Its lower reaches are frequently interrupted by dams and locks and, as one nears Pittsburgh, its banks become increasingly industrialized, detracting from the river as a canoe route. The upper sections, however, make for interesting canoeing.

Practically the entire section of the Delaware River between Hancock, N. Y., and Trenton, N. J., provides canoeing for all classes of paddlers. The up-river area, during the spring run-off, supplies wild water for the experts. Most of the river, though, is gentle and extremely scenic. It has numerous rapids rated Class I and II which are a challenge to novices seeking experience. Care should be exercised, however, at Skinner's Falls below Callicoon, Foul Rift below Belvidere, the Lambertville dam, and at Scudder's Falls near Washington Crossing. April, May, and June see the most suitable water levels, although many sections are runable and attractive all summer.

Except for five major obstructions, the Susquehanna River can be run all the way from Sunbury, Pa., to Havre de Grace, Md., the upper segments at their best early in the season. Total distance is about 145 miles and the overall drop is only 206 feet. Except for the Harrisburg section, the route is quite scenic; the shores of Conowingo reservoir unusually so. The five obstructions referred to (and which must, naturally, be portaged) are the dams at Harrisburg, York Haven, Safe Harbor, Holtwood, and Conowingo.

The West Branch of the Susquehanna River has retained much of its original wilderness character, particularly in the Clearfield to Keating region. Even the railroad tracks which parallel it detract little from its attractiveness. For much of its 215-mile course from Mahaffey to Northumberland it flows through rugged, hilly country.

Apart from some severe rapids found between Shawville and Clearfield, the river is generally easy to run, with numerous access points and camping sites.

The North Branch of the Susquehanna provides about 350 miles of cruising and running, starting at Cooperstown, N.Y., and terminating at its confluence with the West Branch at Sunbury. The upper river is at its best during April and May. Its numerous rapids, all upstream of Sunbury, are generally not difficult to run, except for Red Rock Rift, near the Big Bend bridge, which may attain Class III turbulence at high water.

Perhaps the most carefree trip in Pennsylvania is on the Juniata River, from Ardenheim to its junction with the Susquehanna, the 100-mile course running through picturesque mountain country. It is best traveled on high water to avoid minor obstructions, although there are no rapids. A more apt term for a run down the Juniata is "float trip."

Far more exciting is the run down the Lehigh River from Clifton to its confluence with the Delaware. Between the several dams are found numerous rapids rated as high as Class IV, the river dropping about 1290 feet during its 100-mile course. Although not always flowing through an attractive environment (coal mining and industry are heavily represented along its shores), the Lehigh at spring run-off provides white-water thrills.

These are but a few of Pennsylvania's major water courses. There are dozens of other streams for shorter excursions where, in most instances, thrilling wildwater running is possible during the early high-water season, usually during April and May. These may include:

Bear Creek from Rt. 115 to the Lehigh River reservoir, a 5-mile run, strictly for experts when the pitch is right, with the difficulty rating set conservatively at Class III;

Beech Creek, a 25-mile mountain pitch, rated Class III, between Kato and the junction with Bald Eagle Creek, and dropping more than 500 feet! Definitely wild water, usually at its best in April and May;

Big Schuylkill Creek, from Beaver Run to U.S. Rt. 209, a 23-mile maelstrom of springtime fury, rated up to Class IV;

Black Moshannon Creek, reaching the height of watery turmoil (up to Class V!) during March and April, with a drop of 800 feet in less than 19 miles between Black Moshannon State Park and state route 58;

Brandywine Creek, a challenging stream in the spring, dropping about 130 feet in about 18 miles between Lenape and Wilmington, Del;

Brodhead Creek, with a drop of 225 feet in 12 miles from the Stites bridge to the confluence with the Delaware, is a noted Pocono white-water course;

Casselman River, from Garrett to Confluence, about 30 miles of ideal white-water during April and May, with a drop of more than 550 feet! Exciting and scenic, rated up to Class III, possibly IV at high water;

The Clarion River from Ridgway to the Allegheny River, is a comparatively gentle stream, ideal for beginners seeking Class I rapids experience;

Clearfield Creek provides close to 30 miles of novice and intermediate water between Madera and the creek's mouth on the West Branch of the Susquehanna;

The Conemaugh River serves up a variety of water, up- and downstream of the city of Johnstown, with rapids ranging from Class I to III;

Kettle Creek, rated Class I and II is a delightful 33-mile run from Ole Bull State Park to Westport, with a drop of more than 500 feet;

The Lackawaxen River is well suited for beginners below Honesdale. Below Hawley, however, the stream becomes exuberant, creating wild rapids;

The Little Juniata River, from Nealmont to Frankstown, drops 190 feet in 15 miles, just enough to be interesting to novices and intermediates;

Little Pine Creek, between English Center and Waterville, provides about 13 miles of running with moderate rapids which may become heavy at high water;

Loyalsock Creek, from U.S. Rt. 220 to Montoursville, a distance of about 50 miles, nearly 1000 feet of which account for Class IV waters and an impassable pitch some miles below the Rt. 220 bridge; for experts only;

Moshannon Creek from Winburne to Karthaus drops about 550 feet in some 27 miles, the gradient consistently gradual, thus affording good running for intermediate canoemen;

Penn Creek, in the attractive area between Coburn and Selinsgrove, provides rapids of Class I and II difficulty during its 50-mile run, dropping about 575 feet;

Perkiomen Creek, in April, is a beginner's stream, swift enough to be interesting, yet not dangerous; Class I rapids and four easy portages around dams;

Pine Creek, from Galeton to the West Branch of the Susquehanna, traverses one of the most scenic regions in the entire Appalachian chain. It includes Class I and II rapids, some almost continuous above Blackwell; below Blackwell, there is much "flat water";

The Raystown Branch of the Juniata River, from Mann's Choice to the junction with the Frankstown Juniata, is a beautiful trip with no severe rapids, although one short carry is necessary at the dam above Hawn bridge;

The Schuylkill River from Pottstown to Philadelphia, although crossed by numerous dams requiring portaging, is an excellent stream with a swift current and a few rapids rated at Class II;

Sherman's Creek, from a point ½ mile below state Rt. 274 to the Susquehanna River, is an easy run with some swift water;

The Tioga River, from state Rt. 660 to the junction of the Cohocton River, some 35 miles, has numerous small rapids and riffles, rated at Class I;

Tobyhanna Creek, from Pocono Lakes to the Lehigh River, a short run somewhat under 12 miles, provides swift water and rapids of medium difficulty, Class I and II.

NOTE: Although I have not mentioned this in the case of each stream cited, it should be pointed out that most of Pennsylvania's white-water streams are best run during March and April, some in May, when spring run-off is at its height, or following a heavy rainfall. At other times, many of these courses become impassable because of low water. Remember, too, that difficulty ratings may change as water levels fluctuate.

Several canoe groups, all associated with the American White Water Affiliation, are active in Pennsylvania. These include: the Pittsburgh Council of the American Youth Hostels, Inc., Monroeville; the Buck Ridge Ski Club, Chadds Ford; the Delaware Canoe Club, Easton; the Delaware Canoe Club of Bucks County, Holland; Explorer Post No. 32, State College; the Penn State Outing Club, also of State College; the Sylvan Canoe Club, Pittsburgh; and the Wildwater Boating Club of State College.

Rhode Island

Rhode Island officials certainly do not neglect canoeing even though the tiny state's canoe waters are rather limited. They have published a study entitled *Pawcatuck River and Wood River* (see Appendix) describing launching spots, portages and campsites. What's more, they have even included the portages on the state's highway map something, which, to my knowledge, no other state has done!

Three trips are possible on the Pawcatuck and Wood rivers. The first starts at One Hundred Acre Pond in West Kingston and proceeds through Thirty Acre Pond into the Chepuxet River, to Worden Pond, then down the Pawcatuck to Westerly or Watch Hill.

Another trip originates at Usquepaug Village and follows the Queens River to its junction with the Pawcatuck.

A third possibility calls for starting in Exeter at Rt. 165 in the Arcadia Management Area, then running down the Wood River to the Pawcatuck through Barberville, Hope Valley, Woodville, and Alton.

These are leisurely, flat-water trips and there are portages on the Pawcatuck at Kenyon, Shannock (2), Carolina, Burdickville, Bradford, Potter Hill, White Rock, and at Westerly. Access areas are numerous. At the Carolina and Burlingame Management Areas there are campsites, described briefly in the booklet *Camping in Rhode Island* (see Appendix).

The Narragansett Chapter of the Appalachian Mountain Club, Cranston, is active in Rhode Island and is a member of the American White Water Affiliation.

South Carolina

Except for the superb *Appalachian Water* by Burmeister (see Bibliography), there exists little literature describing South Carolina waters from the point of view of the canoeist. Fortunately, Burmeister has included several fine South Carolina runs in his Volume II, and this book should be consulted before attempting any of the streams which are being suggested here, unless of course, the canoeman has prior knowledge of the water.

The Broad River, starting at the Lake Lure dam in North Carolina (the paddler will cross into South Carolina just above Gaston Shoals dam), provides a variety of white water ranging from Class I to IV, as far as the junction of Turkey Creek, a distance of about 100 miles. Below that point, to Columbia, the river, impounded by several dams, tones down considerably. Access points are numerous all along the route, however, so that any section can be run conveniently.

Those interested in flat-water canoeing through a marsh area will enjoy the Congaree River, which meanders a leisurely 53 miles from Columbia to U.S. Rt. 601.

The Catawba, Wateree, and Santee watercourse offers more than 500 miles of varied water, much of it in the form of impounded lakes with an assortment of rapids between them. Trips can be started as far up as Old Fort, N.C., and run as far as tidal water on the Intracoastal Waterway. Since there are no fewer than 20 access points along the route, a canoeman can choose any segment or any type of water he prefers.

The Chattooga River, flowing from Georgia, joins the Tallulah at Tugaloo Lake, to form the Tugaloo River. This creates a variety of runs. The Chattooga, starting at Rt. 28 (in Georgia), provides awesome white water, up to Class V, during April and May. Not only are wild rides possible, but the scenery is superb. The Tugaloo River is a gentler stream, some sections backed up by dams to form lakes. The total distance from Rt. 28 in Georgia to U.S. Rt. 123 in South Carolina (take-out point) is about 52 miles.

The Chauga River, although it offers only about 19 miles of running, with a drop of more than 200 feet, is primarily a wild-water trip, possible for only a short time in the spring. Its rapids are rated up to Class IV, with the upper sections downright violent at high water! Put-in is at a point northeast of U.S. Rt. 76, with take-out about a half-mile north of the confluence with the Tugaloo River.

South Dakota

One of the most delightful canoe trips anywhere is on the Little White River which flows through the Rosebud Sioux Indian Reservation in South Dakota. The trip, a possible 115 miles, can be made in daily sections from a base camp in Ghost Hawk Park, near Rosebud. It is charmingly described in an article entitled "Canoeing Crazy Horse Canyon" by Dean Norman in the Winter 1967/68 issue of *American White Water*, the journal of the American White Water Affiliation.

"I will go a long way to find a place where I can paddle my canoe through wild country all day," the author states, "and camp alone wherever I decide to camp. The Little White River is such a place."

The river is swift and there are rapids. Dean Norman didn't classify these but apparently they were not difficult. He recommended putting in some 12 miles below the Bennett/Todd county line and taking out above the dam at White River, some 78 miles downstream. The trip can be started at the county line. However, most canoemen do terminate the trip at the dam near White River, due to a very difficult portage. Were it not for this, another 25 miles to the main White River would be possible. Day trips from Ghost Hawk Park, on any section of the river are possible and car shuttles can be arranged either at the park or at the Rosebud Indian Agency office at Rosebud.

In Tennessee, everyone seems to get involved in canoeing, directly or indirectly. The Game and Fish Commission issues float maps; legislators have established a Tennessee Scenic Rivers System for which the Tennessee Scenic Rivers Association had campaigned; the state university, cooperating with local Kiwanis clubs and chambers of commerce, sponsors the canoe race on the Big South Fork of the Cumberland River.

Among the float maps issued by the Game and Fish Commission (see Appendix), one describes the Buffalo River, which has been included in the state's scenic rivers system and also in the Federal system of scenic and wild rivers. Beginning near Henryville, in Lawrence County, the Buffalo affords some 110 miles of canoeing to its mouth at the junction of the Duck River in Humphreys County.

Another float map includes the Little Tennessee River and charts a 35-mile trip from Lenoir City to a point below the Chilhowee Dam, below Tallassee. However, I understand that this trip is about to be destroyed by the construction of another dam.

Another map charts the Harpeth River in Heatham County. The section covered by the map includes many huge "oxbows," through which the river winds a distance of some 26 miles to attain an airline distance of only 8 miles!

Still another map issued by the Game and Fish Commission is one which includes all waterways in the state. On this, "pastoral" float streams are indicated, as well as those streams which provide white-water running.

Other streams, too, which are included in the state's scenic rivers system and which offer white-water canoeing, are Roaring River, Spring Creek, and Blackburn Creek, all part of the Cumberland River watershed; the Duck River, a tributary of the Tennessee River; the Nolichucky, French Broad, and Hawassee Rivers, which flow out of the Great Smoky Mountains in the east.

The Obed, with a put-in area at the Catoosa Wildlife Area, is a sporty stream which includes Class III and IV rapids at certain water stages.

In western Tennessee, the Hatchie River is an outstanding example of a bottomland wilderness river.

Canoe groups active in Tennessee and members of the American White Water Affiliation are the Bluff City Canoe Club, Memphis, and the East Tennessee White Water Club of Oak Ridge.

Texas

The very vastness of Texas prevents any one man's becoming an authority on all of its navigable waters, but two men have between them somehow managed to attain this status.

Bob Burleson, a Temple attorney and dedicated canoeman, has written a comprehensive treatise on the Rio Grande River in New Mexico and along the Texas-Mexico border and, at this writing, is working with the Sierra Club in compiling a guide to Texas waterways.

E. O. Kindschy, outing chairman for the Sierra Club of Houston, is probably better versed on East Texas streams than any other person.

The Rio Grande, of course, is Texas' most famed river. In the vicinity of Big Bend National Park it is best run between October and March, the summer months in the canyons being extremely hot. This route is not for beginners, unless they are accompanied by sluice-tested experts. Travel is under wilderness conditions through deep canyons and much heavy white water. Any trip through this remote area should take on the proportions and planning of an expedition.

Central and East Texas rivers offer good canoeing, a favorite stream being the Guadalupe River, north of San Antonio. This is a spring-fed river, running through hill country with fast water.

The Upper Brazos, southwest of Fort Worth, is a shallow and easy-to-run river, with more canoeing available below Waco.

The Little River, crossing Highway 81 about halfway between Waco and Austin, just south of Temple, is another canoeable stream.

The Trinity River, running southeast from Dallas for several hundred miles, has many canoeable sections, serviced by numerous highway access points. The Trinity flows through the western edge of the famed Big Thicket country. Along its eastern boundary, is the Neches River, canoeable all year in the area north of Beaumont.

Perhaps the best source of canoeing information in Texas is the Texas Explorers' Club of Temple, an affiliate of the American White Water Affiliation; and the Sierra Club of Houston.

Utah

Although Utah's Green River has attained fame as a rafting waterway, canoeing is not a dominant sport on Utah's rivers. However, some sections of its major streams are canoeable.

The Green River, from Flaming Gorge Dam to Brown's Park, varies from easy-to-navigate to Class III, IV, and V rapids. Below Brown's Park to Dinosaur National Monument impassable rapids are found, while from Ouray to Green River there are approximately 100 miles of difficult and dangerous water. The only section encouraging to canoeists is from Green River to Mineral Canyon, rated as "easy."

The Colorado River, from Cisco to Fisher Valley, is also considered easy, although at Fisher Valley there are dangerous rapids. From Fisher Valley to Potash, below Moab, it is an easy and scenic trip. Take-out should be made at Potash, however. From here to Lake Powell, the river is treacherous.

On the Jordan River, from Saratoga Pumps to Camp Williams, good novice and intermediate water is found.

The Bear River, between Evanston and Great Salt Lake, varies from easy to difficult, with some dams to be portaged.

For flat-water canoeists, Lake Powell and Flaming Gorge Reservoir offer unusual scenic beauty, with the former administered as a national recreation area by the National Park Service.

Vermont

Barring some long stretches on the Connecticut River, which it shares with New Hampshire, Vermont has few flat-water streams, particularly on its east-flowing watersheds. Running water, in Vermont, likes to plunge downhill. This detracts from the state's attractiveness so far as novice canoemen are concerned, but for lovers of wild water the Green Mountain state's springtime waters are a veritable bonanza. During the summer, however, most peter out to relative trickles coursing among rock-strewn stream-beds. There are, of course, some sections of placid water on otherwise tumbling streams but, all in all, Vermont must be considered a white-water man's country.

The Connecticut runs some 235 miles between Vermont and New Hampshire during its 450-mile course to the sea. On high water early in the season, when mountain streams are pouring off their melted snows, skilled canoemen put in near Pittsburgh, New Hampshire. However, for novices and intermediate paddlers using the river during the summer, West Stewartstown, N.H., is preferable as a launching point, offering more water and fewer hazards. For a well-detailed description of tripping on this river, read *Canoeing on the Connecticut River* (see Appendix). For canoeing in other parts of Vermont, there is no guidebook comparable to the *A.M.C. New England Canoeing Guide* published by the Appalachian Mountain Club (see Bibliography).

One of the state's most famed rivers is the West, on which are held the Eastern Slalom Championships and the West River Slalom Races, in the vicinity of Jamaica. Below West Townshend, however, the West River gentles considerably for about 20 miles, bubbling only occasionally with easy rapids.

The White River, scene of canoe races conducted by the Ledyard Canoe Club of Hanover, N.H., is exciting white water early in the season between Grantville and Rochester. From Rochester to Stockbridge are about 8 miles of Class I and II rapids, good canoeing for intermediate paddlers, as is the section between Stockbridge and Bethel if care is used on some of the unusually sharp bends. The final 28 miles to the Connecticut are marked by ledges and swift water, negotiable in most places.

The Black River for about 10 miles above Whitesville is not difficult, but there are dams requiring portages. Below Whitesville for some 8 miles, good running for intermediates and experts is provided by rapids rated up to Class III.

Between Lyndonville and its juncture with the Connecticut, the Passumpsic River provides one of the longest flat-water runs in Vermont—22 miles. This quiet water, however, is the result of impoundments by several dams, around which carries must be made.

Other streams running into the Connecticut, predominantly white-water with occasional flat sections, include the Wells River, Williams, Saxton's, Ompomponoosuc, Nulhegan and the Ottauqueechee—the latter including the notorious "Queechee Gulch," which has tempted many a white-water expert but which has never been run, at least by an open canoe.

On the western slope of Vermont forming the Lake Champlain watershed, rivers are somewhat more gentle. One of these is Otter Creek, which deserves a more impressive designation than "creek." For close to 75 miles, it provides pleasant canoeing through attractive country, starting near Wallingford and continuing northward to Lake Champlain. Above South Wallingford, canoeing is possible only at high water levels.

From Montpelier to Lake Champlain at Burlington, the Winooski River is a moderate stream, not difficult to run. However, there are at least two danger spots and one or two difficult portages. The *A.M.C. New England Canoeing Guide* should be checked before attempting a run here. On-the-scene scouting, too, is advisable.

The Lamoille River, from Morrisville to Lake Champlain, a distance of about 55 miles, involves a great variety of water, mostly gentle but with a few difficult spots. The guidebook should be studied and local scouting done.

An international trip is possible on the Missisquoi River, which crosses into Canada and back into Vermont. Canoeists must check with Immigration and Customs offices. The stream provides both smooth-as-glass water and impossible-to-run rapids, thus requiring more guidebook study and local scouting.

Other streams and small Vermont rivers on the west slope offer white-water and placid trips, in alternating sections. These may include, according to water level, the Mettawee, Poultney, Castleton, and the Lemon Fair rivers.

Canoeing groups with headquarters in Vermont include the Canoe Cruisers of Northern Vermont, Burlington; and the Norwich University Outing Club, Northfield. Both are connected with the American White Water Affiliation.

Virginia

Randy Carter's book *White Water Canoeing* describes some of the rivers of eastern West Virginia and of Maryland, but it is in Virginia that this guidebook excels, along with the twin volumes of *Blue Ridge Voyages* by Corbett and Matacia (see Bibliography). Studying these three books won't make an expert of a novice, but it will certainly alert him to numerous canoeing possibilities in Virginia.

Among Virginia's rivers which should be investigated, first in the above guidebooks then with personal scouting, is the Rappahannock, including its headwaters, the Hazel and Thornton Rivers, from Sperryville to Fredericksburg. Much flat water is available, along with rapids graded up to Class III.

The North Fork of the Shenandoah River is canoeable from a point 3 miles below Mt. Jackson to Front Royal, with difficulty ratings to Class II. This is an early season run, with several access points en route.

The South Fork of the Shenandoah, with some difficult rapids, can be negotiated from Port Republic to Rt. 613 at Bentonville. The pitch of the water is usually good except during mid-summer.

Cedar Creek, from Star Tannery to Rt. 635, is a fast-flowing stream with rapids up to Class III.

Big Walker Creek, for some 19 miles between Rt. 100 near Poplar Hill and New River, is a relatively easy run early in the season.

The Cheat River, starting at Rawlesburg and ending at Highway 73 near Morgantown, is an expert's trip, with rapids designated up to Class V.

The Clinch River, with put-in sites at Highways 19 and 460 near Tazewell and take-out at Kyles Ford, Tenn., has several other access points en route and is rated up to Class IV.

Some sections of the Cowpasture are excellent beginner's water, while others challenge experts with Class IV rapids. The upper reaches of the river offer especially exciting white-water sport. Put-in is at Rt. 614 and take-out at the confluence with the James River, with several interim access points.

Goose Creek, from Rt. 50 to Rt. 7, is rated Class II and III, best run early in the season or following a substantial rain.

The Hazel River, from a point near Boston to Monumental Mills, is a lovely beginner's cruise, except for a difficult carry around a dam near the confluence with the Thornton River.

There is a great variety of water on the North, Middle, and South forks of the Holston River in Washington, Scott, Smyth, and Wise counties. Difficulty ratings range from Class I to V.

The Jackson River, between Highway 220 and Covington, is an "early stream," exciting even for experts. Pitches, especially in the lower segments, rate up to Class V.

The New River is Virginia's largest, running northward across the state from North Carolina into West Virginia, its water level usually holding up well through the summer. Experts run some sections but, due to its great size, dams, and hazardous rapids, it is not especially popular with canoeists.

The North Anna River, canoeable for about 23 miles between the Smith Mill bridge and Rt. 1, is a relatively easy-to-run stream, particularly its upper sections. It does, however, boast a few rapids of Class II and III difficulty, with one segment rated Class V. It should be scouted.

The Nottaway River is probably Virginia's most idyllic canoe stream, running entirely through forests between highways 609 and 619. Most of it is flat water but there are rapids rated at Class III in the lower reaches.

While the upper sections of the Rapidan River, above Rt. 29, are Class V wild water, the area between Rt. 29 and the river's juncture with the Rappahannock above Fredericksburg, is mostly flat water, usually canoeable until mid-summer.

From Elliston to Roanoke, the Roanoke River is generally small and not particularly fast, though some rapids rate a Class I or II designation, ideal for intermediate canoemen or beginners under supervision.

The Russell River, from Haysi to Elkhorn City, Ky., can be run by topnotch experts who don't mind lining and portaging through its terror-inspiring rapids, 10-foot waterfalls and 5-foot standing waves. This is canoeing for novices and intermediates to observe, not attempt!

It should be borne in mind that many of the foregoing river runs are seasonal possibilities only. Summertime low water may quickly reduce a navigable segment of river to a mere streambed dotted with damp rocks.

Nor do all of Virginia's rivers inspire terror. There is much easy canoeing, particularly on coastal streams. One of these is the Mattaponi, from the Bowling Green road down to Aylett.

Another is the Pamunkey River, especially popular between Highway 11 and Lille Point, a good two-day trip.

Too, there are numerous tidal and marsh streams, which may appeal to the canoeing fisherman and nature observer—such streams as Mt. Landing Creek, north of Tappahannock; Big and Little Totuskey Creeks, below Warsaw; and Farnum Creek, Nomini and Occupacia creeks, all joining the Rappahannock.

Other similarly interesting waterways are Gray's Creek near Jamestown; Ward's Creek, entering the James River below Hopewell; and the Floridieu Hundred Creek near Fort Powhatan.

Two groups, active in Virginia canoeing, and members of the American White Water Affiliation, are the Coastal Canoeists of Newport News, and the University of Virginia Outing Club, Charlottesville.

Washington

To quote one state official, "Washington's rivers, for the most part, are quite fast-flowing and only the more intrepid canoeists tackle these to any degree." However, there are a few flat-water areas, notably certain segments on such rivers as the Stillaguamish, Skagit, Columbia, and Cowlitz.

Generally, though, Washington's rivers are not gentle. Floods frequently change river characteristics, log jams and snags appear and disappear, so that river cruising maps maintained by some canoeists and kayak river-runners constantly need updating.

Within 40 miles of Seattle are several accessible rivers which are run mostly in decked canoes or in kayaks. These include the close-by Duwamish, Class I; the Cedar River, Class II; the Sammanish, Class I; the Snoqualmie, Class I to IV.

Farther out from Seattle, but within 40 miles, the Pilchuk River is rated Class I and II; the Skykomish, I and II; the Green, II to IV; the Puyallup, I to III; and the Misqually, II to III.

These ratings change with water levels of course, so that advance scouting is a prerequisite. The best approach to canoeing in Washington for a novice is to affiliate with a group such as the Washington Kayak Club, 5622 Seaview Avenue, Seattle 98107. The club's former president, Wolf G. Bauer, has done considerable mapping of rivers run by the club's members, and they in turn are encouraged to keep their own maps up to date as they note changes in river conditions. Thus, the club has a vast store of river knowledge.

West Virginia

Here again we encounter the names of Carter, and Corbett and Matacia, for in their books *White Water Canoeing* and *Blue Ridge Voyages* (see Bibliography), they have described thoroughly the canoeing streams of eastern West Virginia.

Few of this state's streamways are placid waters for any extended distance, so that these books, along with the waters themselves, should be studied before canoe cruises are launched.

The pamphlet *Boating Facilities of West Virginia* (see Appendix), while designed to serve anglers, may be helpful to the flat-water canoeman who wants to locate easily paddled streams and access points.

West Virginia's canoe forte, however, is white-water running. The national white-water championships, for instance, are held near Petersburg on the North Fork of the South Branch of the Potomac River, which rates as Class IV early in the season when the races are held.

The North River, a tributary of the Cacapon, is an example of a small white-water stream, mostly Class I and II, at its best during the early spring run-off. The most popular run is from the bridge at Rt. 50, to the river's junction with the main Cacapon, a distance of approximately 24 miles.

The Cacapon, from Wardensville to Great Cacapon, is considered West Virginia's most beautiful canoeing river, but, alas, it's not for novices! The 80-mile run includes pitches up to Class III, although most of the stream averages between Class I and II. It, too, is an early stream.

The South Branch of the Potomac is usually broken up into a series of separate runs, although the entire length can be run with portages and considerable skill. Between Franklin and the South Branch's confluence with the main Potomac, difficulty ratings vary from Class I to VI. Carter's *Canoeing White Water* should be studied before attempting any part of this run. Volume II of *Blue Ridge Voyages*, too, includes a well detailed strip map.

The North Branch of the Potomac, from Circleville to Royal Glen Dam, a distance of some 35 miles, is a much smaller river than the South Branch, but its difficulty rating of III to IV provides lively action until early June, after which it is generally too low to run.

The Greenbriar, for some 40 miles between Durbin and Hinton, has little placid water. It's for canoemen who can handle Class II to IV pitches.

The "Paw Paw Bends" of the Potomac, between Paw Paw and Little Orleans, offer 20 miles of relatively easy paddling in wild country, unless high winds come up. There are some ledges but rapids are generally considered easy to navigate.

Two groups associated with the American White Water Affiliation are active in West Virginia. These are the Mountainlair Outing Club of Morgantown, and the West Virginia Wildwater Association of South Charleston.

Wisconsin

Wisconsin is another of the Midwest states which has recognized canoeing as a sport by establishing regular canoe routes and publishing an excellent guidebook, *Wisconsin Water Trails* (see Appendix). The state's numerous canoe cruising routes include:

The Manitowish River Canoe Trail, on which two separate segments are accessible: High Lake to Rest Lake, a 30-mile cruise with two portages but no rapids; Rest Lake to Flambeau Flowage, about 25 miles with no portages but two Class I rapids.

The Turtle River Water Trail originates at North Turtle Lake, but there is rough going to Cedar Lake, which is considered a better starting point for the 25-mile trip to Flambeau Flowage. There are some rapids and a few portages.

The Flambeau River Water Trail, from Flambeau Flowage to Park Falls, includes eleven rapids, some of moderate difficulty; from Park Falls to Ladysmith are some of Wisconsin's finest white-water runs which can be shot by skilled canoemen; Beaver Dam is an exception and is considered dangerous; from Ladysmith to the Chippewa River is all smooth paddling except for dams and portages at Port Arthur and Thornapple.

The South Fork of the Flambeau River Water Trail originates at Round Lake and runs to the North Fork of the Flambeau, alternating between smooth water and rapids, some of which, notably Rocky Carry and Carpenter's, can be tricky. The trip is not recommended for novices.

On the Big Elk River, from Musser Dam to the South Fork of the Flambeau, are several easy-to-run rapids, at least for intermediate or better canoemen.

The Bear River trip, from Flambeau Lake to the Flambeau River is an ideal beginner's cruise, without rapids and requiring about one day.

Another easy trip is on Trout River, from Trout Lake to Manitowish, easy because there is little current, so little, in fact, that the trip can be made in either direction.

The Wisconsin River Trail has two portages, both short, between Lac Vieux Desert to the Vilas-Oneida county line but no dangerous rapids. From there to Merrill, it is easy paddling except for Whirlpool Rapids below Rhinelander. From Merrill to Nekoosa, several paper mill dams require portaging; otherwise, this section presents no problems. From Nekoosa to Prairie du Sac there are some 35 miles of smooth paddling, with no rapids or dams to portage until Pettenwell Dam Flowage is reached. From Prairie du Sac to the Mississippi River, sand bars may be encountered at low water but no portages.

The Tomahawk River, from Minocqua Lake to the Wisconsin River, combines slow shallows with deep, swift runs. Half-Breed Rapids, about midway, should be portaged.

From Highway H to the Wisconsin River, Lemonweir River presents the usual shallow-water minor hazards but is generally an easy trip.

There are five short portages on the Baraboo River between Highway G and the Wisconsin River but no rapids or extensive swift water.

The Chippewa River, from Shanagolden via Chippewa Lake to the Mississippi River, presents one difficult set of rips below the dam at Raddisson and a long carry at Jim Falls dam. There are several other portages, too.

The St. Croix River, one of the trips the author made in 1959, may be run from Solon Springs to Highway 70, with alternating rapids and smooth water. The rapids are not severe, mostly Class I. From Highway 70 to the Mississippi, much of the river flows over a sandy bottom. There is a carry at Taylor's Falls.

The Totogatic River, from Nancy bridge to the Namekagon River, is marked by shallows and easy rapids, with the lower end of the run through Dismal Swamp.

An easy, three- to four-day trip is afforded by the Yellow River from Highway 70 to the St. Croix River. The Clam River also flows to the St. Croix, from Clam Lake, and provides a pleasant trip without serious difficulty except for two small rapids and an occasional blow-down.

Some 66 miles of interesting water exist on the Bois Brule River, between Stone's Bridge and Lake Superior but included are some rather severe rapids.

The Brule River, from Nelma to the Menominee River, flows through wild country, providing a two-day trip over some shallow, rocky, but not difficult stretches. There are, however, dangerous rapids at the mouth of the Michigamme River.

The Menominee River, from Brule River to Green Bay, includes several stretches of bad water which should be portaged, but otherwise this is an excellent fast-water trip.

The Wolf River, from Post Lake to Shawano, is strictly for experts. Below Shawano, to Lake Winnebago, it is novice water with no dams or rapids.

The Fox River, from Portage to Wolf River, follows an old fur trade route. Abandoned locks may require short portages but, except for these, the trip is not difficult.

The Waupaca Chain of Lakes includes some twenty-three connected lakes in Waupaca County of central Wisconsin, the trip being predominantly a flat-water cruise. From the lakes to Wolf River, via the Waupaca River, is a short trip, with some rapids below Parfreville.

The Peshtigo River, from Highway C to Green Bay, runs through wild country with a few dams requiring portages, plus some rapids too difficult for novices.

The Rock River, from Highway 49 to the Illinois state line, runs within the famed Horicon Marsh Wildlife Refuge. This is an easy trip with few portages but refuge officials should be consulted before starting.

The Yahara River, from Lake Mendota to Rock River, is a novice trip which traverses Madison's "Four Lakes." The Black River, from Lake Arbutus to the Mississippi River, poses problems in the vicinity of the Black River Falls dam, where there are rapids, but below this point it is easy going all the way.

Groups which are active in Wisconsin canoeing, and members of the American White Water Affiliation, are the John Muir Chapter of the Sierra Club, Wauwatosa; and the Wisconsin Hoofers of Madison.

Wyoming

Within Yellowstone National Park is one of Wyoming's most attractive canoe trips, a relatively short one ideally suited to novice skill. It runs from Lewis Lake through the Lewis River to Shoshone Lake, in the park's southwestern section.

By way of contrast, the white-water expert will enjoy the Class III rapids to be found on the Hoback River, running along U.S. Highways 187 and 189, southeast of Jackson. Medium water height provides the best runs.

The Greys River, which empties into Palisades Reservoir of the Snake River at Alpine, has lengthy sections which are relatively placid and safe for open canoes. The lower river, below Lynx Creek particularly, has some dangerous stretches rated up to Class V or worse.

Below Dubois, the Wind River provides some white-water running, much of this section visible from U.S. Highway 26-287. Further downstream, Class V rapids occur.

Below Jackson Lake, the Snake River presents some 12 miles of flat-water canoeing through scenic country. The next 40 miles see the current accelerating although developing no hazardous rapids.

Some 60 miles of cruising are possible on the Green River, starting at the bridge west of Cora, near Pinedale, to a point about 5 miles below Big Piney. There are rapids in the vicinity of the Warren bridge and occasional barbed wire fences, strung across the river, are hazards.

During high-water stages, or generally up until about July 15, the upper Platte River offers good running. Below Grey's Reef on the lower Platte is more excellent canoe water.

Canada

It is in Canada, one of the largest countries on earth, with more fresh water than any other, that the ultimate in canoe cruising can be attained. So vast is the intricate network of waterways, that a canoeman might travel from ice-out to freeze-up every year during his lifetime and seldom retrace or recross his route.

Obviously then, to detail Canada's canoeable waters even briefly would require several volumes, a task which has yet to be undertaken. However, the Federal government and several of the provinces have issued booklets, maps, and other information covering the more popular established trips (see Appendix).

Except in the Yukon Territory, where canoe rentals are not generally available, outfitters can supply partial or complete gear. The Hudson's Bay Company, alert to modern trends, offers a U-Paddle canoe rental service through which a canoe may be picked up at one post and returned at another (see Appendix).

Preliminary investigation of canoe trips in Canada can best be made by contacting the Canadian Government Travel Bureau or the Hudson's Bay Company (see Appendix).

Organized canoeing in most of the Canadian provinces is represented by the Canadian Canoeing Association, 32 Sedgewick Cres., Islington, Ontario.

Several Canadian canoeing clubs are associated with the American White Water Affiliation. These include: The British Columbia Kayak and Canoe Club, Vancouver, B.C.; the Dogwood Canoe Club, also of Vancouver; the Fourth Weston Scout Troop, Weston, Ont.; the Mohawk Rod and Gun Club, Toronto, Ont.; the Montreal White Water Club, Montreal, P.Q.; the Ontario Canoe Cruisers, Toronto, Ont.; the Ontario Voyageurs Kayak Club, Don Mills, Ont.; and the Viking Ski Club, Quebec City, P.Q.

Alberta

From Rocky Mountain House on Rt. 11, to Edmonton, the Saskatchewan River provides a 250-mile cruise which follows an early fur trade trail, now running through settled country.

Somewhat longer is the 350-mile trip, via the Athabaska River, which starts at Jasper in Jasper National Park and terminates at Athabaska, about 95 miles north of Edmonton. Several highway crossings en route provide access or take-out points to shorten the trip.

For a cruise which should well take on the proportions of an expedition— 760 miles—the starting point is Waterways or Fort McMurray on the Northern Alberta Railway, 300 miles north of Edmonton. This water trail crosses the entire Province of Saskatchewan and terminates at The Pas in Manitoba, travel being via the Clearwater River, Lac La Cloche, Lac Ile La Crosse, and Churchill River.

British Columbia

One of the most scenic canoe trips in British Columbia is in Bowron Lake Provincial Park whose 464 square miles encompass a 70-mile circuitous route through Bowron, Indianpoint, Isaac, Lanezi, Sandy, and Spectacle lakes, most of these connected by navigable waterways or fairly short portages. Seven to ten days should be allowed.

Also along a former fur trade route, a more extensive trip is possible from Summit Lake, 30 miles north of Prince George, down to the Peace River to Fort St. John on the Alaska Highway. From there, the cruise may be extended down the Peace to the town of Peace River in Alberta, the entire distance totalling 510 miles. Initial travel is via Crooked River to McLeod Lake, then through the Pack River to the Parsnip River which flows into the Peace at Finlay Forks. At Peace River Canyon there is a 15-mile portage, not as ominous as it sounds, since the river at this point is paralleled by a road over which local farmers can usually supply truck transportation.

The North Thompson River, from Clearwater to Kamloops, is pleasantly navigable through sparsely settled country, following Highway No. 5. Large sandbars make ideal campsites.

The Canoe River, aptly named, is navigable for 80 to 90 miles from Valemount to the river's confluence with the Columbia River at Boat Encampment, providing a four- or five-day trip. The current is slow, though some sections present hazards.

About 90 miles of the Columbia, between Windermere and Golden, is suitable for canoes. From Golden to Revelstoke, however, the river is highly hazardous except for the last 45 miles below Downie Creek. Downstream from Revelstoke, it is possible to paddle to the United States border, local canoemen favoring the section between Revelstoke and Robson, although much of this is lake paddling.

The Fraser River, a big and muddy stream, flows quietly for 115 miles through farm lands before reaching salt water at New Westminster. Campsites occur frequently.

Manitoba

While the province of Manitoba lies astride many of the major Canadian canoe routes, not all traverse deep wilderness. The Red River trip, from Emerson on the U.S. border to Winnipeg, for example, follows Highway No. 75 through settled country for 70 miles.

The Whiteshell–Caddy Lake trip, a 105-mile circle route in Whiteshell Provincial Park, originates at Caddy Lake on Highway No. 4, and proceeds northward on the Whiteshell River to the Winnipeg River, then into Eaglenest Lake. From there, a carry into Crow Duck Lake follows, another into Whiteshell Lake, then a return to the Whiteshell River, retracing the outward route back to Caddy Lake. The cruise may, of course, be made in the opposite direction by leaving the Whiteshell River at Little Whiteshell Lake. Since all travel is through a forest reserve and among precipitous cliffs, this is an especially scenic cruise.

One of Manitoba's adventuresome trips originates at famed Norway House, at the head of vast Lake Winnipeg and follows a wilderness trail via the Nelson and Hayes rivers to York Factory on Hudson Bay, a distance of 350 miles. Since heavy rapids and difficult portages occur frequently on the Nelson, this is a trip for highly skilled canoemen. Shallow tidal waters which must be crossed along the west shore of Hudson Bay can be dangerous too. Nevertheless, this is one of the great Canadian canoe trips.

By way of contrast, one of Manitoba's easy canoe cruises covers 120 miles from Cranberry Lake, north of The Pas, to Wekusko Lake. Both ends of the trip are accessible by automobile or train and much of the paddling is through beautiful Grass River Provincial Park.

An extension of this trip, from Wekusko Lake to Wabowden on the Hudson Bay Railway, is possible for about 90 miles. The Grass River is followed for a considerable distance and the return to Wekusko or to The Pas can be made by railway.

Pukatawagan Falls on the Churchill River is the goal of a 140-mile trip which can be made without portages. The first leg of the cruise is downstream on the Churchill from Lake Pukatawagan with a stopover at Highrock Lake that night. Pukatawagan Falls is then reached the next day. The return trip, however, retraces the route.

These are but a few of the numerous cruises in northern Manitoba. Maps and Canadian canoeing literature will suggest dozens of others.

New Brunswick

Although New Brunswick has an interesting network of riverways, many of them in wilderness settings, canoeing and canoe trips have not attained the popularity enjoyed in other provinces, except that canoes are used extensively for Atlantic salmon fishing. Also, a New Brunswick law requires non-residents to be accompanied by a licensed guide when entering forest lands. This has discouraged canoeing visits.

One of the most noted salmon rivers, however—the famed Miramichi—provides a 120-mile excursion from Juniper, on Rt. 107, to salt water at Newcastle.

Another lengthy trip, 204 miles, is possible on the St. John River from Grand Falls in northern New Brunswick, to the port of St. John on the Bay of Fundy. The lower river, however, will find the canoeman navigating among ocean-going vessels.

The St. Croix River, which forms the boundary between New Brunswick and Maine, also provides trip opportunities.

Newfoundland

Although Newfoundland has fine canoe waters, its geography and development pose problems to canoeists. Access to its northerly-flowing rivers is via Rt. 1 which crosses the island but, in most instances, the headwaters of these rivers cannot be reached by road. Hence, most canoe trips must retrace their routes, with the first leg invariably an upstream haul.

An example of such a problem is the Upper Exploits River trip, which starts at Buchans Junction, proceeds 40 miles to the head of Indian Lake, then via Lloyd's River into Lloyd's Lake and King George Lake. From here, the cruise must retrace its course, total distance amounting to 150 miles. All in all, it can be seen why Newfoundland has not been able to exploit canoe trips as a recreational attraction.

Newfoundland has jurisdiction over Labrador where vast tracts are still relatively unknown, and through which undoubtedly flow attractive canoe waters. Trips into this country, however, are arduous and sometimes dangerous. As a result, licensed guides are required of all non-residents who venture into this region. Inquiries regarding Labrador should be addressed to the Newfoundland agency listed in the Appendix.

Northwest Territories

Any mention of the Northwest Territories to a canoeman will probably bring to mind the mighty Mackenzie River and its numerous tributaries, providing thousands of miles of cruising water in an exciting setting. The very name "Northwest Territories" conjures up limitless spaces, brawling rivers, vast forests, and the enthralling tundra lands, to say nothing of historic struggles for survival and fabulous journeys made against seemingly unbeatable odds. There is no doubt: "Northwest Territories" is synonymous with "adventures."

A prime example is the Mackenzie River trip which may well cover close to 2000 miles! It can be started at Fort McMurray (Waterways) in Alberta with an initial run of 250 miles to Fort Smith, near the Northwest Territories-Alberta line. Not to be overlooked on this leg is a 16-mile portage near Fort Smith. This section is via the Athabaska River to Athabaska Lake, crossing the lake at its western end to the Slave River. From Fort Smith, on the Slave, to Great Slave Lake is 180 miles; and 90 miles more to Hay River on the south shore of Great Slave Lake. From Hay River, to the outlet of the lake which forms the actual source of the Mackenzie, it is another 90 miles. Fort Simpson, on the Mackenzie, lies 160 miles downstream and, from there Aklavik, on the Mackenzie delta, lies another 1000 miles of river! The very vastness is entrancing.

There is a drawback, however. Much of the Mackenzie is highly commercialized, with about a quarter-million tons of freight hauled over its waters each summer.

Experienced canoemen—experienced not only in canoeing but in wilderness travel—will find the almost limitless region east of the Mackenzie far more appealing. Canoe travel in this area is vividly described by Eric W. Morse in two articles, "Fresh Water Northwest Passage," published in June 1965, and "Summer Travel in the Canadian Barrens," May 1967, both in the *Canadian Geographical Journal*. Reprints are available from the Northwest Territories Tourist office, Ottawa, Ont. (see Appendix).

Much of the information included in these articles is invaluable to anyone contemplating canoe trips on such rivers as the Thelon, Hanbury, Lockhart, Snare, Camsell, Great Bear, Mackenzie, Rat, Bell, Porcupine, and Yukon, the latter four in the Yukon or Alaska. Those familiar with the geography of the Northwest Territories will recognize the sequence of these rivers as a 3000-mile east-west route from Hudson Bay to the Bering Sea.

Nor are these the only rivers in the Northwest Territories which beckon to adventurous canoemen; there are also the Liard, Nahanni, and Coppermine rivers and their tributaries.

Another pithy and informative work is the article "Across the Barrens by Canoe," by Orris C. Herfindahl, which appeared in *North* magazine, issue of September-October, 1956. In this the writer describes a four-week, 500-mile trip down the Hanbury and Thelon rivers to Baker Lake post. A reprint is available from the Northwest Territories Tourist Office.

Nova Scotia

Like New Brunswick, Nova Scotia requires that non-residents be accompanied by a licensed guide when traveling on its forest lands; also, the sport of salmon fishing on its rivers is more important to the local economy than canoe trip outfitting. However, a few canoe trails have been established.

Three of these originate at the Shannon River bridge at Squirreltown Station. The first is routed via Alma Lake, Ponhook Lake, and the Medway River to the town of Medway, a distance of 60 miles. The second follows the same route through Alma and Ponhook lakes but there branches into Lake Rossignol to the Liverpool River for an 82-mile trip to Liverpool.

The third is a full-circle trip, via the Medway River, Lake Rossignol, Kejimkujik Lake, Liverpool River, and Alma Lake, returning to the starting point, the Shannon River bridge.

Crossing the peninsula in a northerly direction is a 74-mile cruise, starting at Halifax and terminating at Truro, at the head of the Bay of Fundy. The passage includes the Dartmouth locks, Banook Lake, Micmac Lake, two more locks at Port Wallace, then the Porta Bella locks into Lake William, Lake Thomas, the Wellington River, Shubenacadie Lake to Maitland. From that point, the course is along the eastern shore of Cobequid Bay into the Salmon River to Truro.

From Hubbard Cove to Windsor, a distance of 40 miles, another trip is feasible via Dauphinee Mill Lake, Westhaver Lake, the Ponhook lakes, and the St. Croix River.

A 105-mile cruise is available, too, from St. Peter to Strathlorne, via the Bras d'Or lakes to Badeck, through St. Patrick's Channel to Lake Ainslie and Strathlorne.

Ontario

Nowhere have canoe routes been as extensively developed as in Ontario, the province being literally criss-crossed with waterways ideally suited to canoe cruising, whether the aim is an afternoon's leisurely excursion or a full-fledged Hudson Bay expedition.

Any canoeman living in the relatively congested southeastern part of the province can easily enjoy the 125-mile Kingston to Ottawa trip, via the Cataraqui River, Rideau River, and the Rideau Lakes chain. Then there is the 112-mile cruise from Pembroke to Ottawa on the Ottawa River, some portages involved. This can be extended 95 miles by starting at Mattawa, north of Algonquin Provincial Park.

Another "neighborhood" excursion runs from Trenton on Lake Ontario to Gamebridge on Lake Simcoe, a distance of 175 miles, via the Trent River and Kawartha lakes. Numerous canal locks will be encountered.

Still another easily accessible trip is the 49-mile run from Huntsville to Algonquin Park Station on Cache Lake, via Fairy and Peninsula lakes in the Lake of Bays chain, the Oxtongue River, Tea, and Smoke lakes.

Fort Frances, on the Minnesota border, is the starting point of the 150-mile trip to Sioux Lookout, located at the junction of Rt. 72 and the Canadian National Railway, the route crossing the following lakes: Rainey, Sphene, Manitou, Sandy, and Minnitaki.

In the Timagami Forest Reserve are several trips, including a 120-mile circuit from Timagami Station through Lake Timagami, north through Lake Evelyn, the Mattawabika River, the Montreal River, then to Lake Anamanipissing and back to Timagami Station.

It is the vast watersheds flowing northeasterly into Hudson Bay and James Bay that stir the imaginations of canoeists. Literature of the North is rife with descriptions of such great rivers as the Albany, the Missinaibi, the Mattagami, and the Abitibi. Trips of 200 miles to James Bay are possible on the latter three, all accessible via Highway No. 11 or, in the case of the Abitibi, via the Ontario Northland Railway. One of these trips starts at Mattice, on Rt. 11, and travels 203 miles to Moose Factory via the Missinaibi River. From Island Falls to Moose Factory, over the Abitibi, is about 150 miles. Via the Mattagami River from Jacksonboro, James Bay is 204 miles downstream.

These are all, of course, downstream cruises. Any attempt to return to the starting point by means of upriver canoe travel would prove a formidable task; and since there are no automobile roads to Hudson Bay, the return must be made either by chartered flight or by railroad to Cochrane or other points.

One of the longest and most exciting trips in Ontario is from Sioux Lookout to Fort Albany on James Bay, a distance of 637 miles. Passage is through Pelican Lake, Lac Seul, then over the height of land to Lac St. Joseph and into the Albany River, at the mouth of which lies Fort Albany. Arduous toting over the height of land from Lac Seul to Lac St. Joseph can be eliminated by

driving the outfit over Rt. 599 from Savant Lake off Rt. 17 directly to Osna-
burgh House on Lac St. Joseph.

These trips, of course, are for experienced bush travelers or those accompanied by experts. And they are only a few of numerous trip possibilities in
Ontario's northland. One has only to examine a detailed map to visualize dozens
more.

Not to be overlooked are the comparatively leisurely cruises established in
Quetico Provincial Park, the Canadian counterpart of the Superior National
Forest Boundary Canoe Waters in Minnesota. Travel from one park to the
other, by canoe, is common. The Canadian Quetico Outfitters, Ltd. has a comprehensive bulletin describing these trips (see Appendix).

Quebec

Not only does Quebec have enticing canoe waters but there are the fascinating French and Indian names to master; tongue-twisters like Kanikawinika
and Chibougamau, Montagnais and Chute-aux-Outardes! Canoeing in Quebec
is a linguistic challenge, too.

Until 1965, little printed information on Quebec canoeing was available, at
least from government agencies, and there were few designated recreational
canoe routes. This is now being remedied.

Laurentide Park, north of Quebec City, is now the site of the newly established 60-mile Metabetchouan River trip, run with ease in four days. Starting
at Camp Montagnais, 15 miles east of Kiskissink over a gravel road, canoeists
paddle southward through a chain of lakes and streams to the Metabetchouan
River, then northerly to the bridge of the Kiskissink-Camp Montagnais road.
Some 14 portages are encountered but none requires more than 20 minutes of
toting.

Three canoe circuits were set up in La Verendrye Park, in southwestern
Quebec, during the summer of 1966. These range from 10 to 35 miles in
length and from one to five days' duration. Each bears the unimaginative and
prosaic designation of "A," "B," or "C" and each starts at Auberge "Le Domaine," 200 miles northwest of Montreal and 70 miles from Mont Laurier.

Circuit A is the easiest; 15 miles long, it runs through Lac des Loups, Baie
Menard, Kearney Bay, Lac Jean-Peré, back into Lac des Loups and return to
Le Domaine. There is only one portage, 1/3-mile, and the trip is "recom-
mended for beginners."

Circuit B is the longest, 35 miles, with four portages totalling one mile, and
is somewhat more difficult than Circuit A. From Le Domaine, it traverses Lac
des Loups, Lac Jean-Peré, Lac Antostagen, Poulter Lake, des Rapides River,
then back into Lac Jean-Peré and Lac des Loups, to the starting point.

Circuit C's 25-mile circumference is interspersed with three portages, adding
up to 3/4-mile of carrying. Despite its being rated "difficult in spots," this
loop features relatively easy paddling much of the way. It runs through Lac
des Loups, Lac Antostagan, to the Canadian International Paper Company's
Camp No. 15, to Lac Richet, then back into Lac des Loups to Le Domaine.

These are the extent of presently designated canoe routes in Quebec's parks
but plans call for the development of more in all provincial parks where there
is suitable canoe water.

One of Quebec's most extensive trips, comparable to some of Ontario's, is
the 380-mile water trail from Lake Mistassini, via the Martin and Rupert

rivers, to Rupert House on James Bay. Lake Mistassini can be reached by car over a secondary road from Lake St. John (Lac St. Jean).

Starting at St. Filicien or Robertval on Lake St. John is the 238-mile run to Lake Mistassini, via Nihabau and Chibougamau lakes, and returning to the starting point via Lac Le Meule and Rivière du Chef.

The Quebec Provincial Council of the Boy Scouts of Canada has established several canoe routes within the province. One of the most extensive of these is the 250-mile circuit which starts at the foot of Lake Peribonca, runs northward along the Peribonca River to Lake Onistagan, followed by a portage into Lake Manouan, the trip terminated by a run down the Manouan River to Tchitogoma Lake. Two weeks should be allowed.

Another scout trip runs within the Kipawa Forest Reserve in western Quebec, starting its 140-mile circuit at Lake Kipawa, proceeding easterly to Hunters Lake, through Long Narrows, portaging by Red Pine and Ragged chutes (about 6 minutes' carrying), then northerly through Brennan Lake, along the Kipawa River to Wolf Lake, Ogascanan Lake, Sasaginaga Lake, Ascoe Lake, Five Mile Lake, into the Sasaginaga River to Lake Ostaboning, then southward back into Kipawa Lake. The unusual clarity of Kipawa waters and the scenic beauty of this region make this trip a favorite.

Several other routes have been mapped by the Boy Scouts of Canada in the Saguenay, Temiskaming, and Rouyn-Noranda districts with information about them available from the Montreal headquarters (see Appendix).

Saskatchewan

Probably no state or provincial agency has so thoroughly detailed canoe routes as has the Saskatchewan Department of Natural Resources. At least twenty-four trips have been mapped and a brochure prepared for each, including minute descriptions of portages and rapids. The Churchill River trip, for example, from Ile-à-La-Crosse to Otter Rapids, a distance of 240 miles, requires a 16-page mimeographed booklet.

Although the trip is routed through virtual wilderness, both ends are accessible by car. Ile-à-La-Crosse is reached via Rt. 155, north of Green Lake 140 miles (Green Lake is west of Prince Albert National Park). The take-out point, Otter Rapids near Otter Lake, is 50 miles north of La Ronge, near the northern terminus of Rt. 2. This is a trip for experts, however, since much of it is through large lakes connected by swift and sometimes dangerous passages. At least two weeks should be allotted to cover it.

Once at Otter Lake, canoeists may continue on to La Ronge by water, three routes being available, running from 64 to 90 miles and requiring five to six days.

Also starting at Otter Lake, the 100-mile Pelican Narrows trip travels through Otter Lake, part of the Churchill River, Trade, Frog, and Wood lakes to Pelican Narrows. The latter is located at the northerly end of Rt. 135. Thirteen portages are required during the week's trip.

Within the boundaries of Prince Albert National Park, a 100-mile circular canoe route has been established. This starts at Waskesiu Lake, runs through Waskesiu Narrows into Kingsmere Lake and includes an unusual portage by a miniature rail system operated by the park. From there, the trip proceeds through Ajawaan, Sanctuary, Lavallee, Wabeno, Wassegam, Tibiska, Crean, and Heart lakes, back into Waskesiu Lake, the starting point.

A tremendous variety of canoe water exists in Saskatchewan; the lengthy and arudous trip from Cree Lake to Black Lake via the Cree River, an example of the more difficult. For an easy jaunt, there is the Saskatoon to Nipawin trip, 220 miles through settled country via the South Saskatchewan and the Saskatchewan rivers, with only two portages.

Yukon Territory

The Yukon's canoe routes are long and remote. With the reduction of commercial river traffic—most of this now going over the highways—the rivers are once more deserted. Waters in the Yukon average about 50 degrees even during a hot summer; lakes may not be ice-free until the middle of June and freezing temperatures and snow can be expected by the first of September. The rivers are large, supply points are few and far between. A canoe cruise should, therefore, include at least two, preferably three craft. Early September sees grizzlies feeding on salmon in the shallows so that the Department of Travel suggests that a rifle be carried during this period, *to be used only in emergency.*

These are the factors, however, that challenge adventurous canoemen, urging them northward. Experience will minimize danger but the element of it remains. A Yukon trip cannot be dull!

There are compensations for the difficulties, though. From Whitehorse to Dawson City, via the Yukon River, there are no portages during the 450-mile run and the river gradient is only 1 foot per mile! Since this is a former route of the majestic sternwheel steamers, there is available a published log of the river between Whitehorse and the Tanana River (see Appendix).

A 200-mile trip can be made from Quiet Lake on the Canol Road, via Big Salmon Lake, down the Big Salmon River to the Yukon and Carmacks. The gradient on the Big Salmon averages about 6 feet per mile and there are no portages. The trip may be terminated at Carmacks or continued down the Yukon another 250 miles to Dawson City.

From Johnson's Crossing, on the Alaska Highway, to Carmacks constitutes another 200-mile cruise, via the Teslin and Yukon rivers, without portages and with an average gradient of only 2.5 feet per mile.

For the canoeman who is an explorer at heart, there is the enchanting challenge of the old Hudson's Bay Company pre-gold rush route from the Liard River northerly into the Pelly and Yukon watersheds, eventually ending up at Dawson City, about 1000 miles from the start. This fur-trade route has been used little, if any, during the past 60 years and undoubtedly presents difficulties that would prove insurmountable to anyone but seasoned wilderness travelers.

The trail starts at Watson Lake, just north of the British Columbia border on the Liard River. The first 200 miles are upstream to the Frances River, up this to Frances Lake, then along the west arm of Frances Lake into the Finlayson River and Finlayson Lake. Here the height of land is reached where there is a 5-mile portage to Campbell Creek. From here it is downstream into the Campbell River and into the Pelly. About 30 miles southeast of Ross River, on the Pelly, there is a portage around Hoole Canyon. The Pelly River then runs into the Yukon, northwest of the town of Minto, about halfway between Whitehorse and Dawson City. From this point, it is all clear sailing to Dawson.

One interesting facet of canoe tripping in these regions during the early summer is that lanterns are not needed. There is daylight for more than twenty hours a day from the first of June until about mid-July!

Appendix

Information Sources By State—U.S.

ALASKA

Bureau of Land Management
P.O. Box 2511
Juneau 99801

Alaska's Gulkana Basin and *Alaska's Gulkana Float Trail* (free).

Bureau of Sport Fisheries
U.S. Fish and Wildlife Service
P.O. Box 500
Kenai 99611

Maps of Swan Lake Canoe Route in Kenai National Moose Range (free).

ARKANSAS

Ozark Wilderness Waterways Club
P. O. Box 8165
Kansas City, Mo.

Publishes bulletins and runs organized canoe trips on Ozark streams.

The Ozark Society
P.O. Box 38
Fayetteville

Information on Buffalo River.

Publicity & Parks Commission
State Capitol
Little Rock 72201

General information on Arkansas streams.

Harold Bly
Box 343
Upper Eleven Point River Association
Pocahontas

Information on Eleven Point River.

CONNECTICUT

Appalachian Mountain Club
5 Joy Street
Boston, Mass. 02108

A.M.C. New England Canoeing Guide ($5). Best source of information on Connecticut canoeing. Other publications, also.

Connecticut Development Commission
State Office Building
Hartford

Information on Connecticut and Housatonic Rivers (free).

Farmington River Watershed
Association, Inc.
24 East Main Street
Avon 06001

27 towns in Connecticut and Massachusetts, concerned with Farmington River, make up membership.

DELAWARE

State Development Department
45 The Green
Dover

Folder *Boating—Camping—Fishing*. No details on rivers but shows access points (free).

FLORIDA

Citrus City Chamber of Commerce
Inverness 32650

Sponsors annual canoe races on Withlacoochee River.

Game & Fresh Water Fish Comm.
Information and Education Division
Farris Bryant Building
620 South Meridian Street
Tallahassee 32304

Will supply information on specific riverways upon request.

GEORGIA

Folkston–Charlton County Chamber
of Commerce
P.O. Box 276
Folkston 31537

Information folder and map of Okefenokee Swamp canoeing waters (free).

IDAHO

Fish and Game Department
600 South Walnut
Boise 83707

Folder *Idaho Fishing Regulations* (free). Map shows highway access points to rivers but little other detail.

Forest Supervisor
Salmon National Forest
Salmon 83467

Folder *The Salmon—River of No Return* (free). Includes maps and details of river.

Department of Commerce &
Development
State House
Boise 83707

Booklet *Idaho Water Fun* (free). Not a canoeing publication but may prove useful in locating riverways and access points.

ILLINOIS

Illinois Department of Conservation
Boat Section
106 State Office Building
Springfield

Booklet *Illinois Canoeing Guide* (free). Describes 23 established canoe routes.

American Indian Center Canoe Club
c/o Leroy Wesaw
2209 North Campbell
Chicago 60647

Conducts annual canoe races on Lake Michigan. Information on canoeing in Chicago area.

American Youth Hostels
Metropolitan Chicago Council
2210 North Clark Street
Chicago 60614

Publishes newsletter *By-Ways*, announcing organized canoe trips.

Great Lakes Chapter, Sierra Club
Jean Leever, Chairman
10240 Huntington Court
Orland Park 60462

Monthly newsletter covering outdoor events, including canoeing.

The Illinois Paddling Council
Dan Malkovitch, Editor
111 East Church Street
Benton 62812

Publishes regular column on canoeing "Currents" in *Outdoor Illinois*.

The Chicagoland Canoe Base
4019 North Narragansett Avenue
Chicago 60634

Chicago area canoeing information.

INDIANA

Department of Conservation
612 State Office Building
Indianapolis 46209

Booklet *Canoeing Trails in Indiana* (free). Describes 16 established canoe routes.

IOWA

Conservation Department
East 7th and Court Streets
Des Moines

Booklet *Iowa Canoe Trips* (free). Describes 13 established canoe routes.

KANSAS

Department of Economic Development
State Office Building
Topeka 66612

Brief information regarding Little Arkansas River at Wichita.

Ozark Wilderness Waterways
P. O. Box 8165
Kansas City

KENTUCKY

Kentucky Rivers Canoe Club
P.O. Box 986
Bowling Green 42101

Co-sponsors Barren River Canoe Marathon.

Scott County Chamber of Commerce
Oneida, Tenn., 37841

Co-sponsors Angel Falls—Devil's Jump Canoe Race on Big South Fork River in Tennessee and Kentucky. Other co-sponsors are Universities of Kentucky and Tennessee; Oneida (Tenn.) Kiwanis Club.

LOUISIANA

State Parks and Recreation Commission
Old State Capitol
P.O. Drawer 1111
Baton Rouge

Folder (free), describes state parks which include canoeable waterways.

MAINE

Department of Economic Development
Tourism Division
Augusta 04330

Booklet *Canoeing in Maine* (free). Describes 29 established canoe routes.

Great Northern Paper Co.
6 State Street
Bangor

Sportsman's map (free). Shows details of Allagash, Chesuncook, Chamberlain canoe country.

Maine Forest Service
Augusta 04330

Booklet *Maine Forest Service Campsites* (free). Describes location of some 300 free campsites, many along established canoe routes.

Rangeley Lakes Region Chamber
    of Commerce
Rangeley

Detailed map (free). Shows established canoe routes in Rangeley Lakes–Aziscoos area.

Scott Paper Co.
Winslow

Sportsman's map (free). Shows Moosehead, Upper Kennebec waterways.

St. Croix Paper Co.
Woodland, Baileyville

Sportsman's map (free). Shows Grand Lake canoe area.

State Parks & Recreation Commission
Augusta 04330

Information (free) on Allagash Wilderness Waterway.

Stratton Chamber of Commerce
Stratton

Sponsors annual canoe race on Dead River

MARYLAND

Louis J. Matacia
7414 Leesburg Pike
Falls Church, Virginia 22043

Blue Ridge Voyages Vol. I ($1.75) and Vol. II ($2). Describe canoeable waters in Maryland and adjacent states.

MASSACHUSETTS

Appalachian Mountain Club
5 Joy Street
Boston 02108

A.M.C. New England Canoeing Guide ($5). Best source of information on Massachusetts streams.

New England Electric System
441 Stuart Street
Boston 02116

Booklet *Down River* (free). Excellent detail on Connecticut River from source to Connecticut line, including section in Massachusetts.

Westfield River Watershed Assn.
P.O. Box 232
Huntington 01050

Information on Westfield River.

MICHIGAN

Huron–Clinton Metropolitan Auth.
1750 Guardian Building
Detroit

Detailed maps (free) showing campsites, portages, access points on Huron River.

Forest Supervisor
Huron National Forest
Cadillac

Folder *Huron National Forest* includes map of Au Sable River and others. Little detail, however.

Michigan Tourist Council
Steven T. Mason Building
Lansing 48926

Booklet *Michigan's Canoe Trails* (free). Excellent detail describing 59 established canoe routes.

MINNESOTA

Cook County Civic Council
Grand Marais

Canoeing information in Arrowhead country.

Crow Wing Canoe Trail Committee
Box 210
Sebeka

Map and folder (free) Crow Wing Canoe Trail.

Ely Chamber of Commerce
Room 117
Community Building
30 South 1st Avenue, E.
Ely

Information on Quetico – Superior wilderness canoe routes and numerous outfitters in area.

Department of Business Development
State Capitol
St. Paul 55101

Information on canoe routes and outfitters.

Forest Supervisor
Superior National Forest
Duluth

Folder *Boundary Waters Canoe Area* (free) includes map. Little detail, however.

MISSISSIPPI

Supervisor
De Soto National Forest
Box 1291
Jackson

Folder *Black Creek Float Trip* (free). Includes map.

MISSOURI

Division of Commerce & Industrial
  Development
Jefferson Building
Jefferson City 65102

Missouri Ozark Waterways ($1). Highly detailed guide to 37 major canoe trips on Missouri highland waterways.

Highway Planning Division
State Highway Department
Jefferson City 65102

County highway maps useful for locating access points to most waterways (small charge).

MONTANA

Department of Fish and Game
Helena

Booklet *Montana Boating, Floating* (free). Brief details on float trips and access points.

NEBRASKA

Game, Forestation, and Parks
  Commission
State Capitol
Lincoln 68509

Booklet *Nebraska Boating Guide* (free). Includes small scale map showing canoe waters.

NEW HAMPSHIRE

Appalachian Mountain Club
5 Joy Street
Boston, Mass. 02108

A.M.C. New England Canoeing Guide ($5). Best source of information for New Hampshire canoeing.

White Mountain Region Association
of New Hampshire
Lancaster 03584

Conducts canoe races on Androscoggin
River at 13-Mile Woods section.

Department of Resources
and Economic Development
Concord 03301

Canoeing on Connecticut River booklet
(free). Also issued by State of Vermont.
Describes portages, rapids, etc.

NEW JERSEY

Department of Conservation
P.O. Box 1889
Trenton 08625

Booklet (free) describes trips on following rivers: Hackensack, Passaic, Ramapo,
Warrogue, Millstone, Raritan, Rancocas,
Wading, Great Egg, Delaware, and
others.

Rutgers University Press
30 College Avenue
New Brunswick

Exploring the Little Rivers of New Jersey,
by James and Margaret Cawley ($4.50
clothbound; $1.95, paperback). Highly
detailed description of New Jersey waterways.

Upper Raritan Watershed
Association, Inc.
P.O. Box 44
Far Hills 07931

Information on Raritan River.

NEW MEXICO

Texas Explorer's Club
Bob Burleson, Pres.
Box 844
Temple, Texas 76501

Best authority on Rio Grande River in
New Mexico and Texas.

NEW YORK

Conservation Department
Division of Lands and Forests
Albany 12226

Recreation Circular No. 3 *Adirondack
Campsites* (free) describes campsites
along Adirondack canoe routes. Recreation Circular No. 7 *Adirondack Canoe
Routes* (free) includes map and canoe
route details.

NORTH DAKOTA

Fish and Game Department
Bismarck

Booklet *Opportunities for Outdoor Recreation at Wakopa* (free). Brief details
and map of specially developed 4-mile
canoe trail. Folder *Why Not Wakopa?*
(free) includes more detail, plus map of
same area.

OHIO

Department Natural Resources
Publications Section
1500 Dublin Road
Columbus 43212

Booklet *Ohio Canoe Adventures* (free).
Map and some details on several river
trips up to 162 miles long.

Neshaminy Valley Watershed Association, Inc.
8 West Oakland Avenue
Doylestown 18901

Information on protection and development of Neshaminy watershed.

Pennsylvania Fish Commission
Box 1673
Harrisburg

Booklets (all free) *Fishing and Boating in Pennsylvania, Fisherman's Guide to Pennsylvania Waters and Access Points, Boating Guide to Pennsylvania Waters.* Not canoeing publications but helpful.

Pennsylvania State University
College of Agriculture
Agricultural Experiment Station
University Park

Stream Map of Pennsylvania ($1) shows virtually all waterways.

Pittsburgh Council, American Youth Hostels
6300 Fifth Avenue
Pittsburgh

Canoeing in the Pittsburgh Area, mimeographed booklet describes canoe waters —lakes and streams.

Wissahickon Valley Watershed Association, Inc.
473 Bethlehem Pike
Fort Washington 15222

Organized to restore, improve and conserve natural resources of Wissahickon valley.

Development Council
Roger Williams Building
Hayes Street
Providence 02908

Folder *Camping in Rhode Island* (free) includes brief information on Pawcatuck River Canoe Trail.

Department Natural Resources
Veterans Memorial Building
Providence 02903

Folder *Pawcatuck River and Wood River* (free). Well detailed for canoeists.

Game and Fish Commission
Room 600
Doctors Building
Nashville 37203

State wide map *Tennessee Recreational Waters* (free) classifies streams as white water or pastoral float trips. Folder *Buffalo River Float Map* (free), excellent detail. Map *Little Tennessee River Float Waters* (free), some detail. Map *Harpeth River Float Trip* (free), large scale (1 mile = 2 inches) contour map.

Scott County Chamber of Commerce
Oneida 37841

Co-sponsors Angel Falls—Devil's Jump Canoe Race on Big South Fork River in Tennessee and Kentucky. Other co-sponsors include universities of Tennessee and Kentucky; Oneida Kiwanis Club; Pine Knot, Ky. Kiwanis Club.

Tennessee Scenic Rivers Association
P.O. Box 3104
Nashville 37219

Seeks to classify Tennessee rivers with an eye to preserving natural beauty and navigability.

Texas Explorers Club
Bob Burleson, President
Box 844
Temple 76501

Information on Rio Grande River Canoe-ing.

Superintendent
Big Bend National Park

Folder *Big Bend National Park* (free) includes some information on section of Rio Grande River within park.

Vermont Development Commission
Montpelier

Booklet *Vermont Canoeing* (free) describes Connecticut River canoe route.

Board of Recreation
Montpelier

Booklet *Canoeing on the Connecticut River* (free), details on canoe route from Stewartstown, N.H. to Massachusetts border.

Appalachian Mountain Club
5 Joy Street
Boston, Mass. 02108

A.M.C. New England Canoeing Guide ($5.). Best source of information for Vermont canoeing.

Commission of Game and Inland
    Fisheries
Box 1642
Richmond 23213

Canoe Trails of Eastern Virginia (free) reprint of article in *Virginia Wildlife*; excellent suggestions on canoeing possibilities.

Louis J. Matacia
7414 Leesburg Pike
Falls Church 22043

Blue Ridge Voyages (Vol. I, $1.75; Vol. II, $2). Well detailed.

Randy Carter
158 Winchester Street
Warrenton 22186

Canoeing White Water ($4.75). Outstanding guidebook to canoe waters of eastern West Virginia, Virginia and Great Smoky Mountain area.

Washington Foldboat Club
5622 Seaview Avenue
Seattle

Local information on navigable streams in Washington with regard to foldboating but applicable to canoeing.

See "Randy Carter" and "Louis J. Matacia" listings under Virginia.

Wisconsin Conservation Department
Box 450
Madison 53701

Booklet *Wisconsin Water Trails* (free). Excellent details with maps on 48 established canoe routes.

Outing Director
The Wisconsin Union
University of Wisconsin
800 Langdon Street
Madison 53706

*Guide to White Water in the Wisconsin
Area by Andres Peekna,* 1967 ($1.25).

American White Water
Membership publication,
American White Water Affiliation

"Hoback, Grey's and Wind Rivers of
Western Wyoming," by Oz and Dorothy
Hawksley, Sept. 1966, p. 4. Excellent
report of running these rivers.

Superintendent
Yellowstone National Park 83020

Booklet *Wilderness Boating on Yellowstone Lakes* (free).

Information Sources—Canada

Canadian Government Travel Bureau
Ottawa, Ontario

Booklet *Canoe Trips in Canada* (free).
Some details on canoe trips in each
province, plus general information.

Northern Stores Department
Hudson's Bay Company
Hudson's Bay House
Winnipeg 1, Manitoba

Folder *U-Paddle Canoe Rental Service*
explains canoe trip equipment rental
system.

Government Travel Bureau
331 Highways Building
Edmonton

At this writing, officials are gathering
canoe trip information.

British Columbia Travel Bureau
Department of Recreation and
Conservation
Victoria

Information on Bowron Lake Provincial
Park canoe routes; also other routes.

Tourist Development Branch
Department of Industry and Commerce
Winnipeg 1

Canoe Trips in Manitoba details major
canoe routes (free). *Manitoba's Northland* folder includes map of northern
canoe routes (free). *Manitoba's Whiteshell* includes map of canoe routes in
Whiteshell Provincial Park (free).

New Brunswick Travel Bureau
Box 1030
Fredericton

Narrative description of canoe routes on
St. John and Miramichi rivers; little practical detail.

NEWFOUNDLAND AND LABRADOR

Department of Mines, Agriculture
and Resources
St. Johns, Newfoundland

At this writing, province is exploring possibilities of canoe-trip literature.

NORTHWEST TERRITORIES

Northwest Territories
400 Laurier Avenue, West
Ottawa 5, Ontario

Canoe route pamphlet in preparation at this writing. Reprint *Across the Barrens by Canoe* (free) by Orris C. Herfindal, describes 4-week canoe trip down Hanbury and Thelon rivers. Reprint from *Canadian Geographical Journal,* May, 1967, "Summer Travels in the Canadian Barrens" by Eric W. Morse (free). *Must* reading for anyone planning an extended Canadian cruise. Reprint from *Canadian Geographical Journal,* June, 1965, "Fresh Water Northwest Passage" by Eric W. Morse, describes trip from Hudson Bay to Bering Sea. Highly informative.

ONTARIO

Department of Tourism and Information
185 Bloor Street, East
Toronto 5,

General information on Ontario canoe trips.

Canadian Quetico Outfitters, Ltd.
Kawane

Free bulletin describing trips in Quetico Provincial Park. (Also available from Canadian Government Travel Bureau.)

QUEBEC

Department of Tourism, Fish and Game
Parliament Building
Quebec City

Booklet *Canoe Routes in La Verendrye Park* (free). Details 3 trips in park; other booklets in preparation at this writing. Map *Metabetchouan River Canoe Trip* (free). Describes 60-mile trip in Laurentide Park.

Boy Scouts of Canada
2085 Bishop Street
Montreal

Campsite Directory includes map references and details of 8 canoe trips in Quebec.

SASKATCHEWAN

Information Branch
Department of Natural Resources
Government Administration Building
Regina

Pamphlets issued for each of 24 established canoe routes include utmost detail.

Chief Ranger
Prince Albert National Park
Waskesiu

Information on numerous canoe trips within park.

Department of Travel and Publicity
Box 2703
Whitehorse

Suggested Canoe Trips—Yukon Territory, mimeographed description of several trips, including regulations and equipment suggestions (free).

The Whitehorse Star
Box 1149
Whitehorse

Yukon River Log, covering section between Whitehorse and Tanana River, revised 1957, $1.50.

National and Regional Information Sources

American Camping Association, Inc.
Bradford Woods
Martinsville, Indiana 46151

New canoeing manual for organized summer camps in preparation at this writing.

American Canoe Association, Inc.
400 Eastern Street
New Haven, Connecticut 06513

Official clearing house for most canoeing activity in the United States. Publishes *American Canoeist* quarterly.

American Forestry Association, Inc.
919 17th Street NW
Washington, D.C. 20006

Conducts group canoe trips on Allagash River in Maine and in Quetico — Superior country of Ontario and Minnesota.

American Red Cross

Two publications available from local chapters and bookstores: *Canoeing* ($1.25); *Basic Canoeing* (40¢).

American River Touring Association, Inc.
1016 Jackson Street
Oakland, California 94607

Conducts river trips on Stanislaus River (Calif.), Grand Canyon (Ariz.), Middle Fork of Salmon (Ida.), Rogue (Ore.). Also offers *A Guide to Rafting and Shore Camping* ($1), by Lon Elliott.

American White Water Affiliation
Harold G. Kiehm, Chairman,
    Membership Committee
2019 West Addison Street
Chicago, Illinois 60618

An association of 83 local canoe and related groups with world-wide interest in white-water canoeing. Also publishes *American White Water* quarterly.

American Youth Hostels, Inc.
Room 202, YMCA
1528 Locust Street
St. Louis, Missouri

Sponsors organized trips on Ozark streams.

Appalachian Mountain Club
5 Joy Street
Boston, Massachusetts 02108

Individual chapters conduct canoe training courses; sponsor group trips. Club also publishes: *AMC New England Canoeing Guide* ($5); *Whitewater Handbook for Canoe and Kayak,* by John T. Urban ($1.50).

Boy Scouts of America

Offers canoe training at most of its summer camps; publishes booklet *Canoeing* by W. Van B. Claussen (35¢), available from Boy Scout outfitters.

Canadian Canoeing Association
32 Sedgewick Crest
Islington, Ontario

Performs similar functions in Canada to those of American Canoe Association in U.S.

Connecticut River Watershed Council
497 Main Street
Greenfield, Massachusetts 01301

Publishes *The Connecticut River Guide* ($2).

Delaware River Basin Commission
Box 360
Trenton, New Jersey 08603

Information on Delaware River in New York, New Jersey, and Pennsylvania

Delaware River Watershed Association
P.O. Box 44
Far Hills, New Jersey 07931

Works to improve, preserve Delaware River watershed.

Girl Scouts of the U.S.A.
830 Third Avenue
New York, N.Y. 10022

Offers canoeing instructions at many of its summer camps; canoeing information in handbooks.

Grumman Boats, Inc.
Marathon, New York 13803

Publishes booklet (free) listing agencies in U.S. which rent aluminum canoes.

Interstate Commission on the
   Potomac River Basin
203 Transportation Building
Washington, D.C. 20006

Concerned with development and preservation of Potomac River.

Minnesota–Wisconsin Boundary Area
   Commission
619 2nd Street
Hudson, Wisconsin 54016

Concerned with development and improvement of waters between the two states.

National Watershed Congress
1025 Vermont Avenue, N.W.
Washington, D.C. 20005

Correlates watershed improvement efforts through U.S.

National Wildlife Federation
1412 16th Street, N.W.
Washington, D.C. 20036

Conservation group strongly concerned with preservation of scenic and wild rivers.

New England Camping Association, Inc.
29 Commonwealth Ave.
Boston, Mass. 02116

Publishes *Canoeing Standards, Graded Classification, Canoeing Manual* ($1.50), for use by organized summer camps. New manual in preparation at this writing.

New England Electric System
441 Stuart Street
Boston, Massachusetts 02116

Publishes *Down River* (free). Account of Connecticut River trip from Pittsburg, N.H., to Mass.–Conn. line. Narrative includes much detail.

Sierra Club
1050 Mills Tower
San Francisco, California 94104

Strongly concerned with preservation of free-flowing rivers; conducts organized river trips. Publishes frequent bulletins.

United States Canoe Association
c/o Charles Moore
6338 Hoover Road
Indianapolis, Indiana 46260

U.S. Army Engineers District
Lake Survey

Publishes catalog (free) of U.S. Lake Survey charts including outflow rivers,

630 Federal Building
Detroit, Michigan 48226

Lake Champlain, New York State Barge Canal System, and Minnesota-Ontario border lakes.

The Wilderness Society
Western Regional Office
5850 Jewell Avenue
Denver, Colorado 80222

Conducts western float trips.

The Wilderness Society
729 15th Street, N.W.
Washington, D.C. 20005

Active in struggle to preserve wild and scenic rivers. Publishes *The Living Wilderness* quarterly, which often includes material on free-flowing rivers.

Map Sources

U.S. Geological Survey
Washington, D.C. 20242

U.S. Geological Survey
Federal Center
Denver, Colorado 80225

Free indexes available, showing published topographical maps of each state. These indexes contain lists of special maps, addresses of local map reference libraries, map dealers and Federal map distribution centers.

U.S. Army Corps of Engineers. This agency has several field offices throughout the U.S. from which local maps may be obtained.

U.S. Army Corps of Engineers
P.O. Box 1538
Albuquerque, New Mexico 87103

P.O. Box 1715
Baltimore, Maryland 21203

Foot of Bridge Street
Buffalo, New York 14207

P.O. Box 905
Charleston, South Carolina 29402

219 Dearborn Street
Chicago, Illinois 60604

P.O. Box 1027
Detroit, Michigan 48231

P.O. Box 1600
Fort Worth, Texas 76101

P.O. Box 2127
Huntington, West Virginia 25701

P.O. Box 4970
Jacksonville, Florida 32201

1800 Federal Office Building
Kansas City, Missouri 64106

P.O. Box 867
Little Rock, Arkansas 72203

P.O. Box 17277
Foy Station
Los Angeles, California 90017

P.O. Box 59
Louisville, Kentucky 40201

668 Federal Office Building
Memphis, Tennessee 38103

P.O. Box 1169
Mobile, Alabama 36601

P.O. Box 1070
Nashville, Tennessee 37202

P.O. Box 60267
New Orleans, Louisiana 70160

111 East 16th Street
New York, New York 10003

6012 U.S. Post Office & Court House
Omaha, Nebraska 68101

Custom House
2nd & Chestnut Streets
Philadelphia, Pennsylvania 19106

564 Forbes Avenue
Manor Building
Pittsburgh, Pennsylvania 15219

628 Pittock Block
Portland, Oregon 97205

Clark Tower Building
Rock Island, Illinois 61202

P.O. Box 1739
Sacramento, California 95808

180 New Montgomery Street
San Francisco, California 94105

P.O. Box 889
Savannah, Georgia 31402

1519 S. Alaskan Way, South
Seattle, Washington 98134

906 Oliver Street
St. Louis, Missouri 63102

1217 U.S. Post Office & Custom House
180 E. Kellog Boulevard
St. Paul, Minnesota 55101

P.O. Box 61
Tulsa, Oklahoma 74102

P.O. Box 60
Vicksburg, Mississippi 39181

Building 602
City-County Airport
Walla Walla, Washington 99632

424 Trapelo Road
Waltham, Massachusetts 02154

P.O. Box 1890
Wilmington, North Carolina 28402

W. A. Fisher Co. Virginia, Minnesota	Maps specifically drawn for canoeists of the Superior – Quetico Boundary Waters Canoe Area of northern Minnesota and southern Ontario.
Prentiss and Carlisle, Inc. 107 Court Street Bangor, Maine	County maps of Maine, showing all major riverways and streams.
Appalachian Mountain Club 5 Joy Street Boston, Massachusetts 02108	Maps of all canoe routes in New England.
Trygg Land Office P.O. Box 628 Ely, Minnesota 55731	All types of maps covering northern Minnesota, including canoe routes.
Penn State University Box 600 University Park, Pa. 16802	Large map of all streams in Pennsylvania.
Map Distribution Office Department of Mines and Technical Surveys Ottawa, Ontario, Canada	Free indexes available, showing published topographical maps of Canada.

General provincial maps, county maps and legal survey plans are available from the following Canadian agencies:

Department of Mines and Resources
St. John's, Newfoundland

Department of Mines
Halifax, Nova Scotia
(Provincial and county maps)

Department of Lands and Forests
Halifax, Nova Scotia
(Legal land surveys)

Department of Lands and Mines
Fredericton, New Brunswick

Surveys Branch
Department of Lands and Forests
Quebec City, P. Q.

Surveys and Engineering Division
Department of Lands and Forests
Toronto, Ontario

Director of Surveys
Department of Mines and Natural
  Resources
Winnipeg, Manitoba

Controller of Surveys
Department of Natural Resources
Regina, Saskatchewan

Director, Technical Division
Department of Lands and Forests
Edmonton, Alberta

Director of Surveys and Mapping
Department of Lands and Forests
Victoria, British Columbia

In the United States, other sources of maps may include:

State park departments
State forestry agencies
Conservation departments
Tourism promotional agencies
Timber and pulpwood companies
Chambers of Commerce

Canoe clubs and associations
College outing clubs
State and municipal libraries
Sporting goods stores; book stores
Canoe outfitters

Canoe Manufacturers

Aero-Craft
Division of Harwill, Inc.
St. Charles, Mich.

Aluma Craft Boat Co.
Division of Alpex Corp.
1551 Central Avenue N.E.
Minneapolis, Minn. 55413

Alumidock, Division of Metallic Ladder
  Mfg. Corp.
2 Sheldon Street
Randolph, N.Y. 14772

Appleby Mfg. Co.
Interstate 44
Lebanon, Mo. 65536

Bemidji Boat Co.
Bemidji, Minn.

Cadorette Canoes, Inc.
P.O. Box 518
Grand Mere
P.Q., Canada

Cape Cod Shipbuilding Co.
Narrows Road
Wareham, Mass. 02571

Chestnut Canoe Co.
Fredericton
New Brunswick, Canada

Chicagoland Canoe Base
4019 North Narragansett Avenue
Chicago, Ill. 60634

Delhi Mfg. Co.
Delhi, La.

Feather Craft, Inc.
450 Bishop Street N.W.
Atlanta, Ga. 30318

Fleet Products Co. Inc.
1930 Placentia
Costa Mesa, Calif. 92627

Grumman Boats
Grumman Allied Industries Inc.
Marathon, N.Y. 13803

Industrial Fiberglas Products
Ludington, Mich.

Lakeview Boat Co.
P.O. Box 51
Sunnymead, Calif. 92388

Lincoln Fiberglas Division
Lazott Co. Inc.
Milk Street
Westboro, Mass. 01581

Lund Boat Co.
P.O. Box 10
New York Mills, Minn. 56567

Mirro Aluminum Co.
1516 Washington Street
Manitowoc, Wis. 54220

Monark Boat Co.
P.O. Box 210
Monticello, Ark. 71655

Mountain Ash Fiberglas Co.
Hudson, N.Y.

Northway Canoes
10015 Green St.
Hebron, Ill. 60034

Old Town Canoe Co.
Old Town, Maine 04468

Ouachita Marine & Industrial Corp.
P.O. Box 420
Arkadelphia, Ark. 71923

Pioneer Mfg. Co.
Middlebury, Ind. 46540

Richland Mfg. Co.
Richland, Mo. 65556

Rivers & Gilman Moulded Products Co.
Hampden, Maine

Riverside Fiberglas Canoe Co.
Box 5595
Riverside, Calif.

Ross Canoe Co.
Loretteville
P.Q., Canada

Sanco Equip. Corp.
24 East 13th St.
New York, N.Y. 10003

Sawyer Canoe Co.
4496 North U.S. 23
Oscoda, Mich.

Schneider Boat Co.
3133 W. Lisbon Ave.
Milwaukee, Wis. 53208
(Kits only)

Shell Lake Boats
Shell Lake, Wis. 54871

Smoker Lumber Co. Inc.
New Paris, Ind.

Sportspal Inc.
Drawer T
Emlenton, Penn. 16373

Starcraft Corp.
Goshen, Ind.

Stowe Canoe Co.
Stowe, Vermont

Trailcraft Inc.
Box 517
Glasco, Kan. 67445
(Kits Only)

Voyager Products, Inc.
25755 D'Hand T Court
Mount Clemens, Mich. 48043

Viking Sports Craft Co.
P.O. Box 8393
Columbus, Ohio

White Canoe Co.
Old Town, Maine 04468

Wooster Marine Engineering
P.O. Box 112
Schooley's Mountain, N.J.

Tent Manufacturers and Importers

Avis Products
2820 West Maple Road
Troy, Michigan 48084

Alp Sport
P.O. Box 1081
Boulder, Colorado 80301

Alaska Sleeping Bag Co.
701 N.W. Dawson Way
Beaverton, Oregon 97005

Thomas Black & Sons
930 Ford Street
Ogdensburg, New York 13669

Bishop's Ultimate Outdoor Equipment
6804 Millwood Road
Bethesda, Maryland 20034

Camel Manufacturing Co.
329 S. Central Avenue
Knoxville, Tennessee 37902

Camp and Trail Outfitters
112 Chambers Street
New York, New York 10007

Camp Trails
3920 West Clarendon Avenue
Phoenix, Arizona 85019

The Coleman Company
Wichita, Kansas 67201

Colorado Outdoor Sports Corp. (Gerry)
P.O. Box 5544
Denver, Colorado 80217

Columbia Tent and Awning Co.
1314 Rosewood Drive
Columbia, South Carolina

Duluth Tent and Awning Co.
1610 West Superior Street
Duluth, Minnesota

Eureka Tent and Awning Co., Inc.
35 State Street
Binghamton, New York 13902

Fulton Cotton Mills
Box 1726
Atlanta, Georgia 30301

Hettrick Mfg. Co.
Tayorsville Road
Statesville, North Carolina 28677

Hirsch-Weis Canvas Products Co.
5203 S.E. Johnson Creek Boulevard
Portland, Oregon 97206

Johnson Company
3100 W. Randolph Street
Bellwood, Illinois 60104

Hans Klepper Corp.
820 Greenwich Street
New York, New York

Laacke and Joys Co.
1433 North Water Street
Milwaukee, Wisconsin 53202

Morsan Tents, Inc.
810 Route 17
Paramus, New Jersey

National Canvas Products Corp.
P.O. Box 2268 Central Station
Toledo, Ohio 43603

Outdoor Imports, Inc.
6363 Van Nuys Boulevard
Van Nuys, California 91401

The Ski Hut
1615 University Avenue
Berkeley, California 94703

Walter E. Stern, Tentmaker
254 Nagle Avenue
New York, New York

Thermos Division
King-Seeley/Thermos Co.
Norwich, Connecticut 06360

H. Wenzel Tent and Duck Co.
1280 Research Boulevard
St. Louis, Missouri 63132

Webb Manufacturing Co.
Fourth and Cambria Streets
Philadelphia, Pennsylvania 19133

Bibliography

A.M.C. New England Canoeing Guide, 500 p., 1968, Appalachian Mountain Club, 5 Joy Street, Boston, Mass. 02108. $5.00.

Appalachian Water by Walter F. Burmeister (Vol. I, 279 p.) (Vol. II, 289 p.), 1962, The Canoe Cruisers Association, Washington, D.C. Out of print but invaluable if copy can be obtained from local library.

Bark Canoes and Skin Boats of North America by Edwin Tappan Adney and Howard T. Chapelle, 242 p., Smithsonian Institution; available from U.S. Government Printing Office, Washington, D.C. 20402. $3.25.

Basic River Canoeing, 104 p., 1968, The Buck Ridge Ski Club, 32 Dartmouth Circle, Swarthmore, Pa. 19081. $1.25.

Blue Ridge Voyages by H. Roger Corbett and Louis J. Matacia, Jr., 1965–1966; Vol. I, $1.75; Vol. II, $2.00; Blue Ridge Voyagers, 1515 N. Adams Street, Arlington, Va. 22201.

The Camper's Bible, Bill Riviere, 176 p., 1961, Doubleday & Co., Garden City, N.Y. $1.95.

Camping and Outdoor Cooking by Rae Oetting and Mabel Otis Robinson, 259 p., 1958, T. S. Denison and Company, Minneapolis, Minn. $4.95.

Canoeable Waters of New York State by Lawrence I. Grinnell, Pageant Press, 101 Fifth Ave., New York, N.Y. $5.00.

Canoeing, 1956, 425 p., American Red Cross, available through local chapters. $1.75.

Canoeing, Boy Scout Merit Badge Library, 1939, Boy Scouts of America, New Brunswick, N.J. 35¢.

Canoeing by Carle W. Handel, 96 p., 1956, A. S. Barnes Co., 11 East 36th St., New York, N.Y.

Canoeing Manual, 96 p., 1958, New England Camping Association, 29 Commonwealth Ave., Boston, Mass. 02116. $1.50.

Canoe Camping by Carle W. Handel, The Ronald Press Co., 15 East 26th Street, New York, N.Y. $4.00.

Canoe Trails Through Quetico by Keith Dennis, 84 p., Border Lakes Outfitting Co., P. O. Box 569, Ely, Minn. 55731. $3.50.

Canoe Trails in Indiana, Department of Conservation, 612 State Office Building, Indianapolis, Ind. 46209. (Free).

Canoeing White Water: a guidebook to rivers of Virginia, eastern West Virginia and the Great Smoky Mountain area by Randy Carter, 5th edition, 1967, 195 p. Available from the author, 158 Winchester St., Warrenton, Va. 22186. $4.75.

Elements of Canoeing by P. Van Pulling, Ann Arbor Press, 327 Maynard St., Ann Arbor, Mich.

Exploring the Little Rivers of New Jersey by James and Margaret Cawley, Rutgers University Press, New Brunswick, N.J. 08903. $4.50 clothbound; $1.95 paperback.

Family Campers Cook Book, Bill Riviere, 1965, Holt, Rinehart and Winston, New York, 1965, 244 p. $4.95.

Floating, Fishing and Historical Guide to Yellowstone State Waterway by Ray E. Burdge, 2047 Custer Ave., Billings, Mont. 26 p.

Guide to White Water in the Wisconsin Area by Andres Peekna, 1967, Outing Director, Wisconsin Union, University of Wisconsin, 800 Langdon Street, Madison, Wis. 53706. $1.25.

Illinois Canoeing Guide, Boat Section, Illinois Department of Conservation, 106 State Office Bldg., Springfield, Ill. (Free).

Iowa Canoe Trips, Iowa Conservation Dept., East 7th and Court Sts., Des Moines, Iowa. (Free).

Know Your Canoe by Morehouse and Fancher, Western Division, American Canoe Association, 8224 S. Woodlawn Ave., Chicago, Ill.

Michigan Canoe Trails, Michigan Tourist Council, Steven T. Mason Bldg., Lansing, Mich. 48926. (Free).

Missouri Ozark Waterways by Oz Hawksley, Division of Commerce & Industrial Development, Jefferson Bldg., Jefferson City, Mo. 65102. $1.00.

New Way of the Wilderness by Calvin Rutstrum, 276 p., 1958, The Macmillan Co., 60 5th Ave., New York, N.Y.

North American Canoe Country by Calvin Rutstrum, The Macmillan Co., 60 5th Ave., New York, N.Y.

The Outdoor Guide by Luis M. Henderson, 350 p., 1950, The Stackpole Co., Telegraph Bldg., Harrisburg, Pa.

Outdoorsman's Cook Book by Arthur H. Carhart, The Macmillan Co., 60 5th Ave., New York, N.Y.

The Canoe by Robert E. Pinkerton, The Macmillan Co., 60 5th Ave., New York, N.Y.

White Water Handbook for Canoe and Kayak by John T. Urban, 1965, 76 p., Appalachian Mountain Club, 5 Joy St., Boston, Mass. 02108. $1.50.

The Lonely Land by Sigurd F. Olsen, 273 p., describes 500-mile canoe trip on Canada's Churchill River. Border Lakes Outfitting Co., P. O. Box 560, Ely, Minn. 55731. $4.95.

White Water Sports by Peter Dwight Whitney, 1960, The Ronald Press, 15 East 26th St., New York, N.Y. $4.00.

Journals

American White Water, quarterly journal of the American White Water Affiliation, issued to members, $3.50 annually, 456 Hawthorne, San Bruno, Calif. 94066.

American Canoeist, quarterly journal of the American Canoe Association. Annual subscription $2.00; 1217 Spring Garden St., Philadelphia, Pa. 19123.

Glossary

Access point Streamside or lakeshore location where watercraft may be launched or landed.

Aft Toward the stern or rear.

Air lock Suction within a canoe when it is overturned in the water. Makes craft difficult to right.

Air tanks Air-tight chambers along sides of a sponson canoe to lend stability; also in ends of aluminum and some Fiberglas canoes for buoyancy.

Back ferry To back paddle, with canoe at angle to current during downstream run in order to set over or cross.

Backlash Standing waves at foot of powerful chute or sluice created when fast-flowing water strikes relatively still water.

Back wave See Backlash.

Banana boat Decked canoe or kayak-type craft with upswept keel line, designed for high maneuverability.

Bang plate Metal strip on leading edge of cutwater, bow and stern, to protect hull.

Beam Width of craft at its widest point.

Bilge The interior of a canoe located below the waterline.

Bilge keel Extra keel, one each side, located just inside the chine, used to protect fabric on canvas canoes.

Blade The flat section of a canoe paddle.

Boil Water swelling upward, usually upon striking underwater object. Also called a "pillow."

Bow The front end of a watercraft.

Bow plate Same as Bang plate.

Bow seat Seat located at front of canoe.

Brace stroke   Stroke during which canoeman leans far out of his canoe to effect a quick turn. Primarily a white-water stroke.

Bracket   Device for attaching outboard motor to pointed or double-ended canoe.

Bridle   Line run loosely under forward end of canoe from gunwale to gunwale to which is attached a towing line.

Broach   Turning broadside to oncoming waves or current.

Bucket seats   Seats set lower than gunwale, usually on aluminum canoes.

Buoyancy chamber   Same as Air tank.

Cane seats   Wooden-framed seats with woven cane filling, usually on wood-and-canvas canoes.

Canoe pole   Pole used to propel canoe in shallow water.

Carry   A portage, where canoe and/or outfit is carried around stream obstruction or between two waterways. Also, the route followed.

Channel   Navigable route among obstructions in a stream.

Chine   The curving section of a canoe's sides where it bends or merges into the bottom.

Chute   Accelerated section of a stream, often compressed between two or more obstructions and dropping faster than adjacent current.

Classification   A rating applied to a stream or section of current describing its navigability.

Dead man   Log, anchored at one end, afloat at the other, usually found on streams where log drives have occurred.

Deck   Triangular section fitted between the gunwales at the bow and stern of paddling canoes; in the case of canoes used for white-water, running "deck" applies to a full covering to prevent water coming over the sides.

Decked canoe   Canoe with full covering as described above.

Depth   The depth of a canoe, measured vertically amidship; sometimes the depth is measured at the ends, which may be misleading.

Difficulty rating   Same as Classification.

Displacement   The weight of water displaced by a watercraft, its cargo and crew.

Double blade   Paddle with a blade at each end, usually used in a kayak and sometimes in a decked canoe.

Draft   Depth of water required to float a craft or the vertical distance between the waterline and the keel.

Drip rings   Leather or metal rings on the shaft of a double paddle to prevent water from running down the shaft.

Drop   A sudden pitch or unusually sharp dip in a section of rapids.

Dry pack Waterproof bag for carrying clothing. Used by white-water canoemen.

Duffek stroke Similar to Brace stroke.

Eddy Section of a current, downstream of a major obstruction, where water tends to flow in circular course.

Eddy line Fine line between a swift downstream current, and a circulating or upstream current within an eddy.

Falls Technically, the free-falling of water in a vertical or almost vertical plunge. However, in some parts of the country, heavy rapids are often termed "falls."

Fast water Generally conceded to mean rapids but can be applied to swiftly flowing water without obstructions.

Feather To bring paddle forward with one edge leading, thus reducing resistance by water or air.

Ferry Holding canoe at an angle to the current and paddling so that canoe sets over across the current.

Flare The section of a canoe paddle where the shaft widens to become the blade.

Flat water Lake water or river current where no rapids exist.

Flotation Styrofoam or similar substance placed in aluminum and Fiberglas canoes to provide buoyancy.

Floor boards Removable slats set in the bilge of canoes to protect ribs and planking.

Foldboat Collapsible kayak-like watercraft.

Following sea Waves which overtake a craft from astern.

Fore Toward the bow or front of a watercraft.

Forward ferry Paddling forward, with canoe at an angle to current, to set over or cross stream.

Freeboard Height of a canoe's side above waterline, measured amidship.

Freighter Large canoe used for hauling heavy loads.

Gauging station Streamside device for measuring flow of water.

Gilpoke Lumberman's term for a log protruding into a stream; used to deflect logs during river drive; a hazard to canoemen.

Gradient The average rate of drop in a river, generally expressed in feet per mile.

Grip Top of a canoe paddle shaft, shaped roughly to fit the hand.

Gunwale Strips along the top of a canoe's sides, extending from bow to stern.

Hanging stroke Similar to Bracing stroke.

Haystack   Same as Backlash.

Head   Volume of water or sudden rising of river level as a result of opening dam gates.

Heavy water   Large volume flow of water in rapids section, creating greater-than-average turbulence.

High brace   Similar to Brace stroke.

Hoe-handle grip   Lack of a grip on canoe paddle shaft, such as used by early Indian canoemen.

Hog   A canoe is said to "hog" when it is overly bow-heavy; also applies to craft whose keel line is higher amidship than at either end.

Hull   The main body of a canoe.

Inboard   Within the inside line of a canoe; within the gunwales.

Inwale   The inside gunwale.

Kayak   A decked watercraft with one or more cockpits for occupants, usually with a vee or semi-vee bottom and low ends.

Keel   Strip along the bottom center of a canoe, running from stem to stern, designed to prevent side-slipping.

Knob   The grip on a canoe paddle.

Ledge   Projecting stratum of rock which confines or partially dams stream flow.

Lee   Section of waterway sheltered from wind.

Lining   Guiding a canoe downstream through rough or shallow water by means of a rope or line.

Lob tree   Old time portage marker consisting of tall tree with upper limbs removed.

Low brace   Brace stroke with entire paddle almost flat on surface of water.

Open gunwale   Characteristic of wood-and-canvas canoes, sections between rib ends within the two gunwales are open, permitting quick draining when craft is overturned on land.

Outboard   Outside of the canoe's hull lines.

Outer stem   Outside curved section at each end of craft, corresponding to contours; formerly used on some wood-and-canvas canoes.

Outwale   Outside gunwale.

Overall length   Extreme length of canoe, as opposed to waterline length.

Painter   Length of rope attached to either or both ends.

Pick pole   Canoe pole.

Pike pole   Also a canoe pole.

Pillow   Bulge on surface created by underwater obstruction, usually a rock.

Pitch   Steep section or sharp drop in a rapids.

Planking   Longitudinal strips which form hull, attached to ribs in wood-and-canvas canoe.

Poling   Propelling a canoe with a pole.

Pool   Slowly moving, deep water.

Port   The left side of a canoe, facing forward.

Portage   See Carry.

Power face   The side of a paddle blade which pushes against the water during a stroke.

Prospector   Type of Canadian canoe somewhat wider and deeper than conventional canoes of same length.

Pudding stick   A stiff paddle, with little give in its shaft.

Rapids   Swiftly flowing water, tumbling with some degree of force among obstructions and creating turbulence.

Ribs   Curved strips which run from gunwale to gunwale forming the hull's shape; on wood-and-canvas canoes.

Riffles   Swift, shallow water running over a gravel or sand bottom and creating small waves. Could be termed gentle rapids.

Rips   Moderate rapids.

River rating   See Classification.

Rock garden   Navigable rock-strewn rapids.

Rocker   Upward sweep of keel line toward both ends of canoe, characteristic of river craft.

Rollers   See Backlash.

Sag   Much like Hog.

Scouting   Appraising rapids before running.

Set over   Same as Ferry.

Setting pole   Same as Canoe pole.

Shaft   The handle of a canoe paddle, between the blade and grip.

Shake out   To empty a swamped canoe while remaining in the water.

Sheathing   The planking in a wood-and-canvas canoe.

Sheer   The general lines of a canoe, usually observed along the gunwales.

Shoe keel   Shallow, wide keel for use on river canoes which may also be used on lakes; side slip is minimized somewhat with minimum of interference while making broadside moves in current.

Side push   Pushing canoe broadside, usually with draw, push, or pry stroke.

Slack water   Stream flow without rapids or riffles.

Slalom   A zig-zag course, usually set up in rapids, for competition.

Slat seats   Seats made of hardwood slats, usually found in some Canadian canvas-and-wood canoes.

Slough around   To veer erratically, out of control.

Sluice   Similar to Chute.

Snubbing   Stopping or slowing a canoe's momentum with a canoe pole, while running downstream.

Souse hole   A frothy, highly-foamed eddy, or a depressed surface of water downstream of a large obstruction, generally in a fast-flowing stream.

Splash out   Same as Shake out.

Sponson   See Air tanks.

Spray cover   Temporary fabric deck used on open canoes during white-water running, to keep craft from taking on water.

Spray skirt   Fabric sleeve which encloses paddler's waist and is attached to spray cover.

Standing wave   See Backlash.

Starboard   Right-hand side of watercraft, facing forward.

Stem   The extreme bow; curved section of frame which forms cutwater.

Stem band   Same as Bang plate.

Stern   Rear or back of watercraft.

Stern plate   Same as Bang plate.

Stern seat   Rear or back seat in a canoe.

Throat   Flaring of the paddle shaft where it starts to form the blade.

Thwart   Cross braces, running from gunwale to gunwale, for reinforcement.

Tip   Bottom end of canoe paddle blade.

Tow ring   Ring attached to forward cutwater or forward deck, for attaching tow rope.

Tracking   Towing canoe upstream by hand with line.

Trim   The manner in which a canoe rides on the water.

Trip leader   The canoeman in charge of a trip.

Trough   Depression between waves.

Tumblehome   The inboard curvature of a canoe's sides from the bilge to the gunwale.

War canoe   Large canoe designed for many paddlers.

Waterline   Level of the water on the canoe's sides when carrying normal load.

Waterline length   Length of canoe measured at waterline.

Way   Forward or rear motion; momentum.

Wet suit   Protective suit, close fitting, which serves to insulate against cold water in case of upset.

White eddy   Pool at the foot of a drop over which water flows, creating a marked backflow on the surface; usually highly aerated and somewhat less buoyant than other water surfaces.

White water   Rapids.

Windward   Direction from which wind is coming.

Yoke   Device, attached permanently or temporarily amidship, and usually padded to protect shoulders; for portaging canoe.

Index